THE STORY
of BRISTOL BAPTIST COLLEGE

THE STORY
of BRISTOL BAPTIST COLLEGE

Three Hundred Years of Ministerial Formation

Ruth Gouldbourne
and
Anthony R. Cross

Foreword by Stephen Finamore

◆PICKWICK *Publications* · Eugene, Oregon

THE STORY OF BRISTOL BAPTIST COLLEGE
Three Hundred Years of Ministerial Formation

Copyright © 2022 Ruth Gouldbourne and Anthony R. Cross. All rights reserved. Except for brief quotations in critical publications or reviews, no part of this book may be reproduced in any manner without prior written permission from the publisher. Write: Permissions, Wipf and Stock Publishers, 199 W. 8th Ave., Suite 3, Eugene, OR 97401.

Pickwick Publications
An Imprint of Wipf and Stock Publishers
199 W. 8th Ave., Suite 3
Eugene, OR 97401

www.wipfandstock.com

PAPERBACK ISBN: 978-1-5326-6251-5
HARDCOVER ISBN: 978-1-5326-6252-2
EBOOK ISBN: 978-1-5326-6253-9

Cataloguing-in-Publication data:

Names: Gouldbourne, Ruth [author]. | Cross, Anthony R. [author]

Title: The story of Bristol Baptist College : three hundred years of ministerial formation / Ruth Gouldbourne and Anthony R. Cross.

Description: Eugene, OR: Pickwick Publications, 2022 | Includes index.

Identifiers: ISBN 978-1-5326-6251-5 (paperback) | ISBN 978-1-5326-6252-2 (hardcover) | ISBN 978-1-5326-6253-9 (ebook)

Subjects: LCSH: Bristol Baptist College—History | Baptist universities and colleges—United Kingdom | Baptists—History | Baptists—Education (Higher) | Clergy—Training of—United Kingdom

Classification: BX6206 G68 2022 (print) | BX6206 (ebook)

VERSION NUMBER 021722

To all who have made the College all that it has been, is, and will be;
students, staff, volunteers, and supporters.

In memory of Anthony Cross (1962–2021)

CONTENTS

Foreword by Stephen Finamore | ix
Preface | xi
Acknowledgments | xiii
List of Illustrations | xiv

1 TO BEGIN AT THE BEGINNING | 1

2 THE FIRST HUNDRED YEARS | 16

3 CONTROVERSY OVER THE ROLE OF EDUCATION | 44

4 THE SECOND CENTURY | 55

5 PHYSICAL HOMES OF THE COLLEGE | 113

6 THE LIBRARY | 129

7 THREE HUNDRED YEARS, NOT OUT | 132

Afterword | 209
A Note on Sources | 211
Index | 213

FOREWORD

ONE OF THE MANY lovely things about being a college principal is that you occasionally get invited to lead worship and preach at church anniversary services. One of the things I sometimes say on such occasions is that we should treat them as though we were walking over a busy road. It is not a time for rushing. It is a time for pausing and looking both ways before you cross and as you go. It is a time to look to the past and to see which of its practices, values, and goals remain relevant. And it is an opportunity to look the other way, to the future, and to ponder what God might have in store for the next leg of the journey.

    It occurred to me that I might say something along these lines in any words I might be asked to say in introducing a new history of the Bristol Baptist College in celebration of a significant anniversary – or two. It never crossed my mind that the anniversary would be an occasion of far more pausing and reflecting that any of us bargained for. 2020 was supposed to be a year for celebrating the anniversary of the appointment of the first college principal—or president – and that of the foundation of the Education Society. We expected to look back and learn from three centuries of ministerial education and to look forward to all that we might do to continue the work. Instead, we found ourselves in lockdown, with all our activities forced online, and reflecting on what God might be teaching us through what was, for our generation at least, a unique experience.

    The lockdown affected nearly everything, including the capacity of the authors to fully complete the research they had started. Yet it did allow us to engage in some serious thinking. We were able to consider the college's story and to see how it impacts the present. And we could see which of its values and practices have stood the test of time and so must inform its future. Perhaps most significantly, we gained a fresh appreciation of our own fragility and just how dependent we are on God for everything. These things helped us to plan how we should emerge from lockdown. It became abundantly clear that our story really matters. It is a sign of God's continuing faithfulness to his people and to his mission. I am deeply grateful to the authors, Anthony and Ruth, both such great friends to the college, for their commitment to researching the details of the college's past and to presenting them as such an accessible story. It really helps us 'look both ways' by telling us about the past and prompting thoughts about the future. I would like to pay a particular tribute to Anthony who did most of the research for this project and who, very sadly, died before the work was completely finished. He was a terrific scholar and good friend with a range of wonderful publications of which this book may be the last. Anthony had an abiding love for the college where he had trained. We will miss him very much. We continue to keep Jackie and the family in our prayers.

It's a story to which everyone associated with the college has contributed. We have all played our part in shaping it and in our turn, we have been shaped by the college. Every year, a group of students and perhaps a staff member or two moves on and others take their places. The college changes and yet it stays the same. There is a line of succession that takes us all the way back to the beginning of the story. For all the differences, there is a continuity that ties together, as part of the greater communion of saints, all those associated with this college. It's a story, a community, a tradition, a strand of spiritual DNA that makes us one and tells us we belong. In writing the history Anthony and Ruth have done us a great service and we owe them our thanks. It's a terrific tale. It's a book that can be read with profit by many. But for those of us who carry the seal of the college in some way, those of us who have been a part of its life, the book is important, because like all really significant stories, it helps to tell us who we are.

Revd Dr Stephen Finamore
Principal, Bristol Baptist College

PREFACE

PERSONAL INTRODUCTION

The writing of any history itself takes place within an historical context, and it is appropriate at the beginning of this work to recognize that. The originating history for this retelling of the Bristol College story is the three hundredth anniversary of its emergence as a functioning academy. Other histories have been written at various points, usually significant anniversaries, and it is worth pausing for a moment to ask why now and why another? We believe that this particular work, drawing as it does on the significant and exhaustive research into people, places, and events undertaken by Rev Dr Anthony Cross offers something unique. This current volume draws on that work, and presents it in a condensed form and without the valuable footnotes and examination of sources. Sadly, that material is not going to be available, and this book is lesser as a result. However, it is to be hoped that this book might give direction to somebody else who will restart the research and explore the resources on which the original work has been based. This volume is a book written 'for the family'; it is designed primarily for those who have been part of the College's life and want to know more of the 'family history'.

The immediate history of this book is also the reminder that plans can be made, but then life happens. The intention was that this would be published towards the end of 2020. However, at the beginning of 2020, the world entered a pandemic, and the UK entered a lockdown, and life became complex. Apart from anything else, it became impossible to access the archives in the College or to have the meetings and conversations that, until that point, had been part of the research and writing process.

On a more personal level, towards the end of 2019, Anthony Cross had some periods of ill health, which meant that resources for the writing were already proving hard to assemble and work on. As the year progressed, he was to become more seriously unwell, and this has meant that his work on the material was seriously curtailed. Since the present volume was to be written on the basis of his immense research, and since it only became clear that he would have to make a pause in that research in the time that travel, access to archives, and generally doing research work was impossible, it is important that I note that the last part of this book in particular is not all that we had hoped it would be.

As the time came to finish the book, Anthony died. This is a loss not only to the family to whom he was devoted, and to whom we extend our sympathy, but to the field of Baptist research in so many ways. There are other places where Anthony's work is noted and appreciated, and proper honour paid to his unique and invaluable contribution in so many fields. Here, I want personally to note my tribute and my indebtedness to Anthony. We worked together on several projects and his tireless research, his careful writing, his care, and attention to footnotes so that other researchers could also do the work, as wells as his abilities to make badly drafted typescript into a coherent book were all gifts I treasured and I miss – never more so than in the writing of this book.

How the material is organized

Anthony Cross' research is detailed, meticulous, and fully footnoted. It is also three volumes long. At his request, I have produced here a shorter version, designed to be easily accessible. To that end, at his request, I have omitted footnotes.

The research in this book is Anthony's. I have condensed, cut, and pasted, omitted so much that is fascinating and valuable, and have attempted to keep the depth of the story he wrote, while meeting the constraints of length. I hope he would have thought I did it justice.

ACKNOWLEDGMENTS

Thanks for this volume must first be given to Revd Dr Anthony Cross, on whose work it is based.

We are grateful too to those who have contributed their memories and have shared in conversation about the story here.

Particular thanks to Michael Brearley, who has continued the wonderful tradition of helpful librarians of the College, going above and beyond. Not only has he helped Anthony in accessing archives and records, he has also supplied photographs, corrections, and he has even written the section on the twenty-first century. Michael's willingness to bring the history up to date, and his grace in doing this at short notice and with little time has been invaluable.

Thanks to those who have read this as an ongoing project, especially Derek Murray, Stephen Copson, and Kerry Birch.

Thanks to Brian Haymes for encouragement and support in the long stretches of research and through complexities.

Thanks to Robin Parry at Wipf & Stock Publishers for being so gracious in the matter of deadlines and changing contracts.

Thanks to Fran Brealey for managing the administrative side at College.

Thanks to the congregation at Grove Lane Baptist Church in Cheadle Hulme, who have given me space and time to write this, and encouragement, even when they didn't know it.

Thanks to Ian, for again, showing infinite patience.

ILLUSTRATIONS

College entrants 1878.
Questions to Applicants.
Grant to present students for London University degrees.
Study, Stokes Croft.
Rules for College Students; mid nineteenth century.
College Reunion 1886.
College Football Team 1906.
Principals Culross and Henderson 1895.
Procession at the opening of Woodland Rd Building.
John Sutherland Whitewright.
Appeal leaflet for Stokes Croft.
Subscribers to the Appeal for Stokes Croft.
Stokes Croft Lecture Room.
Study Corridor, Stokes Croft.
Dining Hall, Stokes Croft.
Proposed building in Woodland Rd.
Building in Woodland Rd.

1

TO BEGIN AT THE BEGINNING

To tell the story of an institution over time is first of all to ask the question, to what extent is this the same institution? What, if any, are the enduring characteristics that allow us to speak of an identity that reaches from then, whenever then is, to now, whenever now is.

So, we want to consider to what extent there are characteristics that are recognizable, and that stretch from the Academy of 1720 through to the Bristol Baptist College of 2020 and beyond?

After all, we cannot point to a continuing physical presence—the College has occupied several different buildings and has existed in various physical forms in these three hundred years.

In order to grasp something of how it is the same institution, we will be using the themes represented by The Bristol Tradition; the formation of *lively*, *zealous*, *able*, and *evangelical* preachers of the gospel, if anything, has been the identity that has held together through the years, and the differing patterns of community life and learning and formation.

The themes have taken different patterns in different contexts, but they do, together with a commitment to a breadth of sympathy and engagement both within the denomination and across denominations, offer us a continuity of identity, when other aspects are changing.

To explore the way the themes have been shaped, addressed, and expressed, we will tell a roughly chronological story in three parts that correspond (more or less) to the three centuries of the College history, together with some reflections on particular aspects of ongoing features.

College life is the life of people brought together in particular roles and for particular purposes. Therefore, we will be navigating this story by means of the people who have lived it: for each century, we will use the succession of presidents and later principals as a framework, and we will also be looking at the stories of tutors and, more significantly, students. And since this is specifically a history of the College as an institution as well as accounts of those who have formed it, we will, insofar as we can, tell something of the educational process and content.

Inevitably, there are easy bits of the story to tell, and harder bits. Some parts are hard because there is little documentation or records are incomplete. Other parts are hard because of the story itself—controversy, broken relationship, distress, and anger. This is always true when telling history—as is the complexity that arises when we move from history as recorded in the archives into history as we remember it . . . and we will remember different parts and remember it differently. We trust, especially as you read the sections that deal with parts of College life you remember, that you will recognize the story we tell. We also trust that you will recognize that we are telling a story as we are able; it may not be what you remember, but in all things, we have tried to be true to the documents, records, and accounts that we have.

At the heart of all of the life of the College has been the city of Bristol—the institution started in the centre of the city and has remained in the city ever since. This in itself is unusual, and points to something about a commitment to stability that has been significant in the ongoing life of this community.

However, Bristol was not always what it is now.

IN THE BEGINNING . . .

Context

In 1720, Britain had a population of just over eight million. England and Wales together had a population of about five million. Over the next century, the national population was to grow to about nine million, as economic, agricultural, and social conditions improved enough to support a growing populace. At the beginning of the century, Bristol was a port city of a little over twenty thousand inhabitants, the second city of the country, though by the 1740s, it was to be overtaken by Liverpool. Cities on the whole at this time were young places; as they grew, and they grew fast in this century, it was because young men and women moved in from the country to become apprentices and to seek work. Cities were not particularly pleasant places, but they were the places of engagement and possibility. One of the possibilities that they offered—and which the Academy took up—was that of greater religious freedom, simply because of greater numbers of people.

Nationally, the Parliaments of Scotland and England had been brought into Union in 1707, and the new United Kingdom was still trying to work out who it was. In 1715 and 1745 there had been uprisings in an attempt to restore the Stuarts to the throne, but now George I was King, and there was a determined effort to build a 'British identity'. This was to be Protestant—but Protestant by a particular definition. The established church in England, the episcopal Church of England was in power and protective of its position. The link between crown and church was perceived to be important to the stability of both.

It is true that being Baptist was easier than it had been forty years previously, but it was still precarious. King Charles II, who became king when the monarchy was restored after the Civil War and the Commonwealth, had undertaken as part of The Declaration of Breda—the basis on which he was welcomed back to the country—to allow "freedom of religion in areas where it did not disturb the common peace." However, it soon became clear that this did not extend to the kind of freedom that had been enjoyed under the Commonwealth. Between 1661 and 1665 four Acts of Parliament were passed which are known as the Clarendon Code, and which curtailed toleration of religious dissent. The Corporation Act of 1661 and the Act of Uniformity in 1662 excluded Dissenters from municipal and church office respectively, unless they received the sacrament according to the Book of Common Prayer. This act also excluded Dissenters from the Universities—in England, from Oxford and Cambridge. In Oxford, a student could not be admitted without affirming the Thirty-Nine Articles and in Cambridge a student could not be awarded a degree without a similar religious test. The Conventical Act, also of 1662, forbade more than five people to meet together for worship other than according to the Book of Common Prayer and the 5-Mile Act in 1665 made it illegal for Nonconformist ministers to live or visit within five miles of a town or any other place where they had ministered. An Act of Toleration was passed in 1689, but this was not the repeal of these laws, and simply allowed some freedom around them. As far as the universities were concerned, the position did not change until the middle of the 1800s.

So, as the country was working out who it was, and how to be that, those who were religious dissenters were on the outside and unable to take part in the academic, political, and professional life of society. However, as we will see below, this did not mean inactivity on their part. Rather, it encouraged and shaped the development of an alternative and separate culture. This was true in several areas, including educational. That is the context in which we are particularly interested.

Intellectually, the very early flickers of the period we refer to as the Enlightenment, and what contemporaries called The Age of Reason, were emerging. Isaac Newton and John Locke were writing in the 1680s and their ideas were beginning to influence general thought—and theology—as our story begins. So, our exploration of the forms of and intentions behind the training of ministers has its roots in a period in which thinking about thinking was becoming important. The philosophers of the day—René Descartes, Blaise Pascal, John Locke—were concerned to understand how people know what they know, what constituted knowledge and therefore what learning looked like. This was, of course, thinking within a restricted environment, namely those who were identified with the intellectual elite. But the influence of such thinking had its impact in more general thinking about what it is to learn and to teach.

John Locke, for example, who died in 1704, had developed a powerful and influential theory of mind. He argued that, far from having certain ideas inherent within us, people were born as 'blank slates', and knowledge was derived from sensory experience and determined by those experiences. This empirical approach to knowledge and therefore to education was one of the new ideas that were part of the cultural context within which the Academy was first mooted and then actually begun. As a theory of knowledge, it raises interesting issues about how things are known and, in particular, how that which is beyond sense experience—for example, the topics of theology—is to be known. As we consider the story of the Academy, one of the themes that emerges in various guises is the necessity for and importance of education. It is possible to misread this discussion and to see it as an opposition between those who valued education and those who had little or no time for it. And it is true that this played a part in the discussion. But there is also a debate taking place, some of the time at least, about what it means to learn; whether learning takes place via books and study, or through experience and the Spirit's leading. Or, indeed, whether these positions have to be oppositional, or whether the Spirit can be active both through experience and through books.

It was also a time of rapid technological change. It was in 1712 that Thomas Newcomen first unveiled his steam-driven engine, which was to facilitate the pumping of water in deep mines—and when he was not inventing steam-driven machinery, Newcomen was a Baptist minister in Dartmouth. His connections with other Baptist churches, especially in the Midlands, helped spread the word—and the use—of his new invention. In the second half of the century, the new developments in spinning technology eventually led to the foundation of the factories, and many nonconformists, including Baptists, were involved in the owning and management of the new mills which became such a powerhouse of the economic changes in the nineteenth century. The professions still being closed to them, industry became an important part of nonconformist life, and this was just beginning to be the case as the Academy was beginning its life. As well as the importance of technology, the networks and family links that both support and emerge from these activities are important. One of the powerhouses of Britain's development of new technology in what was becoming the industrial revolution was the networks that allowed ideas and inventions such as Newcomen's engine to be spread.

It was a time of writing, especially politically. Governmental control of the press had ended in 1695 with the cessation of the Licensing Act, and political battles were often fought out through pamphlets, many of them anonymous. Journalism was a new discipline, with the beginning of the first daily newspaper in 1702. Periodicals were a growing phenomenon, and within their covers, the pattern of the essay grew. Alexander Pope was writing, both reviews and poetry, Jonathan Swift was composing satire, and David Hume was writing essays that undermined assumptions about faith. The novel was just being invented, while William Hogarth's series of engravings, The Harlot's Progress and A Rake's Progress were to be created and made widely available through the printing of the engravings.

This area of discourse was one that Dissenters took up with enthusiasm. This was an area in which they were equally free to participate and where they could attempt to influence public debate in ways that they could not otherwise. Pamphlet 'wars' between people of different theological positions, within the dissenting communities and between Dissenters and Conformists were heated by our standards, but were an important part of public debate. Many of those involved with the Academy at various points in its history were, as we will see, caught up in these debates. The capacity to take part in them and to present ideas well and powerfully therefore became increasingly important.

Economically, 1720 was the year of the South Sea Bubble, the collapse of shares that had the impact of significantly reducing the national economy. Those caught in the South Sea Bubble crash were by no means the only ones affected; there was a series of at best chancy and at worst fraudulent investment opportunities. Agriculture was still fundamental to the national economy, but trade was increasing and what we might now call 'financial services' were beginning to emerge. The Bank of England had been founded in 1694. In 1720, Isaac Gervaise published a treatise entitled *On the System or Theory of the Trade of the World*, in which he argued that credit was dangerous and undermined trade. Economics as an area of study was being shaped into the discipline that we now know, with all that that implies for how a society organized itself, and the underlying assumptions shared by those in that society; assumptions that were present within the churches as well as in other parts of the community. How people thought about money, and how people thought about how money should be used, was changing at this point.

The education that was available was largely determined both by religious conviction and class or economic capacity. The universities, as we have seen, were closed to those who were not in communion with the established church. There were the great public schools, all Anglican foundations, and only available to boys from wealthy families, with a curriculum of Classics. If such children did not board at these schools, they were tutored at home. For boys of the middle classes, there were the Grammar Schools, also concentrating on Latin and Greek. They were also just beginning the study of mathematics and natural philosophy—what becomes science. For those without the resources, or who needed to begin earning early to help support the family, there were the 'dame schools', teaching reading, and sometimes writing, and basic arithmetic. These charged a small fee, and for children who did attend, attendance would often be sporadic (in country areas, governed by the harvest, for example) and ending when it became possible for a child to be economically active. The charity schools which did not charge any fee, trained boys and girls 'for their station in life'.

In order to understand what the Academy was doing, not only when it started, but for much of its life, it is important to recognize just how limited basic education was for many of those who were part of the community it was established to serve.

The establishment of the Academy at the point when it happened was shaped by the politics of the time, and in particular, the repeal of the Schism Act in 1719. The Schism Act had been introduced in 1714, and was explicitly to stop Dissenters from running academies or schools. The Act required that anybody who was going to run a school, or be a tutor in a school, had to be licensed by the bishop, and had to receive the sacrament within an Anglican Church at least once a year. This brought the running of schools into line with the practices of the universities, and was another way of restricting the presence of Dissenters in the public life of the country. However, the Act was never enforced, since on the day when it was due to become law, Queen Anne died, and the Hanoverian house succeeded. Queen Anne had been a supporter of the Tories and of the High Church Anglican party, and with her death and the Hanoverian succession, power shifted. The Schism Act was lost, and was formally repealed in 1718 with The Religious Worship Act. This made it possible for Dissenters to open their own educational establishments.

Baptist context

It was among Dissenters that Baptists took their place. Emerging from several contexts within the reforming movement of the sixteenth century, Baptists look to two main origins. One being the English-speaking separatist community in Amsterdam, some of whom became convinced of the biblical warrant for believers' baptism, and began a congregation based on this conviction. In 1612, part of this community returned to England, and their continuing life is the beginning of the General or Arminian Baptists.

In the 1640s, a number of separatist congregations in England who maintained a Calvinist theology came to similar convictions about the nature of baptism, and gradually formed themselves into congregations around this theology. This is the beginning of the congregations of Particular Baptists.

By the time we reach the 1700s, these two expressions of Baptist life were present and established in several parts of England. The Particular Baptists were the most numerous, both in size of congregations and in number of churches.

The distribution of congregations across the country was not even: Baptists were concentrated in London, in the Midlands, and in the West Country. There were a significant number of Baptists of both persuasions in Bristol, and several churches in the city and the surrounding villages.

And so our story begins.

FOUNDING OF THE ACADEMY

Or does it?

Usually, we date the founding of the College to 1679, and claim that it is the oldest continuing dissenting academy in the country.

But of course, Dissenters had been educating their young people in a variety of ways before this: there were schools in various parts of the country run by ministers, often as a way of supplementing their income as well as providing education for those who were excluded from the schools attached to the parish churches. It was the proliferation of such schools that lay behind the introduction of the Schism Act. With the exclusion of Dissenters from the places of education following the Act of Uniformity in 1662, the dissenting community began to organize education within its own boundaries, including educating those who were going to become ministers. Teaching was also a way of earning money that was compatible with leading a church, and those who were ministers were often those with education. There were a significant number of people who had been excluded from the established church with the imposition of uniformity who were well educated. They not only valued their own education, but they were also committed to passing on these riches, and so got involved in setting up schools (one reason why the 5 Mile Act was so significant). Even prior to this, there were those in the dissenting community who were involved in providing education: Hansard Knollys, who was a leading Baptist minister of the seventeenth century was running a school in London in the 1640s, while Edward Terrill himself, whose deed of gift lies behind the founding of the Bristol Academy, was a school teacher in Bristol.

There had even been the intention to start some kind of training institution for ministers, based in London; a meeting was called in 1675, but it may not have happened. Certainly, when the churches invited did meet in 1677, education was not on the agenda, but that it was called is an indication that there was among some of the churches at least a desire for an 'educated ministry', and with the coming of freer times, this desire grew. The Baptist Assemblies that met following the Act of Toleration in 1689 did consider the issue and some argued for the importance of education. However, there was little money and no energy actually to start anything. There was, though, an agreement. Joseph Ivimey, one of the earliest Baptist historians, records in his history of early Baptists that any money raised amongst Baptists for a wider work was to be split three ways—to support struggling local churches, to send out evangelists, and, thirdly, to assist those recognized by the churches as being "disposed for study, have an inviting gift, and are sound in fundamentals, in attaining to the knowledge and understanding of the languages, Latin, Greek, and Hebrew."

The lack of money is a chronic issue in churches, but the lack of energy came at least in part because the churches were by no means of one mind about the need for education. There were those who argued that God's call and gifting were all that was needed, and indeed, that to add anything to that was in fact to diminish the ministry that would be offered. The Association of the West of England included those who argued,

> It is not the gifts of either the learned or the unlearned, but the blessing of God upon both that makes successful . . . ?

This is our first introduction in the story of the College to an argument that will appear in a variety of forms over the years. The argument here was not simply that education was unnecessary for a minister, rather it was the conviction that education could be detrimental to ministry.

After all, the Baptist churches and ministries that people knew had been thriving without such education, and indeed, it was the so-called educated ministers in the Anglican church who were among those who tried to silence and disempower Baptist leaders, often using their 'educated' skills. The rejection by the powerful in the land of so-called 'mechanical preachers', that is, preachers from the artisan classes, was borne by the Dissenters as a badge of pride and godly affirmation. Thus, this resistance was not simply to education *per se*, but to its association with power, with the elite, and with the oppressor.

Nevertheless, Terrill had signed his deed of gift, money given to the Broadmead church of which he was a member, which they would receive on his death. This money was to be used to support a minister at the church who was "well skilled in the tongues" of Greek and Hebrew, and who would spend time in preparing men for the ministry among Baptists across the country. This emphasis on "the tongues" reflects both the deep-rooted understanding of education as education in the classical languages which dominated schooling and university study at this period, and also the Reformation emphasis on the need to read Scripture as accurately as possible. Among the very early Baptists, the right and the duty to read Scripture for themselves was highly prized. The exploration of Scripture was the centre of worship and of the life of the community. For example, the order of worship that we have recorded from the earliest English speaking Baptist church in Amsterdam looks like this:

> Prayer
> Reading *one or two chapters of scripture*
> Give the sense *and discuss*
> *(lay aside books)*
> Solemne Prayer *by one who then offers*
> Exposition of a text *and prophesying out of the same for one hour or three quarters*
> Prophesying from the same text *for a similar length of time by a second speaker*
> Prophesying *by third, fourth and fifth speakers, as time allows*
> Prayer *by the first speaker* and
> Exhortation to contribute to the poor
> Collection
> Prayer

Knowing Scripture and having access to it in one's own language was a central tenet of reform, and that access was generally recognized as depending on trustworthy translation, and rejection of texts based on the Vulgate alone. Thus, education for ministry was rooted in education in the languages of Scripture. In 1689, the Particular Baptists held their first national

Assembly. Although it was the first time such a gathering had taken place, there was still the complaint that "much of that former strength, life and vigour, which attended us, has gone."

The "neglect of the ministry" was one reason given for such decline, and addressing such neglect comprised several facets, noted as

- Finding ways to help churches to pay a minister well enough so that he could devote all his time to the church, rather than having other demands on his time in order to earn money.
- Deliberately ordaining men to travel and plant churches.
- Seeking out those who were interested in and able to study, and supporting them in that.

It is the last of these that particularly concerns us, and this aspect focused specifically on forms of training in order "to attain to a competent knowledge of the Hebrew, Greek, and Latin tongues, that they may be the better capable to defend the truth against opposers."

However, such education required money, and even those who supported the need for such education found that the lack of money was an obstacle hard to overcome. Many Baptists were not well off, and such money as there was usually went elsewhere.

However, by the time of the next gathering in 1693, the enthusiasm for "acquired parts" and "human learning" was distinctly muted. There was anxiety about an educated ministry for several reasons. The danger that ministers depended on skills learned and on education, rather than on a real and living relationship with Christ, was the primary one. There was also anxiety around the pride that could come from learning, and in particular from a proud assumption that the depths of the mystery of God had somehow been attained by those who were humanly learned. There was a recognition that God might indeed choose to use those with learning, but that God could also choose to use those who were not learned, and the churches needed to be open to whatever it was that God was doing, since the work was God's and not that of humans. Overall, this position, while not absolutely ruling out the need for learning, especially of the biblical languages, was certainly less encouraging towards it.

In the years that followed, there were regularly two Assemblies, one in Bristol and one in London at different times of the year, and they did develop distinctive approaches, not least to the place of education. While the London Assembly maintained an apparent commitment to the position of 1689, there was not the money to support it. In Bristol, although there was the same wariness as exemplified in 1693, there was also a strong enough sense that education, while it could in no way replace the call and gifting of God and must never become a matter of pride, might yet be something which God could use and which therefore ought to be encouraged.

The deed of gift in which the College is rooted was a response to this move, a practical way of addressing a concern for educating ministers and "stirring up the churches".

Edward Terrill made his money as a Scrivener, that is, a writer of documents and legal papers, and as a schoolmaster. He was also a businessman, involved in the sugar trade which was developing quickly at this time. This was a couple of generations before the beginning of the resistance to slavery which was to involve the boycotting of sugar. By the 1720s Bristol was beginning to become the dominant slaving port in England, but even before that it had been one of the main centres from which chattel slaves were transported to Barbados for the sugar plantations. Both sugar and tobacco were imported to Bristol for further processing before being exported both around the country and overseas. The importing and processing of sugar in particular grew rapidly from the middle of the seventeenth century. It was from this wealth that Terrill signed the deed of gift in 1679, making money over to the church following his death, specifically to be used for the task of preparing ministers.

He lived until the mid-1680s, several years after the deed of gift. As a deed of gift rather than a bequest, the money did not become available even on his death, but remained in the care of his widow, Dorothy, who went on to marry the then minster of Broadmead, Thomas Vaux. Dorothy died in 1697. Even then it was over twenty years until the money was available and used for the purpose intended. This accounts of course for the discrepancy in the dates, but also reflects something of the anxiety and disagreement about whether such a project was appropriate. The money had been gifted—but was the will to use it present?

Terrill was not the only person to give towards this project. In 1716, another benefactor, and indeed a trustee of Terrill's will, Robert Bodenham, also set up a trust for the work of education. This was not a novel idea, as even before Terrill's money became available, Broadmead Church was already committed to trying to offer training for ministers using existing funds. They had made a start (possibly in 1710?) by appointing Caleb Jope as assistant to their minister, Peter Kitterell, with responsibility for teaching those who would be ministers. Kitterell had been called to the pastorate at Broadmead in 1707 and served until his death in 1727, with the church declining during his time. He does not seem to have been a successful minister. Jope's role as assistant and teacher also does not seem to have gone well either, and he left for Exeter in 1719.

In 1720, the church invited Bernard Foskett to take up the role of assistant minister and educator, and this time used the Terrill and Bodenham money to pay his stipend. This is the point at which it becomes possible to speak of an institution or organization with sufficient identity and permanency to allow us to see continuity through to our own day.

The themes of the nature of and indeed necessity for education, and the struggle for money will be themes that recur as we tell our story. And a story of three hundred years takes some navigating. So, we will chart our way through by looking at those who carried responsibility for delivering the education, and raising the money; the principals (and at times, other tutors) and also those who benefited from the education and were part of the ongoing funding, namely the students. This is the story of an institution—but an institution is people.Not all those who have made the College what it were covered in the original research, and therefore in this text there are some significant gaps. The story of those who, bringing expertise from many other fields, as they served on committees, fundraising efforts or trusteeship is not told. Nor has there yet been work on those—apart from the two at the beginning—whose generosity has supported the College through the years.

However, an institution is more than just a collection of people who happen to come together. It also has a purpose and an identity; a set of common features that distinguishes it. For the College, these are best summed up in what has come to be known as The Bristol Tradition.

The Bristol Tradition

It is worth outlining the Bristol Tradition at this point in our account, even if it is slightly to anticipate aspects of the story. The Education Society was founded in 1770, and the reasons for and impact of its founding are told below. As part of its founding, a constitution was drawn up. After an "Introduction", the purpose was outlined thus:

> To the end that dissenting congregations, especially of the Baptist denomination, in any part of the British dominions, may, if it please God to succeed our endeavors, be more effectually supplied with a succession of *able and evangelical ministers*

In 1781, Hugh Evans, who had been president of the Academy, as the role was then called, died. His son, Caleb Evans, preached at his funeral and spoke about his father's aim in the Academy, using language that was very much of its time—a culture and period when people were reflecting on the possibility of making a difference through human endeavour and control.

This very Enlightenment approach, that it was possible to manipulate the world and make things happen, comes out in the language of instrumentality. Caleb Evans summed up his father's aim as being

> not merely to form substantial scholars but as far as in him lay he was desirous of being made an instrument in God's hands of forming them, *able, evangelical, lively, zealous Ministers of the gospel*.

This idea of being an instrument, a means by which God made things happen, was present in various parts of Baptist life at this time. It is there, for example, in William Carey's *Enquiry* ten years later. Here in Evans's summary, it is an important affirmation. The four adjectives describing what Bristol-trained ministers were to be are usually the words that we focus on. Each has its own particular weight: *able* speaks directly to training, with the expectation that there were tasks to be performed and they should be performed well, but it also—perhaps primarily—refers to skills in Scripture interpretation and preaching; *evangelical* identified the College as part of the movement emerging from the revival that affected the United Kingdom and the United States in the 1730s and 1740s, most helpful conceptualized nowadays as cross-centred, Bible-centred, expecting conversion and activist in society; *lively* is a term that draws a comparison with the perceived formalism of the established church; while *zealous* draws on the scriptural description of the zeal of the Lord, implying effort and commitment. But there is more here than just a description of what those trained through the Education Society should be. There is also a statement as to how it is to happen. Evans insisted it is not through human skill and endeavour alone, but through God's use of human willingness and ability. In the ongoing debate about the role of education in preparing for ministry, and the balance between the call and gifting of God, or the skills and abilities latent in an individual and honed and developed by education and training, this argument made by Evans takes a position. Clearly, the answer must always be the call and gifting of God.

However, there were at the beginning, and have always been, some who saw the work done within the Colleges as, at best, undermining an existing call and already present gifting, and at worst, 'training' people to be ministers who were not called of God, but who had skills and personality that led them to consider this a good 'job', one that was respectable, or granted power or recognition. Also, it was suggested, there might be people who were pushed into the position in order to gratify the aims and ambitions of others, such as family or church. There has also been, at times, a suspicion of the education and training provided by the College. Has it concentrated too much on intellectual skills at the cost of true and sustaining spirituality, has it in fact been detrimental to a living and lively faith, has it trained preachers and scholars who are out of touch with local congregations?

These discussions occur, quite properly, at various points in the College's story. Such discussion is appropriate, because it is important that the life and work of the College, in modern parlance its aims and objectives, should be kept under review and should be held to account against its 'mission statement' to be an instrument in God's hands to form able, evangelical, lively, zealous ministers of the gospel. By situating it as an instrumental intention, that is, that the College is always and only ever an instrument of God in this work, then many of the objections are overcome. But we, like all of those who have gone before us, are all too aware of the ability of institutions and people within institutions to lose that first phrase, and to concentrate on what 'we' do. Therefore, the questioning of the purpose and place of the institution has always been for its good in its developing life.

The breadth of its purpose is also important and always has been. Six years prior to the statement we have just discussed, in 1775, Caleb Evans had stated that "the education of pious candidates for the ministry" was "the first object of the Institution, the encouragement of missionaries to preach the gospel wherever providence opens a door" being the second. In his shortened version of Evans's 1781 statement, and writing three years after the formation of the Baptist Missionary Society (BMS), Rippon echoed Evans's words when in his summary of "the design" of the Education Society he used the words of its constitution which stated its aim to supply "the dissenting congregations, especially of the Baptist denomination, in any part of the British dominions, if it please God" with "a succession of able and evangelical ministers." To this he immediately added, "and that missionaries may be sent to those places where there is an opening for the gospel." This extract shows that from the outset the Education Society's constitution envisaged training non-Baptists for their respective ministries on the same terms as they prepared Baptist students. In fact, Samuel Stennett commented on how Caleb Evans "cordially embraced" "all who loved the Lord Jesus Christ in sincerity and truth, of whatever denomination," and was always "ready to serve" them "to the utmost of his power."

Thus, alongside the adjectives with which we are familiar in defining the Bristol Tradition there is the presence if not the explicit naming of another facet, that of what we might call 'catholicity': the refusal of a narrow denominational (or, within the denomination, a party) position, and a willingness to embrace all those who embrace the Saviour, and to work together with those of differing shades of opinion for the sake of the Kingdom. This commitment to catholicity takes the form both of cross-denominational work, which has different shapes at different times but which is a nonetheless a consistent presence, and of inter-Baptist work, expressed through a commitment to the connexional life of the denomination, shown in association, union, and societies. We will see as the story progresses that in various ways, the life of the College and the work and vision of those who shaped it and were shaped by plays an important part in the connexional life of Baptists.

This is the identity that is emerging in the early eighteenth century, is articulated in the middle of that century, and has continued to point to the distinctive features of the nature of the College.

So, how did the succession of tutors and principals work with the men who came to Bristol in that first hundred years of the College's life to "form [. . .] scholars [. . .] who would be able, lively, evangelical, zealous ministers of the gospel?

2

THE FIRST HUNDRED YEARS

PRINCIPALS FROM 1720 TO 1825

THIS CHAPTER WILL LOOK at the century covered by four principals, and we will look at several themes within this time. We consider funding and the way in which it changed. We will also see ways in which understandings of education, both its form and necessity, were more fully articulated, and how this was expressed in the Bristol Tradition. We will briefly look at some of those who came to train, and at what it was they learned, asking what was nature of the education provided, and how did it change over these hundred years? We will also tell of the founding of the Education Society—a financial move that allows the articulation of the Bristol Tradition. And it is in the Education Society and in the Bristol Tradition that continuity and identity is located; they emerge from the context we have outlined, and they lead through the years to the place where we currently find ourselves.

Bernard Foskett worked alongside Kitterell and acted as tutor for the young men and as principal of the Academy until 1758. In 1728, when Kitterell died, Foskett became minister at Broadmead, and the church appointed Andrew Gifford as his assistant and tutor to the students. Gifford only stayed a year, and in 1734, Hugh Evans was appointed to the post. When Foskett died in 1758, Hugh Evans became senior minister and principal, and in 1759, he was joined by his son Caleb Evans as tutor and assistant minister. Caleb Evans succeeded his father as principal and served in that post until 1791. He in turn was succeeded by John Ryland, who served as minister of Broadmead church and president of what had by then become the Bristol Education Society until 1825.

Knowing something of those who came to train and what they studied will be important—and in order to understand something of their story, we need to consider what Foskett, both the Evanses, and Ryland each brought to the role of principal.

Bernard Foskett

As we have said, it was following Bernard Foskett's appointment as assistant minister and tutor that the first students arrived—two Welsh men. Thus, the institution began to take shape, a shape at this stage determined by the leadership offered by Foskett.

Academically very able, Foskett had been involved in Baptist churches since his late teens. He was originally planning a career in medicine, but in 1711 he left that in order to work with John Beddome, in the church in Henley in Arden. He had become very friendly with Beddome while he was minister at Horsleydown in Southwark, and since no other form of training was available at the time, it may be that he was effectively Beddome's student, or perhaps we might better say 'apprentice'.

There is not a great deal of information about Foskett as an individual, his personality or his beliefs, but we do know some things. He was firmly within the Calvinist identity of the Particular Baptists, but is also described as "being fond of no extreme"; the capacity to work alongside a range of beliefs and outlooks is thus ingrained in the identity of the Academy from the start with its first tutor and eventual principal.

The statement of faith to which he put his name while working with Beddome is clearly committed to a deep biblicism, to the headship of Christ in the church, and to a traditionally Calvinist statement about the cross and salvation, expressed through predestination. He also used language, later associated with Carey, while he was working with Beddome about seeking to "spread the tent wider, lengthen the cords and strengthen the stakes"—an illustration that his was a Calvinism of the activist kind that sought to work according to means.

Though we know nothing of Foskett's teaching methods, we do know, from comments of Hugh Evans, that he treated the students as individuals rather than having a set course that everybody had to follow rigidly. The studying that students undertook was worked out in line with their interests, abilities and presumably pre-existing education. As we saw above, opportunities for early education could for many people be quite limited, and the education offered at the College could not assume an existing strong foundation in every case.

Foskett was not universally admired. J. C. Ryland, a student in Bristol between 1744 and 1746, notes in his diary in March 1784 that

> [he] should have spared no pains to educate our souls to grandeur and to have enriched and impregnated them with great and generous ideas of God in his whole natural and moral character, relations and actions, to us and the universe. This was thy business, thy duty, this honour, O Foskett! and this thou didn't totally neglect.

Nonetheless, thanks to Foskett's work, first as tutor, then as principal, the Academy was started, and began to acquire some of those characteristics that remain part of the continuing identity: the solid Calvinism that marked it for so many generations, yet open to other theologies and practices; the commitment to Scripture and its exposition; and the involvement in the wider community, as Baptists, through Association, and in evangelism.

Hugh Evans

Foskett became minister of Broadmead and principal of the Academy in 1728. It was not until 1734 that a colleague was appointed who stayed— Hugh Evans. He became, as Foskett had been, assistant minister and tutor. This was the only church that Evans served, and his commitment to both church and College were lifelong. He had come to Bristol from Brecon for medical reasons. He was baptized by Foskett and become a member of the church, and one of Foskett's students.

They appear to have been alike both in theology and temperament, and when Evans succeeded to the principalship on Foskett's death in 1758 it is unlikely that much in the mood and the teaching of the College would have changed.

John Rippon, one of Evans's students later wrote a history of the Academy. He had joined the Academy in 1769 and, along with other students, lived with Evans and his wife and family. The community was small at the time, and operated more as an extended household with apprentices than the kind of institution that it was later to become. This was a common model in various spheres: extended households in order to allow men, especially those who were barred from the universities, to learn a skill or trade. It was a blending of the collegiate and apprentice model, and was very fruitful.

The depth of relationship between the principal (and his wife we assume) and the students is noticeable in Rippon's writing, and it is also clear that the relationships continued after students left Bristol. Evans's continued interest in their ministry and well-being was a mark of the affection that existed between them. Is it here, perhaps, in the expectation of continuing contact even after the years of formal College involvement have ended, that we see the clearest roots of the importance of community that remains a mark of the continuing institution?

Evans was also recognized as a good teacher—and one who was less severe than Foskett. The number of students was low at the time, but the standard of teaching remained important, and there was an expectation that the students would develop their abilities as much as they could.

We only have three published sermons of Hugh Evans, but in them we can trace a theology and worldview that clearly underlay his teaching and practice:

- The able minister must be converted—and able to preach for conversion.
- Thus, the able minister must be a good preacher who can teach the congregation the content of their faith.
- Such teaching must be soundly and deeply biblically based.
- There is an expectant activism in such preaching—there is a task to undertake for God, and that must be done to the best of the preacher's ability.

That is, he was concerned that at the heart of any ministry was a personal experience of Christ, and a trust in the grace of God, together with an impulse and calling to share that. Right at the very beginning then, there was an emphasis on the call and activity of God first, the place of conversion in the life of the would-be minister, and then and only then, the acquisition of those skills and capacities that would enable an individual to 'be useful' among the churches.

Caleb Evans

With Hugh Evans's appointment as senior minister and principal in 1758, another assistant minister and tutor was needed, and Hugh's son Caleb was appointed in 1759 and served, like his father, first as tutor then as principal until 1791. One of those who worked as a tutor with him was Robert Hall, whom we will consider in more detail below.

In Caleb Evans's time, the nature of Calvinism was much debated, and his students were part of this discussion, as we shall see below. It was also under his care that the Bristol Education Society was founded, which changed the relationship between the Academy and Broadmead Church—and therefore other churches. This also changed the nature of the principalship. We shall see more of Caleb Evans's work and influence as we consider all of these topics.

John Ryland

Caleb Evans was succeeded by John Ryland—but by now, it was a different position. As we have seen, Ryland was one of Foskett's students, and having finished his College time, he became pastor in Warwick, and then College Street, Northampton, where he also ran a school.

Ryland was a complex and highly intelligent man, often unpredictable in what he said, and caused some consternation with his views at various points in his ministry.

He came to Broadmead Church following a difficult time between Caleb Evans and Robert Hall, and was inducted as associate minister and tutor in 1794.

Like his predecessors, he was firmly evangelical in his theology, expressing this through the evangelical Calvinism that was emerging in the contemporary debates. Ryland was deeply influenced by the Calvinism associated with Jonathan Edwards and as such was part of the movement that shaped the particular form of Calvinism in the Western Association and the Northamptonshire Association during this period. This was a change for him; he had started out as a follower of John Brine, the significant High Calvinistic preacher and writer, and had been a Calvinist within the high tradition. However, as he noted, Edwards's writings, and conversations with Andrew Fuller and others had encouraged him to change his mind. We will discuss this more below when we look at the controversies over theology. However, in understanding his position as principal, it is important to note not only his position theologically, but also the way in which, as the principal of the only Baptist Academy in the country at the time, he had a particular role in helping to spread this theology, not only through the churches in England, but also because of his association with and support for overseas mission, into the formation and founding of churches in other parts of the world.

He was also convinced that it was important that his students were familiar with those of other convictions, and therefore encouraged discussion across the denominations—again, a pattern that was present from the beginning but became more marked as the Academy took on more of an 'institutional' form. The Bristol Tradition has long included within it an understanding that the church of God is broader than the stream within which the College was established and worked.

Education as important for ministry, and mission and evangelism as central to ministry were also patterns that, having been established, Ryland nurtured and developed in his own way.

These four men in particular, each serving first as tutor and then as principal, shaped and guided the Academy through its first hundred years. Under their leadership, it was firmly evangelical within the Calvinist tradition, committed to Scripture and to preaching, involved in mission as well as the care of established churches, and determined to offer the best and most appropriate education to each of the students who came to share its life.

BEING A STUDENT

Who came to College?

The first question to be asked of anybody coming to College throughout this period was whether he had a lively and experiential faith in Christ—that is, was he truly converted?

This was a matter of some real consideration in the mid-part of the eighteenth century, as the debate within Calvinism known as The Modern Question, was at its height. The Question is simply put: should unconverted people be invited to trust in Christ, or is that to undermine the sovereignty of God, who will call the elect? In this debate, the Bristol Academy was firmly on the side of those who believed in inviting people to respond to the call of Christ—and as such, the expectation was that all those who were training to make such an invitation should themselves have responded to it.

Alongside a "lively faith" a man was expected to have demonstrated a capacity to preach, and a "desire to be useful." Such a desire would be both perceived and encouraged by family and by a local church. Thus, for example, Thomas Llewelyn, one of the very first to be enrolled, joined his local church at sixteen. His gifts and personality were soon noticed in such a way that "both his friends and the church 'felt it their duty to distinguish and encourage him with a view to ministerial usefulness'" Participation within a local church, baptism, and membership were also expected—though in certain cases, this seems to have waived for pragmatic reasons.

What was studied?

The shape of what was studied changed over the century, and was, of course, a matter of controversy and debate. But normally included were the study of languages, Greek and Hebrew, and also Latin and the reading of the Classics; biblical studies encompassing a knowledge of the Scriptures and of the history of the Scriptures; and divinity, which was the systematic study of doctrine and biblical themes. At times during the century, Jewish history and church history, evidences for Christianity (apologetics), and logic, geography, astronomy, natural philosophy, and moral philosophy were all part of what was studied. These latter in particular were areas of uncertainty; should they be included, and if so, how?

In 1771, we have record of what one of the students, a Mr Dunscombe, did that year, in a letter he wrote to family:

> The history of Gallic and Civil Wars on Caesar's commentaries. The first six books of Virgil's Aeneid. Two books of Grotius on the Truth of the Christian Religion. The first three Orations of Cicero. The four Gospels in the Greek New Testament. Abridged: great part of the first volume of Dr Gill's "Body of Divinity" and the first part of Watts' "Logic" Repeated memoriter; Mr Turner's introduction to Rhetoric and the Greek Grammar. Translated into English; Two Centuries of Turretinus; and into Latin thirty chapters of Ecclesiastical History. Wilmott's Particles. And wrote once a week from some passage of Scripture.

Students were also expected—indeed required—to preach in various places, and at certain points in the year, to spend time based in local churches, as well as being involved in itinerant missions. One of the aspects of the developing Evangelical Revival was the interest in and commitment to "going out," and this was a significant part of the way the students exercised their "usefulness" and developed their skills.

Preaching within College for comment and criticism was also part of the curriculum, as was preaching "in the vestry" at Broadmead. This was a midweek sermon which provided a kind of half-way house between "preaching class" and leading Sunday worship for a congregation.

At the beginning of the College's life, it would probably be more accurate to speak of mentoring than a formal College course. As we have seen, students and tutors lived together, and reading and discussion was largely individually tailored and followed the interests, strengths, and needs of the particular student, as well as the resources of those who were tutor and principal at the time.

The intention behind the teaching was to produce ministers who would fulfil the terms of the Bristol Tradition. What such a minister would look like was outlined, for example, in an ordination sermon that Caleb

Evans preached. He highlighted six facets of what a minister would do. They were

> to preach the word, to lead public prayer, to preside over and regulate the singing of psalms, to administer the ordinances of baptism and the Lord's Supper, to rule but not lord over the government of the church and to visit the people.

Though probably encompassed within the understanding of preaching, it is interesting to notice that the role of evangelist was not identified specifically. At this stage among Baptists, the minister was very much the 'pastor-teacher' of the congregation—and also the worship leader! The singing of psalms (hymns were not yet accepted, and indeed, the role of singing was one of the major debates among Baptists) was, we can assume, a significant part of the gathering to worship. One is left wondering if the capacity to lead singing was part of the discerning of a call (though we should also note that making music, both instrumental and vocal was a much more widespread skill in that period).

There were times when the College's course and its method of teaching were not wholly popular, even among those who were teaching there. In 1792, Joseph Hughes, who had been a student at the Bristol Academy in his mid-teens, and then gone to Aberdeen University for further study, was appointed as temporary assistant at Broadmead and as an assistant tutor at the Academy. He stayed on as tutor after Caleb Evans died and was assistant to Ryland in the ministry at Broadmead.

However, his assessment of the Academy's teaching and curriculum was not complimentary.

> Bristol Academy both in its literary and its theological departments, was, while I continued there, and perhaps for forty years afterwards, deficient in system and in stimulants.

Part of this appears to have been to do with the educational attainments of those coming to study; many did not have the benefit of a grammar school training, and so were starting from a low base of training and existing knowledge. There was also the practical limitation of the number of tutors. When Hughes compared his experience in Aberdeen, and later Edinburgh, with his experience both as a student and later as a tutor in Bristol he was aware of the disparity of resources. But he was also anxious about the calibre of students being accepted. In a sermon which he is recorded as delivering to the Bristol Education Society, he is very cutting about the students who see ministry as leading to an easy life; he insisted that the freedom that students had from "normal" duties was not an opportunity for "inglorious repose," but "an impressive summons from your heavenly Master to *arduous*, not to say *severe* exertions."

There was also a shared anxiety about the way in which preaching was taught. A Mr Thompson, who was a retired minister from Clapham, was one of those who backed Hughes to come to the Academy. He wrote to him when he was a tutor, commenting that "the seminary at Bristol" was continuing "to go on in the old absurd method" of sending students out to preach, and then instructing them. To do so, was, he argued, "a disgrace and a reproach to the institution," and he was surprised that "the directors and managers do not see the absurdity." The training in and teaching of preaching has always been a matter of contention!

Other criticisms included that of one of Robert Hall's students, Aspland, who later became a Unitarian. He criticized Hall for elevating classical learning in ways that were unhelpful. Aspland also critiqued the "smallness of mind" of his fellow students. Certainly, he found himself in conflict with them over theological issues. We will look in more detail later at the issues of orthodoxy and heterodoxy in the Academy, but it is an important reflection on the nature of the training, that the issue of just which questions were allowed and which were shut down, if not by tutors, then by fellow students, was noted from the early days.

By the end of the century, the Academy was employing part-time tutors, sometimes laymen, to teach students particular subjects. Some of these tutors were not Baptist, but they brought a particular skill that the students needed. For example, in 1805, a Wesleyan Methodist called Benjamin Donne, was appointed part-time tutor in mathematics. As indicated above, with the teaching of mathematics, as well as the concentration on classics, natural philosophy (science), and astronomy, we can see that the curriculum was rather different from a contemporary one.

What does become clear in looking at what was taught, and how, over this first century, is that the understanding of what resources ministers needed in order to serve the churches well, and how the College should respond to their situation, shifted and refocused as the context changed. At the beginning of the century, there was a great deal of emphasis on languages and on engaging with the debates within Calvinism, and in particular, the Modern Question debate. This debate was heated in the 1730s, with pamphlets and sermons on each side, the sides being whether the gospel could/should be freely offered to non-believers or not. The implications of this question and the different directions in which the different answers led dominated both writing and preaching in many Baptist contexts in the middle years of the century, and therefore shaped the nature of the study undertaken by those who wished to serve the churches.

This did not disappear, but as the century progressed, questions of "evidences for Christianity" and in particular, how faith was to be presented and defended in the developing Enlightenment context, became more and more important. Thus Thomas Exley, appointed in 1809 to teach biblical studies and natural philosophy, was the first tutor from the Bristol Tradition notable for addressing the increasingly complex and controversial relationship between Scripture and science, and as such, to attempt, however unconvincingly as it turned out, an apologetic aspect to his writings, something he would have certainly addressed in his lectures to the Academy's students.

We note several things from this, one being that the scientific and mathematical subjects were taught, in part, as apologetics. The possibility of "reading the book of Creation" as part of the revelation of God was a quite explicit expectation, not only of seminary trained preachers, but of all who shared an early-modern-becoming-Enlightenment mind set. Just as we saw earlier with the Enlightenment understanding of instrumentality as the capacity to shape and indeed change the world through action, so the notion that creation revealed the creator was being widely explored. William Paley, for example, who wrote of God the watchmaker, was writing his apologetics in the 1790s. Thus, these subjects were crucial for any preacher who was going to engage with the debates and issues of the time. However, it is also an indication that those who came to the Academy were not normally very well educated in any rounded sense. There had often been a great deal of prior reading, but most of it seems to have been around scriptural and theological topics. Since, as we have seen, universal education, even for men, was not yet the norm, part of what was going on for those who came to study was a broadening of their understanding, and the development of an all-round education.

This raising of sights and standards of behaviour was to become even more important later, but at this stage, one of the aspects of the physical experience of College is all too easily overlooked. As we have said, students lived first in the home of the principal, and later, as we will discuss below, in community in the College building. Part of the intention of these arrangements was to enable young men to become at ease at table and in the drawing room. Again, this was to become more important in the following century, but in the eighteenth century 'politeness' was a dominating concept: knowing how to behave in company, how to dress, speak, and move were becoming increasingly important. Though most Baptists were not among the elite of society, yet there was an increasing awareness of what it was to behave 'well', and a need for ministers to be able to conduct themselves appropriately. That this was beginning to be part of the College training is clear—and that it was mistrusted, even more so in later years.

So tutors, who were, until the early nineteenth century, all part-time, were not only there to educate in Scripture, doctrine, languages, and history, but in how to speak, walk, eat, and argue.

In 1825, under a new principal, it was decided that all tutors should be full-time, and so things changed, as we will see below.

Who attended?

In this first hundred years, the students came from across England and from Wales. From the 1730s, there had regularly been a student from Wales as part of the College, and from the 1770s, this increased, reflecting the increase in the number of Baptist churches in South Wales in particular. This proved a linguistic challenge to the College, and at times the English-speaking students were less than respectful of their Welsh-speaking colleagues. The presence of Hugh Evans as the tutor and principal was helpful in strengthening these links; he was a fluent Welsh speaker, and it was largely through his presence that these links were established.

There were links too with other establishments in the United Kingdom. Students, though not yet allowed to attend university in England, did study in Scotland, especially in Aberdeen, where the theology faculty had a high reputation. The other major set of links was with the United States of America, where many students travelled, and indeed settled. There were strong links with educational establishments in the USA. One student, Morgan Edwards (see below), was, for example, instrumental in founding a Baptist College on Rhode Island in America, a College that eventually became Brown University. This university then repaid the 'debt' by conferring honorary degrees on various Bristol students, an action that was particularly significant at a time when studying at university was still not possible in England.

There are all sorts of records of those who attended in these first years, and it is to be hoped that somebody else will be able to cover them again in some detail. Here, we will simply look at some examples, one from each principal.

The first student to be recorded in the minute book of Broadmead was one Thomas Rogers, a member of the Pithay Church in Bristol. He was to be supported to the sum of ten pounds a year, and to study under Bernard Foskett. However, he appears to have died within the year, and the next year, the minute book records a similar support for John Philips to be "instructed in Hebrew by Bro Foskett."

The nature of the deed of gift was debated in the church—whether the fund was to allow the training for men who came to the city for that purpose or only those who were already present, and presumably, therefore, part of the Baptist community in the city. Those who came to train in these early years, presumably continued to live at home if they were already resident in the city and to serve the churches where they were already known, attending at set times for teaching in the various subjects.

A student who was there under both Foskett and Evans, and who clearly benefitted from Evans's teaching and the way in which it appears to have broadened the work done by Foskett, was Morgan Edwards. His dates are somewhat confused, but he came to the Academy in the mid-1740s. He studied for two years, and then served a church in Cork, probably for about nine years. This was followed by a year in Sussex and then he moved to Philadelphia, where he served a church for "many years," resigning eventually because "it was not prospering." He continued to preach in various congregations who were without ministers, and then, during the American War of Independence, kept silent (we will discuss issues connected with the War of Independence below). Following the war, he bought and worked in a plantation, and also wrote and lectured, with a particular interest in Baptist history. His involvement in the founding of Brown University was to be very important not just for Baptists in America (and incidentally in the UK) but in the civil life of the new country as a whole. His commitment to education was something that he brought with him to his new country, and to which he was particularly dedicated.

A student who studied under both Hugh and Caleb Evans was John Kingdon, who had listened to and been deeply influenced by Robert Day. He was the minster in Wellington, Somerset, and had trained at Bristol. While Kingdon was still studying, the church in Frome invited him to consider becoming their minister when his studies ended. But he chose not to commit himself, since he planned at least another two years at College; thus, we can see both that settlement could happen at any time during a course, and that a course was now understood to be two or three years. Kingdon's later ministry, which was indeed at Frome, was also deeply involved with the Association—he was president three times, and wrote the annual letter five times. This part of his ministry demonstrates another aspect of the Bristol identity—that of connexionalism. This is something we will see repeated both in those who taught and those were trained, as a deeply important part of being Baptist.

He was also a gifted evangelist, and during his time at Frome, the church experienced what Roger Hayden in his history called "a revival," and a new church was formed.

These snapshots of people who trained under the first four principals show us ways in which the Bristol Tradition was taking shape and being worked out in 'every day' ministry. The training in biblical and classical languages, in preaching, in philosophy and science, and in various other subjects, together with the practical development through living in a home together and working in various churches short and long term was producing those who could rightly be described as able, evangelical, lively, and zealous. They were also shaped by an assumption of catholicity and connexionalism, and mission and evangelism were at the heart of their practice.

BROADENING THE BASE

It was during these hundred years that the Academy was reconstituted from a local church initiative, run by and through the congregation at Broadmead into the Bristol Education Society. This was an initiative of Caleb Evans, and was intended to "further, support and encourage the work of the Bristol Baptist Academy" at a time when "some very worthy people who, from a mistaken view of things, not only call in question the importance of such an education, but even seem to imagine that is rather prejudicial than useful."

In 1770, Hugh Evans as president and Caleb Evans as tutor wrote to Baptist churches around England and Wales to explain their intentions and raise support. They argued that more churches were seeking an educated ministry in order to support their work and mission in a changing context. They pointed out that there were some being trained, but not many, and that there was not sufficient finance to support them for long enough for the training to be effective. People were invited to become "subscribers" to the society, following a model that was widespread at the time. The constitution of the Society laid out its aims, as we have seen:

> To the end that dissenting congregations, especially of Baptist denomination in any part of the British dominions, may, if it please God to succeed our endeavours, be more effectually supplied with a succession of able and evangelical ministers.

Five years later, Caleb Evans wrote that the first aim of the Education Society was the "education of pious candidates for the ministry" and the second "the encouragement of missionaries to preach the gospel wherever providence opens a door."

Again, elements of the Bristol Tradition are clearly expressed here; not just the training of those who are able and evangelical, but the emphasis on mission overseas and on catholicity, on the training being not only for

Baptists and not only for Baptist churches. This, as we might anachronistically call it, ecumenical ideal is not something that could be taken for granted at that time, but is noteworthy, as are the limits within which it worked. This ecumenism was primarily among Dissenters, and definitely among evangelicals who, in Caleb Evans's words, "love the Lord in sincerity and truth."

Twelve trustees were appointed to the Education Society, mainly, though not exclusively, from the West of England and the Academy was institutionally separated from Broadmead Church. However, a strong relationship with the church, and with whoever was its minister, continued. This broadening of the support base was important. No longer an initiative of an individual congregation, the College now began to develop a place within the denomination, indeed as part of the denomination in its own right.

Some students continued to be funded by the Terrill Fund and others were now supported by the Society. There were also students supported financially by the Particular Baptist Fund, based largely in London, and by the Bristol Baptist Fund. And some were, as now, supported by home churches and family.

CONTROVERSIES AMONG BAPTISTS

Calvinist debates

The nature of Calvinist theology was under debate, and this was a debate in which the Academy played a significant part.

We have already seen part of it in reference to The Modern Question, but this is a topic worth taking a longer look at here, since it was a controversy that had a significant impact on Baptist life, and was not only shaped by, but shaped the Academy. The terms used to describe the two sides in this conflict are usually High Calvinism and Moderate Calvinism or warm Calvinism. It is important to recognize that both sides laid claim to be inheritors of the theology of John Calvin—although High Calvinists were known sometimes to accuse their Moderate opponents of being Arminians, and Moderates accused High Calvinists of being Antinomian.

The Modern Question (whether it was right to invite sinners to respond to the gospel invitation) reflected two points over which there was dispute. The High Calvinist position, developed first from the teaching of Tobias Crisp, a minister in the first half of the seventeenth century whose work was republished in 1690, argued for such a high doctrine of election to the extent that it was said God would save the elect without any significant action, such as a response of faith, on an individual's part. This had become the dominant teaching of some significant Baptist preachers in the early eighteenth century, especially, for example, John Gill, minister of Horsleydown in London. The consequence of this teaching was that preaching was not understood to have any invitational impetus; it was to edify believers, but on no account to give the impression that an individual could, by their own action, even by making a faith commitment, respond to the activity of grace in their lives.

In 1737, an Independent minister published a pamphlet *A Modern Question Modestly Answered*, in which he challenged this position. He argued "God does in His Word plainly and plentifully make it the duty of unbelievers to believe in Christ"; that is, it was right and scriptural to preach in such a way that people were challenged to consider the demands of faith.

This by no means settled the question and it became the dominant topic for debate for a long time. It seems that Baptists have in every generation a discussion which divides; one which polarizes opinion over a particular matter, but also provides markers for a whole series of other divisions. To hold a particular position on the major question of the day also determines or indicates where one belongs on a range of other matters. For Baptists and other Calvinists in the first half of the eighteenth century, The Modern Question was that issue.

In identifying the aims of the Academy as the forming of lively, able, zealous, and evangelical ministers of the gospel, the Society placed itself in the party of Moderate Calvinism in two ways. Firstly, the Bristol Tradition identified the Academy with evangelicalism, and the acceptance of means to fulfil the purposes of God. Thus, preaching was expected to be "invitational," and it was accepted that people have the capacity to respond.

Secondly, the commitment to education, and its instrumental aspect was a feature of Moderate Calvinism. Education was not rejected by High Calvinists absolutely; there were many who affirmed the importance of good learning, especially in "divinity" and in Scriptural languages and history. But the anxiety about interfering with the intentions of God and the activity of God did lead to a wariness among some with regard to human learning. We will see this wariness re-emerge in the process of another of the controversies.

One of the leading lights in the development of Moderate Calvinism, or as we might call it evangelical Calvinism, was Jonathan Edwards. His writings were particularly important to Caleb Evans, and he recommended them to his students. He described Edwards as "the most rational scriptural, divine and the liveliest Christian, the world was ever blessed with."

Andrew Fuller, whose pamphlet *The Gospel Worthy of Full Acceptation* was one of the most significant and influential arguments for evangelical Calvinism, was greatly influenced by Caleb Evans's *An Address to the serious and candid professors of Christianity*, in which he explored and explained much of Edwards's theology. Thus, though not a student at Bristol, Fuller was still influenced by the theology being taught there. Together with other writings which moulded his evangelical Calvinism, he developed into one of leading exponents of this theology—and one who helped to provide the theological foundation for the beginning of BMS. In its turn, the thinking and theology of the Academy was shaped by Fuller's writing.

It is this theology which means that the Bristol Education Society, the Academy it supported and the Tradition it nurtured can be firmly placed within the Evangelical tradition. The Evangelical movement was taking shape and developing its identity from the 1730s, just as the infant College was finding its feet. By the time the Education Society was defining aims and expressing its distinctives, Evangelicalism had an established identity. The marks of Evangelicalism, as defined and named by David Bebbington in terms of the Bible, the Cross, conversionism, and activism, can all be seen in the preaching and the teaching of both Caleb and Hugh Evans, and are therefore to be understood as implied in Caleb Evans's use of the term in the definitions of the Education Society.

This was a significant marker for the Education Society in terms of, for example, distinguishing it from The Particular Baptist Fund which was set up in 1717. That fund outlined its theological stance in 1771 in a circular to supporting churches with a definition of those for whom the fund was intended:

> By Particular Baptists are intended, those that have been solemnly immersed in water, upon a personal confession of faith; and who profess the Doctrines of—Three Divine Persons, in the Godhead,—Eternal and Personal Election—Original Sin—Particular Redemption—Efficacious Grace in Regeneration and Sanctification—Free Justification, by the Imputed Righteousness of Christ—and the Final Perseverance of the Saints—according the Confession of Faith that was published in London, by the Calvinist Baptist, in the year 1689.

As Tim Grass, who quotes this in his history of the Particular Baptist Fund comments, "Clearly by now an explicit definition of the term 'Particular Baptist' was felt necessary." And this was so, partly because of the debate over Calvinism itself.

Trinitarianism

This debate about Calvinism was to continue through the hundred years we are currently examining. But it was by no means the only theological dispute that affected Baptists, or even evangelicals. Although in this dispute, the Academy had, on the whole, a clear position that was accepted by everybody, in the debate concerning the nature of Christ, the other question that dominated the later part of the eighteenth century, things were less clear cut.

One of the impacts of the rationalism of the Age of Reason, or Enlightenment, was the questioning of the divinity of Jesus. This was by no means a new question—it had troubled the church at the end of the third century, and led to the calling of the Nicaean Council and the development of the Nicene Creed, which did not, at the time or later, settle the question. However, the debates about the nature of the Trinity, and specifically about the person of Jesus, re-emerge at various points, particularly when there is a challenge to a dominant orthodoxy. For example, among the Radicals in the Reformation, there were those who rejected a trinitarian faith, and similarly, as Dissenters in England were debating a faith not dictated by government fiat and transmitted through the Thirty-Nine Articles, so the question of the Trinity was in the air.

In 1719, representatives from the various dissenting traditions met in London, in the Salters' Hall, to discuss the relationship between Scripture and doctrine, and in particular the issue of the Trinity, famously not defined in propositional terms within the confines of Scripture. Since one of the marks of the dissenting traditions was their challenge to the imposition of creeds, the relationship between the doctrine as defined by credal statements and the "plain words" of Scripture was clearly one that was significant for their understanding of themselves. The debates at Salters' Hall, though provoked by questions about the Trinity, were rather about whether words that were not in Scripture could be used as authoritative tests of people's orthodoxy. The two sides in the debate were defined as "Subscribing," those who would "subscribe" to non-biblical words such as a creed, and "Non-Subscribing," those who insisted on using only biblical words (some of whom still held to a fully orthodox belief in the Trinity, but refused creeds not because of their content, but because of their claimed status).

The further details of this debate itself are not significant for our story here, but this is an indication of the point that was to be a matter of concern for those supporting and looking at the College. The debates in Salters' Hall were provoked by discussions that were happening at a Presbyterian Academy in Exeter, which had caused some anxiety within the Ministers' Meeting in Exeter. The discussion was among those who were exploring ideas and who were being encouraged to think for themselves and question, which led some to question the doctrine of the Trinity. The debate then became around the limits within which such discussions could rightly be held. Clearly, this is a conversation which was to have significant impact on the way in which all Colleges and the work they did was viewed. Could anything and everything be debated, or were some things to be protected?

One of the distinctive features of this time is summed up in the contemporary description of "The Age of Reason": people, educated people, were expected to, and expected to be allowed to, question accepted ideas and seek truth through their own reasoning and experimenting, and not simply to accept teaching on trust. Those who embraced a non-trinitarian faith would describe themselves as accepting Rational Religion or as being Free Thinkers.

For Baptists, with their emphasis on liberty of conscience and the importance of freedom of belief, there was here both a possibility of moving into a different theology, and of suspecting others of doing so. That many General Baptist Churches moved in the direction of Unitarianism is one of the outcomes of this historical process.

It was also an issue within the College. In 1788, the minister of the Baptist church in Frome, Job David, published a letter in which he criticized other ministers in the Western Association, those he called the "Ministers of the Orthodox or Calvinistic Churches." He argued that while criticizing paedo-Baptists for "unscriptural" practices in baptism, they themselves were unscriptural because they preached a doctrine of "a Trinity in Unity," which was not to be found in the Bible. He linked this in particular to the use of doxologies in the trinitarian form which were not directly from the Bible and therefore were importing into worship words that were not authorized by Scripture. David had been a student at the Academy from 1766–71, under the leadership of Hugh and Caleb Evans. It was Caleb Evans who responded to this letter on behalf of the Association, disputing the contention put forward, but also arguing that recognizing the place of mystery in Christian doctrine was a position that Baptists holding an orthodox trinitarian view accepted, while Rationalists such as David rejected such mystery as obfuscation, unnecessary and oppressive.

This was not the first time that Evans had been involved in debates about the Trinity, but it seems to have been the first time that it was with one of his own students. That appears to have struck him deeply. In 1789, he published a pamphlet entitled *Remarks on a Letter Addressed to the Ministers of the Orthodox or Calvinistic Baptists*. In his opening paragraphs, he asked how one of his father's students whom he had also taught as a tutor at the Academy "could now call himself one of our brethren?" Evans continued,

"Is he an orthodox Calvinistic Baptist? Is he a member of the Western Association?" and went on to argue that, in holding these views, he could not be these things.

Evans also wrote the Association Letter in 1789, which, while not directly addressing David's writing, still engaged with the issue. He continued this theme of distancing himself and the Association from the position that David argued for, and he challenged the churches to hold fast to orthodox doctrine as the source of life and warmth of faith.

Nevertheless, there have been those, notably W. T. Whitley in his history of Baptists, who have suggested that the Academy under the leadership of both the Evanses was a place where unitarian theology grew in strength. It is true that there were students, such as Job David who, having studied at the Academy, went on later to embrace Unitarianism or Rational Religion. Another such, Aspland, became such a leading Unitarian that he founded the Unitarian Academy in Hackney.

However, it seems unlikely that it was part of the teaching of the Evanses that the doctrine of the Trinity was to be rejected. Not only was Caleb Evans involved in controversial writings in which he defended orthodox trinitarian belief, the only extant sermons that we have of Hugh Evans also show, albeit implicitly, a non-controversial acceptance of trinitarian doctrine.

Things become more complex when we consider the case of Robert Hall.

Robert Hall was an immense intellect, and something of an infant prodigy, certainly being paraded as a "child preacher" in ways that did little to undermine his sense of superiority. He studied first in Bristol and then in Aberdeen, and then, aged twenty, he was invited to be assistant to Caleb Evans at Broadmead Church and to serve the Academy as classical tutor.

Hall was always committed to liberal and free-thinking politics, and to the practical expression of Christian love and acceptance; this led on occasions to him speaking warmly of those who were not orthodoxly trinitarian. Indeed, at times he was warm enough that he was sometimes suspected, and even accused of agreeing with them, and actually commending Socinianism or anti-trinitarianism.

His time as assistant minister at Broadmead and tutor in the Academy was not easy for anybody. In 1790, he wrote to the church to address five points on which he was regarded as being unorthodox, including that of trinitarianism. Another was his position on baptism: he stated that he would not "rebaptize an adult" a position that was not considered acceptable by his fellow-Baptists.

Shortly after this, he left Bristol, both the church and the Academy, and moved to Cambridge. While there, doubts about his trinitarianism continued to emerge, particularly since he was very admiring of Joseph Priestley, a theologically minded scientist, or a scientifically minded theologian, who was a leading thinker among those Dissenters who became Unitarians. However, from 1799, it is clear that Hall was explicitly trinitarian, and he even spoke of becoming "more settled" in his views.

He only served the Academy for one or two years, admittedly at a time when his views seem to have been at odds with the wider assumptions of Baptists. The impact which he had on the College from that point of view is not clear. But his presence, and the debates that his teaching and writing provoked are important not simply in themselves, but also as indicators of the way in which the debate about trinitarianism was live within and around the College at the time.

However, when we turn to the period in which John Ryland was principal, there is less uncertainty. When he was ordained in 1781 (eleven years after he started his ministry at College Lane, in Northampton) he presented a *Confession of Faith*. This was traditionally trinitarian in form, but he also stated that he "rejected all Doctrines and Practices that are not proved and warranted in the biblical canon." All ancient traditions and new revelations were, therefore, unnecessary if they lacked "Scripture Proof." Thus, he reflected too the debates of the age, and was careful to say no more than he knew he could assent to.

He went on from this to assert that "it would ill become me to explain *how* the three that bear record in heaven are one God."

There were times when Ryland was closely questioned about his doctrinal position, but in the public statements that he made, he was always orthodoxly trinitarian. He used terms that were emerging in the Age of Reason, and reflected what was expressed in the Non-Subscribers' stance in the Salters' Hall debates, namely that human words, in particular about doctrinal assertions, were to be treated with care. But he did not espouse the "free-thinking" position of those who rejected a traditional trinitarian faith.

However, there were students who, at College or later, did either move to theological unitarianism or decide to voice a previously held position of unitarianism. This is not at all surprising and reflects the College's tradition of developing the critical faculties and encouraging those who were students there to think for themselves and not simply adopt a 'party line'. The Bristol Tradition can include the term evangelical and it can be fairly safely assumed that all those who taught within the College at this time were orthodox trinitarians. But the trend was not towards closing down enquiry, but rather opening it up. And so, of course there were those whose theology moved in different directions. In this, the teaching could be said to be successful: men were thinking for themselves and coming to their own conclusions. As a College which was serving a denomination that valued "freedom of conscience," nothing less could be expected.

Ordinances

In addition to trinitarianism and the nature of Calvinism, there were also debates about church order. As we saw briefly in the story of Robert Hall, the issue of baptism was a live one—at its heart was the question of relationships with other believers. Hall refused to baptize an adult who had previously been sprinkled, while still asserting that infant baptism was a distortion of the biblical teaching. This was not yet the most commonly held view, but it was an indication of a changing set of views that were emerging, in particular with the Evangelical Revival. Baptists found themselves in a position of recognizing that there were those with whom they shared a saving knowledge of Christ, and yet they had a different understanding of baptism. This of course had always been the case, but it becomes particularly visible with the impact of revival. Within the Bristol Tradition, with its emphasis on catholicity, and the recognition of fellowship with believers across denominational lines, there was at least the possibility of a position like Hall's gaining ground and there is some evidence that it did.

A similar debate, perhaps even more heated, was also going on with regard to Communion and whether the Table should be open or closed. Again, Hall is at the heart of the controversy, this time in conversation with a man who had been one of his students, Joseph Kinghorn. Their debate was conducted through pamphlets, in the fashion of the times, with Hall arguing that Table fellowship should be open to all believers, regardless of the mode of baptism, and Kinghorn insisting that the Table followed baptism, and therefore only those who were baptized according to the New Testament teaching (at least as Baptists understood it) should be free to come to the Table. This debate continued for about ten years between 1815 and 1826. We see traces of it in local churches at this time, and again, see something of the strain that could emerge within a community that was committed both to biblical loyalty and to free thinking and liberty of conscience.

Baptists have never been known for the unanimity in all things doctrinal—nor always for their capacity to have the debates well. There always appears to be something about which people will feel strongly and want to discuss or argue about. By not having a central statement of faith or a magisterial authority within the community, there is always space for that discussion. At a time when the Academy was not yet fully established, nor completely accepted as a part of wider Baptist life, it is notable that the people involved in the Academy were participating in the debates and taking a role in the wider life of the community. This is a pattern we will see repeated through the generations: the capacity and intellectual rigor of the College being offered as a resource to the wider community, as staff and students alike take part in debates within the College and take their place with this debate among the wider family of Baptists.

POLITICAL AND SOCIAL CONTROVERSIES

The American War of Independence

The commitment to freedom and free conscience was also to have social and political consequences in these hundred years. We have already alluded to the issue of the American War of Independence, when we touched on the story of Morgan Edwards above. He was in the USA at the time of the war and withdrew from preaching and any public pronouncements for that time. This was because he was a supporter of the British cause and was indeed regarded with a great deal of suspicion because of that. He was unusual, as a Baptist, in supporting the Crown. Many Baptists, including many who were connected to the Bristol community, were supporters of the American cause. Although Baptists, especially in this new era of religious toleration, were loyal to the Crown and committed to living within the law, this was in the context of a broader commitment to civil and religious liberty. The issue that sparked the revolt and then the war was to do with the imposition of taxes by the British Parliament on the Colonies—who were not represented in Parliament. Many churchmen and many Evangelicals supported the British cause, partly from patriotic loyalty but also on the basis of the teaching in Romans about submission to lawful authority.

Caleb Evans was one who did not, and he found himself involved in a pamphlet disagreement with a Methodist named John Fletcher. Fletcher insisted on "submission to Scripture" and therefore to established authority. Evans asked where in the Bible were found "the principles of *political slavery*"—and went on to argue that if Scripture did give warrant to the brutality that he saw being practised by the British on the Colonists, then "it would furnish a stronger objection, in my opinion, against the divine original of the sacred code than has ever yet been produced."

This is a startling claim, and one that demonstrates two things. Firstly, it is evidence of the passion with which Evans held to convictions about religious and civil liberty. Secondly, it is a reminder that the nature and status of Scripture was beginning to be questioned, with the dawning of the Enlightenment experiment in following experimental thought wherever it leads.

For now, let us stay with issue of political and religious liberty. Evans was not, nor were other Baptists, arguing for any kind of anarchy. But he did insist that it was legitimate to attack a lawful government when said government was itself attacking civil or religious liberty.

He was not alone in his position—his name is on petitions against the war, showing that he was consciously identifying with a wider movement. Recent historians have identified Evans as one of the leading agitators during the time when there was serious pressure being put on Parliament through petitions in 1775, and one who made his position very public in an attempt to convince others. Evans had contacts in the USA through personal connections. There were several who had been students who went to the Colonies, and we can safely assume that there was a fair amount of sharing of information, so he was not arguing simply on the basis of theory or assumption. There was a significant correspondence in the Bristol press, and Evans became involved directly in a controversy with John Wesley, who strongly opposed the Colonists.

It was not only by petitions and pamphlets that those who opposed the war made their arguments. Dissenters had a long and lively tradition of preaching to engage with the political issues of the day, and the American War was no different. One of those who preached and published sermons against the war was a former Bristol student, Rees David, who was minister in Chacewater in Cornwall. When in 1781 the government announced a day of prayer and fasting on account of the war, David preached against "the hypocritical fast with this design and consequences." This was then published—knowing it would offend some—with the motto on the title page "To all the Friends and Supporters of Civil Liberty."

Others too were engaged in writing and petitioning against the war. The activism that can be seen as part of Evangelicalism clearly had a presence here in peoples' preaching and acting. In a curriculum that emphasized the study of Scripture and the importance of Scripture as the root of preaching, it is also clear that there was an expectation that the Word heard through Scripture was not simply for the individual soul and its salvation, nor even just for personal morality, but also spoke into contemporary situations and dilemmas.

Slavery

This also showed in another, and even more painful social and political issue of the period, that of slavery.

Bristol was one of the ports deeply implicated in the slave trade; it was the place where ships set off for America, and much of the wealth of the city—including of those who were in the churches—came from the slave trade, or from affiliated sources.

In 1783, the Society of Friends became the first Christian community to organize themselves against the trade. Others followed, including Baptists, and as with the war, sermons, and pamphlets played a significant part in trying to convince others.

Support for abolition was voiced more clearly by some than by others. James Dore preached and then printed a sermon in which he concentrated on the text in Ezekiel 27:13, "They traded the persons of men." From this, he produced a sermon which was a passionate cry for abolition. Dore had come to Bristol in 1779, at the age of seventeen, under the tutorship of the Evanses, and was then called to Maze Pond in Southwark, where he preached this sermon. He evidently retained his links with Bristol, since he quoted the resolution passed at the Western Association's Assembly in the same year (1788)

> Agreed, As an Association, thus publicly to express our deepest abhorrence of the Slave Trade, and to recommend it earnestly to the Minsters and Members of all our Churches, to unite in promoting to the utmost of their power every scheme, that is or may be proposed, to procure the ABOLITION of a traffic so unjust, inhuman, and disgraceful; and to the continuance of which tends to counteract and destroy the operation of the benevolent principles and spirit of our common Christianity.

Caleb Evans was involved in this resolution, since he was the one deputed to pass it on to the chairman of the committee for the abolition of the slave trade, together with a donation from association funds.

Others from the Bristol community were deeply involved in the campaign and in making it known. Robert Hall Jr wrote to tell his father that a petition with over eight hundred unsolicited signatures had been sent from the city to Parliament, and in 1788 he wrote two articles pseudonymously in the *Bristol Gazette*, supporting the abolitionists. As not only a tutor at the College but also assistant at Broadmead Church, his position was complicated. As well as the committee in Bristol arguing for abolition there was a committee campaigning against it. Most of the aldermen of the city were on this committee, and that included one John Harris, a senior deacon at Broadmead, and also an influential merchant in the city. It is also worth remembering that Edward Terrill had been involved in the sugar trade, and so implicated in slavery—which is a part of the College history that needs to be remembered, alongside the more positive aspects of involvement with abolition.

However, that said, there is a good history to tell. As well as Evans and Dore, John Ryland was also involved in arguing and campaigning for abolition. His father had long been an opponent of slavery. In his *Reminiscences of John Collett Ryland*, William Jay recorded that at the time of the first opposition to the slave trade, J. C. Ryland

> threw all his impassioned energies into the condemnation of the accursed traffic. One morning I was reading to him some of the reported miseries and cruelties of the middle passage; among others, of a captain who had a fine female slave in his cabin, but, when her infant cried, he snatched him up, and flung him out into the sea; still requiring the wretched creature to remain, as the gratifier of his vile passions. At the recital of this Mr. Ryland seemed frantic, and to lose his usual self-control. He felt this, and paced up and down the room, "Oh, God, preserve me! Oh, God, preserve me!" and then unable to contain any longer, burst forth into a dreadful imprecation, which I dare not repeat. It shocked me, and I am far from justifying it; and yet, had the reader been present to witness the excitement and the struggle, he would hardly have been severe in condemning him.

Two Bristol students commissioned to go overseas with BMS to Sierra Leone were exhorted by Ryland to care for the souls of men "disinterestedly." However, he also warned them not to get involved in local politics, nor to endanger the preaching of the gospel by becoming associated with radical movements. This was a very common position, reflecting the struggle that was going on to come to terms with the horror of the slave trade and the necessity for resistance. Ryland may have objected to the slave trade, but he was also opposed to any overt action that would bring people, in particular church leaders, into conflict with the state.

He was not alone in taking this position. There was resistance to the slave trade in the UK, but in general, including in the churches, it was of a gradualist sort—a desire for change, but without making that change rapid or too threatening to the status quo. There were too many vested interests, not simply in the country as a whole but among Baptist congregations as well. One of the aspects of the story of the College that the research behind this book did not cover in any detail in this work is the role of powerful church members and church families in shaping the life—and supporting the finances—of the College. This is one of the areas in which further study is very important. There is an important story to be told of giving and encouraging—and the valuing of the work—by those who were part of various congregations. That the churches were divided over Abolition is clear from the ways in which we can trace people on both committees in Bristol, for and against. The College's founding finance came from one who benefitted from the trade. Resistance to chattel slavery was by no means clear cut, because there were those who wanted to protect their financial interests. The differences would have been felt in the College, not just among staff or students but among those who provided the finance and who offered leadership through serving on the College Committee, and who were part of the Educational Society.

Maintaining a discreet silence and staying out of the political battle was the position that BMS wanted missionaries to take. Nevertheless, there were those who were serving with BMS who found it impossible to keep out of 'politics'. Baptist involvement in abolition focused particularly on the Jamaica Mission, and the most notable of the BMS witnesses against slavery, William Knibb, was one of those who found that face-to-face contact with the reality of slavery in Jamaica drove him to take exactly the kind of position that Ryland had encouraged those who went before him to avoid. This despite being a member of Broadmead Church under John Ryland. Between these two positions we can see the difference between a theoretical understanding and a face-to-face encounter with the reality. When he came home, Knibb was urged again not to get involved in the politics. However, addressing the BMS Annual Meeting in June 1832, Knibb announced,

> Myself, my wife and my children are entirely dependent on the Baptist mission; we have landed without a shilling and may at once be reduced to penury. But, if it be necessary, I will take them by the hand, and walk bare-foot through the kingdom, but what I will make known to the Christians of England is what their brethren in Jamaica are suffering.

Baptist work in Jamaica had its origins not with BMS but with George Liele, an emancipated slave who was a preacher and leader, and Moses Baker, another freed American slave. Baker had written to John Ryland, asking for BMS help in particular to resist the hostility of the planters. In 1813, John Rowe, a Bristol student was appointed to assist Baker, though he only lived until 1816. Following his work, others from BMS arrived and worked sometimes alongside, and sometimes separately from the Jamaican leaders.

Thus, the two Baptist groups grew, and continued to provoke hostility and resistance. Slaves were prevented from attending the Baptist congregations and punished for their involvement.

Thomas Burchell studied at the Academy from 1819–22 and when he finished there, he sailed to Jamaica. At first Burchell appears to have accepted the "no political involvement" directive, but when he had to return home because of ill health in 1826, he joined those who were telling churches exactly what the conditions in Jamaica were. He even went so far as to criticize the BMS Committee for the position it was taking, and to propose that it withdraw from the Jamaica Mission and allow others to run it.

In 1831, when there was a rumour that freedom was to be granted, which turned out to be untrue, there was what came to be referred to as "the Baptist War," an initially peaceful resistance led by Sam Sharpe, a deacon in one of the Jamaican led Baptist churches. The rising was put down with violence, and over 100 Baptist chapels were destroyed, while 312 slaves, including Sharpe, were executed.

Following this, even though the Slavery Abolition Act was passed on 1833, full emancipation was not granted until 1838, and many missionaries became increasingly critical of the way the new laws were being implemented, leading to increasing tension between missionaries on-the-ground and the BMS at home.

Burchell returned to Jamaica during the uprising and was arrested. He escaped and fled back to England, where he worked with Knibb in the continuing effort to make emancipation work and in publicizing the reality of slavery. Burchell returned to Jamaica in 1834 and stayed for several years before returning to England. He died in 1846.

John Tinson, who was at Bristol 1818–22, also served in Jamaica, and was principal of the College that was founded at Calabar in 1842 after BMS work ceased and the work was taken over by the Jamaica Baptist Union. The questions surrounding the founding of the College in Calabar, its links to the Education Grants and the issue of their proper use are discussed in the essay "Reparations" by Doreen Morrison in *Journeying to Justice,* and should be understood before we are too glad that there was a Bristol heritage in the founding and forming of Calabar College. But there were such links, through Tinson, and the heritage of the shape and intention of formation was part of those links.

CONCLUSION

At the beginning of the period, the Academy started out as an enterprise of one church, with the intention of serving the wider Baptist community but very much rooted in the one congregation, and indeed, in the home of the principal. By the end of this time, it had become a separate organization, and was moving out of the principal's home into its own building.

It had started with only one or two students, and by the end of the first hundred years scores of students had passed through. They had gone on to serve in churches at home and around the world, they had had ministries of hidden practice, and of national and international consequence. The tutors had been of varying ability, but all of them had the ideal of an educated ministry as their intention. The understanding of what that education might be had changed, as debates and matters of controversy had shifted—from intra-Calvinist debates through to the nature of the Trinity. There had been good years and wonderful relationships, and there had been harder times, and broken friendships.

From beginnings at a time when Baptists were just starting to find a secure place in the public sphere, by the end of the first hundred years, Baptists were involved in significant public campaigning around the abolition of slavery, and caught up in the debates about the war with the USA, and taking sides. They were also involved in a series of internal debates—both specifically Baptist and in the context of the wider evangelical community. The language of the Bristol Tradition, which can be traced in fragmentary form from very early had become deeply rooted in the identity and practice of the College, and the sense of community that grew from studying together and sharing lives and ministries had begun to have its impact. As a nation, the UK had fought and lost a war with the former colonies of the USA, had watched with anxiety the revolution in France and had seen the embedding of the new industrialization in the national economy.

Through the work of College graduates across the country and in other countries, the emphases of the Tradition were spreading beyond Bristol, and beyond Baptists.

By the middle of the nineteenth century as our story moves into its second century, new issues were arising, new questions were being asked, and new forms of ministry were being called for.

Before we go on to consider the second century in detail however, we will consider in more detail the issues around education and the nature of training for ministry.

3

CONTROVERSY OVER THE ROLE OF EDUCATION

FROM THE BEGINNING OF the College's existence, we have seen that there is debate around the actual need for training, and even if that need is accepted, what that training and education should look like. As a continuing strand through the history of the College, it seems good to look at the aspects of the discussion not just in their chronological place but as a whole, to trace the recurrent themes and questions.

The need to go on defending the importance of an educated ministry continued well beyond the impassioned pleas of the founding of the Education Society. In 1812, for example, John Ryland addressed the London Educational Society in a piece later published as *Advice to Young Ministers*, insisting that support for education mattered in order to sustain "the hope that our churches may be furnished with a succession of able and faithful ministers."

He summed up his argument with the words, "we think it at least highly expedient that every large body of Christians should possess some learned ministers and the greater their number and attainments, the better."

Together with Samuel Pearce, he published *Duty of Ministers*, which included several sermons preached at ordination services. In one of the sermons, Pearce addressed the issue of time to study:

> A studious habit [. . .] is essential to a stated minister. A lively imagination may serve an itinerant, but when a man becomes stationary and preaches three of four times a week to the same people, unless he be industrious in furnishing his mind, his services will soon become insipid, devoid of solidity, fraught with tautology and unfit for edification. And what is the result? Why,

thoughtful hearers must either abide with dissatisfaction, or in grief retire, whilst the ignorant are kept in their ignorance and remain babes, when under a judicious ministry they might have become "fathers in Christ".

The intention of an educated ministry was always this: to serve the congregations and enable them to grow in faith.

The founding of the Education Society secured—or aimed to secure—the Academy as an institution with financial stability and a stated aim to be of service to, and to be supported by, a wide range of churches. It was not without its detractors and those who saw no need for it. The place of training was debated but not in isolation. It was part of a larger debate among Calvinists in particular about the use of 'means' to attain any end that might be willed by God. The debate surrounding the founding of BMS is another example of this, epitomized in the probably apocryphal story of the young Carey's enthusiasm to establish some agency for the conversion of the heathen and, after his request that this be discussed, the terse reply, "Sit down young man; if God wishes to convert the heathen, he can do it without our help."

Similarly, there was a strong body of opinion that argued that God could make ministers without human learning; God's calling and gifting was sufficient.

In an address to the Education Society, Hugh Evans argued that although only God can make able ministers of the gospel, still

> [a]s he is pleased to make us instruments to effect his purposes, the honour you are ambitious of, is that of being employed by him, in the accomplishment of the great and desirable work of raising up able ministers of the gospel.

The anxieties of those to whom this argument was directed were twofold: that training was doing God's work for God, instead of leaving it in God's care, and that training would give the impression that a man could become a minister through human intervention rather than the call of God. It was exactly parallel to the anxiety expressed in The Modern Question as to whether it was right to invite people to believe, since that might give the impression that an individual had a choice over their salvation. In addition, there was also the anxiety that the offering of training suggested that God's call and gift was not sufficient for ministry.

However, the debate was not simply the ongoing discussion about whether there was the need for training at all, but also a debate about what sort of training. When the College was moving into a purpose-built premises in Stokes Croft in the early 1800s, there was a need to raise funds. This appeal was used not just to ask for funds but to make the case for this form of ministerial training. So, for example, when he was making an appeal for funds at Bunyan Meeting Free Church in Bedford, Ryland argued that, while Bunyan was a gifted and God-used preacher and writer, his successor who had been trained was equally used by God, and the training was not to be despised. He continued by insisting that that the College was not there to "make ministers," but to "make those who were ministers better scholars" so that they could do the work more effectively. He also argued that "we receive none but such as have been already tried & approved by the Chs. as possessing hopeful talents, & us their Judgmt. being called of God to that work:" The Academies seek "to cure" such young ministers "of awkward habits, tones & gestures, wch. by hurting the feelings of some of their hearers, wd. render them less acceptable and so less useful." They also set out to help them to a better knowledge of their own language, and how to arrange and illustrate their ideas, and also the original biblical languages in which the word of God was written. Others "useful branches of knowledge" were taught to assist them "in explaing. & defendg. the truths of Revelatn. or fit them to help support themselves, if the Chs. are unable to do it, by instructing Children."

The aim was not to create ministers where there were none, but to enable those who were ministers to be better able to fulfil their calling.

This approach—the enabling of lively, zealous, and able evangelical ministers of the gospel—underlies all of the defences of ministerial education that surround the College's life, and particularly fundraising for all of its activities. It is apparent right at the beginning of the College, when Foskett argued that only those who were already doing the work would be accepted. The expression of faith was a prerequisite.

However, and in particular as the move to Stokes Croft was being contemplated, there was also a recognition that, in order to hold their own in a context in which congregations were becoming more educated and the complexities of faith appeared to becoming more demanding, there was also the recognition that ministers had to be able to speak in the "dialects" of the day, able to meet arguments from knowledge and to carry themselves well in an increasingly 'polite' society, as Baptists became more a part of wider society.

WHAT KIND OF EDUCATION?

The shape of the arguments for education gives us a very clear sense of the shape of the arguments against. The main arguments against ministerial education included the insistence that where God called, God gifted, and the 'addition' of education ran the risks of undermining true faith and piety—and a dependence on skills and techniques rather than the Spirit. However, the kind of debate that underlies Ryland's appeal is also about the particular kind of education; was it educating a man to be "a man of letters" or a minister of the gospel?

There was significant emphasis on the learning of the classical languages and indeed, reading the classical texts in Greek and Latin, the kind of education that was on offer to those who were attending the universities. This was about providing an education that fitted the temper of the times, and allowed those who taught to take their place among 'educated' people, to discuss not simply theology or matters of faith, but to take part in the debates of the day. Was this what ministerial training should be? The College report of 1806, which was in part laying out the need for the new building at Stokes Croft argued that

> literature is so attentively cultivated in this kingdom and good taste so generally diffused, that the want of literary accomplishments in those who sustain the character of ministers, must be more sensibly felt than at any former period. Though we ever wish to keep in view the far superior importance of experimental acquaintance with evangelical truth and the inward power of godliness to all other qualifications for that sacred office, yet we cannot but wish as many as possible of those who are called out by our churches to the work of the ministry, may receive every assistance we can render them to their discharging it with reputation and advantage.

However, it is clear that there was also resistance to this kind of literary and scientific breadth to ministerial training, and that it was a matter of discussion within the College itself. A generation of tutors, exemplified by Thomas Crisp, as he laid out his program in a sermon at the beginning of his time as principal, had a mistrust of such an education; or at least, saw it as of lesser value. We will discuss Crisp in more detail below, but here to note that, at the start of his role in the College in 1808, he preached a sermon *Christian Ministry an Office of Labour*. In this he laid out his understanding of ministry and therefore what it was to be trained for it. He argued,

> Far be it from us to despise the aids which intellect and literature afford, in the great cause of spreading religion in the world. But those who have been most honoured as the instruments of doing good, have been men whose exertions displayed no extraordinary grasp of intellect; and who, if they had not exerted themselves in the cause of God, might have passed through life, little noticed and little known.

How a minister was to be trained was, of course, dependent on what a minister was for—and on the nature of the churches he was called to serve. In the century after Crisp, the Baptist churches had moved from being small, socially marginalized communities, operating largely within their own circles, to being part of a movement (the free churches) which claimed the allegiance of roughly half the population of England. Education among the general population had also changed significantly. The second half of the nineteenth century saw a rise in interest in education for the sake of the nation's prosperity—with three Acts changing the organization and the content of the educational life of the nation. Moving from being a charitable enterprise, education was taken under governmental control, and made available—and compulsory—for all children.

Thus, those who were going to serve churches of this generation, it was argued, needed to be educated at least to match their congregations.

TRAINING IN A WIDER CONTEXT

The move to Woodland Road in the second decade of the twentieth century was not free of the need for such discussion, especially as part of the intention behind that move was to develop closer links with the university, and there was a continuing fear that what the College was producing was "men of parts" rather than ministers of the gospel. But this move, developing links with Bristol University and with Western Congregational College, as well as showing the enduring commitment to developing able and zealous ministers, also demonstrates the continuing and broadening catholicity of the Bristol Tradition; the intention in the training was not narrowly Baptist or exclusive. This was beautifully demonstrated at the opening of the new building, and in the continuing life in that building, both during the war, and later. Those present at the opening of the new building included representatives from the civic life of the city—the mayor and city councillors—representatives from Bristol University, as well as representatives from various denominations.

The very presence of people from beyond the Baptist constituency was, among other things, an indication of the way that the catholicity of the Bristol Tradition continued to shape not just the content of the teaching, or the life shared by students, but also the outward facing aspects of the College's life; to open a new building and mark such an important 'new start' in the life of the College required the presence of those who represented the wider church.

The presence of civic and university representatives was also important in a similar way. The training of those who would be zealous, able, evangelical, and lively ministers of the gospel included in its remit that those who were so trained would take their place in academic and in civic life. This is a clear move away from a sectarian identity and into a recognition that Baptists had a place in society as a whole. When we remember that the earliest days of the College were at a time when it was only just legal for Dissenters to develop such an institution, the symbolism of these presences becomes clear. It is also an indicator of a change in the nature of training and how it was understood.

The links with the university were particularly important in the move to Woodland Road, and such links indicated a definite move in the understanding of training. The importance of the academic had never been overlooked, but by so visibly and closely aligning with university culture, the paramount importance of the academic was signalled. This was not, of course, without controversy. In the first place, such an assumption required a certain degree of prior education, and this might seem to rule out those students whose backgrounds had not allowed them access to such education. That the College remined accessible, at least in intention, to those who did not come from a context where they had already been able to attain university entrance mattered, and this is demonstrated in many ways through the century, with distinct kinds of courses, the possibility of attaining university entrance through the College courses and teaching to supplement a lack of previous education being part of the College's teaching.

However, it is undeniable that the move to Woodland Road and the identification with the university community did symbolize and indeed claim something important about priorities in ministerial education. Such a priority was not accepted by everybody, and the kind of debate that we have seen previously was to continue. The appointment of Dr Dakin, the first principal to have earned his doctorate and who brought with him the riches of a period of study in German universities, reinforced the academic aspect of training, although, as we will see, not during his tenure at the expense of preaching and pastoring.

Dakin continued, indeed re-emphasized, the place of literature and language in the training (exactly the areas that had caused anxiety in those who feared that College training was more concerned with producing "men of parts" than ministers) precisely because of his commitment to preaching. He argued that "the possession of a living message born of experience" and "some ability to articulate the message for the help of others" were the "two fundamental qualifications for standing in a pulpit as an accredited and efficient minister." Thus, alongside the academic training in theology, history, biblical studies, and biblical languages, he emphasized a breadth of reading.

However, as had usually been the case, he insisted that

> where passion fails no language whether pretty or otherwise will be living. [. . .] Let it be quite understood that the secret of true speech is not beautiful language, but *fitting* language. The art is not in saying the thing prettily, but in saying it aptly. But that can never be done [. . .] without prolonged study of the material language offers and the ways in which it has been used.

Here is one resolution to the dispute about whether training for ministers involved training men to be "men of parts": yes, such training was useful—but only for the end of furthering the capacity to communicate the gospel. This is an early twentieth-century version of the 'means' argument that we have seen elsewhere, namely the recognition that only God can make a minister, and that the experience of saving faith is at the heart of the work. The means of various sorts are only a part of the way the work is to be done.

A NEW-OLD SHAPE OF TRAINING

Over the century that the College lived in Woodland Road, the nature of ministerial training was to change dramatically, and again, not without controversy. The move from Woodland Road to The Promenade reflected the shift from residential training to church-based training as the dominant model which took place during the Woodland Road years. Students were always involved in local churches in a variety of ways. In the very beginning, living in the manse of Broadmead Church and working alongside the minister was a very hands-on form of training. The move away into Stokes Croft diminished this to some extent, and the move into Woodland Road at first continued that change of emphasis. Student presence in churches focused on Sunday preaching, leading missions, offering sustained ministry during the summer in particular. However, with the growing emphasis on the academic, and the changes in church life during the twentieth century, it began to be realized that a more sustained presence with one local congregation might offer benefits and in particular, from the students' point of view, anchor the academic in the day-to-day and personal. A pattern of placements began to be developed, with all the possibilities of wider reflection on that work within an academic context.

We will say more about this as we discuss the life of the College under the principals of the twentieth century, but here it is important to note that this need to anchor training in the local church context was felt acutely as the place in the academic world became more secure. The need expressed in the Bristol Tradition for able and zealous ministers required those who knew how to do ministry as well as how to think, argue and understand the academic context of the faith.

The move from Woodland Road to The Promenade did not seem to involve the same necessity to defend the importance of education *per se*, but it did embody the new emphasis and pattern. The move away from residential training was a major break with the previous assumptions, and requires some close examination, which we will do below. But the move did also continue to demonstrate the aspects of the Bristol Tradition we have already considered; the catholicity is there in the continuing and developing links in the city with the Anglican Trinity College, Methodist Wesley College, and with the West of England Ministerial Training Course, as well as accounting for the new partnership with the Centre of Youth Ministry, itself a partnership organization.

Most significantly, however, was the change in who was coming to train and in the life-position that they brought with them. This had an impact on the way the building was used, but also on the way in which training was understood and the shape it was expected to take. With the significant increase in the age of people coming to train, and the different experiences they were thus bringing with them into the process, the usefulness of recognizing previous experience and finding ways to integrate that into training became increasingly important. While this has a very positive effect in deepening the understanding of a variety of contexts in which congregation members might find themselves and brought into the practice of ministry a broader range of insights and skills than might be expected if people all came into ministry in their early twenties, it also brought a series of challenges to the model of the previous two or three generations. With a shorter 'working life' to offer, many of those hoping to come to College were concerned that they did not spend more years than necessary in a context that was increasingly seen as 'isolated' from the calling to which they were responding. This in itself reflected a difference in the understanding of ministry that had become widespread as the changes of a secularizing society swept through the church. Thus, from a context in which residential training was the norm and church-based training was an exception in order to meet particular circumstances, Bristol, along with other Baptist Colleges, moved to a position in which church-based training was the norm and full-time residential training unusual. This was to profoundly reshape the way in which the courses were organized, as well as the nature of the relationships within the College. By grounding training in the day-to-day life of a local congregation, alongside the support of a senior minister or mentor, and integrating this with an academic course, it can be argued that some of the early patterns of training such as living in the manse and being involved in the life of the church (preaching in the vestry, for example) were being renewed for a new context.

A MINISTRY FIT FOR A CHANGING CHURCH?

As a result of the changes in society and church which we see increasingly from the middle of the twentieth century, understandings of ministry substantially changed to encompass the perception of a different range of skills and activities. While, in theory at least, the study of and training in theology remained important, there was also, as we have seen, a desire to ground academic study in the practice of ministry which led to taking placements more seriously. But it also reflected an increasingly imperative requirement that ministerial formation should include, and might even major on, what might be called the practical skills of ministry. These were understood not only to include traditional pastoral care but also administration, youth work as a particular specialty, and as we moved to the final decades of the twentieth century, leadership, and management skills, and what has come to be called pioneering.

The impact of the 1979 *Signs of Hope* report, responding to concerns aired at the Baptist Assembly in 1977 regarding the decline in numbers and implied decline in spirituality, included challenges to traditional ministerial training, and further raised the importance of broadening the curriculum.

Part of this change involved the lessening of the dominance of theology, and a greater emphasis on 'theology for . . .', that is, skills-based rather than knowledge-based training.

This was further developed in the moves which restructured the Baptist Union at the end of the twentieth century and into the twenty-first. The development of core competencies for ministry and subsequently the 'marks of ministry' model, which are now central to our denominational understanding of ministry, have had their impact on how training is perceived and therefore what is asked for by churches and by students.

While it is incontestable that competency matters, and too many churches have suffered in the past from its lack in ministers, it is also true that this has had a significant effect on the nature of the curriculum, one that it could be argued has meant that what had been considered central before is now peripheral at best, and completely lost at worst. One instance of this is the loss of history as a core subject, and in particular denominational history. While, in an ecumenical context and an ecumenical age, it might well be suggested that denominational history is divisive or unnecessary, it could also be argued that ecumenism is well served when the reason why a denomination has a particular position, or a particular pattern of doing things is understood. This is not to say that nothing can change, and that what has been should always be preserved. But knowing how we got to a place is a helpful part of understanding what happens and how change might be enabled.

There is another aspect of the way in which teaching has changed that has an often-unsuspected effect on the integration of theology and ministry. With the development, usually as a result of the requirements of a validating institution, teaching since the 1990s has been increasingly modular. That is, rather than a continuous course in whatever the subject is over the year, often building up year by year (a certain amount of Greek learned in the first year, for example, and in the second year building on that, deepening the understanding and grasp of the nuances), most subjects are now taught in intensive modules over a semester, and having been assessed by essay, presentation, or examination, are then, as it were, finished and packed away as attention moves to the next set of modules. Clearly, there is building on subjects year by year, but there is also a greater tendency to compartmentalization. There are creative attempts to overcome this, and multi-disciplinary teaching, often made possible because of the ecumenical context that has been so important over the generations and exemplified today in links with Trinity College, can help to overcome this. But it is still true that this is a very different approach from earlier years.

Underlying so many of these changes are changes in what churches want from their ministers, and what ministers perceive themselves as called to be. The impacts of the changes of, for example, the charismatic enriching of the church has broadened the range of those who will preach in many congregations. In addition, leading worship and in particular leading musical worship is now often not only shared between minister and musicians, but often something in which a minister has very little involvement. The development of specialist ministries, such as youth ministry and pioneer ministry, require a distinct set of skills—and indeed, ask different theological questions and therefore require different kind of theological study—from the traditional pastor-teacher minister. There is absolutely no reason why youth ministers, pioneer ministers, chaplains, church planters, and other specialized forms of ministry should not be included in the model of lively, zealous, able, and evangelical preachers of the gospel, and indeed, it remains the intention of the College that they should be. But what shape that should take, and what kind of training and teaching will enable such ministers of the gospel to be formed raises questions that can never be fully answered, since the situation is always changing.

4

THE SECOND CENTURY

CONTEXT

As we move into the next century of the College's life, we again have four principals who guided the College through these years, and they will guide us through this chapter.

In this chapter will we cover 1825 to 1921. During most of this period, Queen Victoria was on the throne; she was crowned in 1837 and died in 1901, being succeeded by Edward VII. During this time, slavery was abolished, Hong Kong was ceded to the British by China, Queen Victoria was acclaimed as Empress of India, the Boer War was fought, and the Balfour Declaration promulgated. These years will also take us through the First World War, and will give us the chance to consider the discussions to accept women as well as men for training.

There were significant political changes: the Catholic Emancipation Act, passed in 1829, changed the role of Roman Catholics in the UK, and the repeal of the Test and Corporation Acts in the previous year changed the place of Dissenters significantly.

In 1832 the First Great Reform Act was passed, opening up Parliament to non-Anglicans, and widening the franchise to small landowners, tenant farmers, shopkeepers, householders who paid a yearly rental of £10 or more, and some lodgers. It defined those who could vote as men (the first time women had been formally banned from voting by virtue of being women!).

The telephone and the camera were invented, railways were built, powered flight took place for the first time, and cars began to be mass produced by Henry Ford. The Eiffel Tower was built in Paris, and the Crystal Palace in London.

The Origin of Species was published by Charles Darwin, *Das Kapital* was published by Karl Marx, and Richard Wagner's *The Ring* cycle was premiered.

There was a famine in Ireland, and a Civil War in the USA, the Luddites were destroying new technology because the new machinery was causing a loss of employment, the Tolpuddle Martyrs were transported for becoming part of a trade union, the Chartists published their demands and within thirty years, Trades Unions were legalized.

Amongst Baptists, several events are important to notice: in 1812 the Baptist Union was formed and in 1832, it was re-formed in a way that has survived; in 1887, it faced a major challenge in the Downgrade Controversy, as the impact of the new theologies became a source of contention; and several other Baptist Colleges were founded—in Stepney (later to move to Regent's Park in London and later still to Oxford), in Rawdon, West Yorkshire, and in Abergavenny, Wales, and finally in 1865, the Pastors' College, later to be named Spurgeon's College, in London.

The identity and practice of Bristol Baptist College is, of course, largely shaped by and expressed through the works and convictions of those who have been principals and tutors of the institution. We have told something of the story of the men who sustained the College through its first hundred years. Now it is time to look at those who led it in this second century. The four principals of the College through these hundred years were Thomas Crisp 1825 to 1868, F. W. Gotch 1868 to 1881, James Culross 1883 to 1896, and William Henderson 1896 to 1920.

Thomas Crisp

In 1825, John Ryland resigned as both minister of Broadmead Church and principal of the Academy. It was at this time that it seemed good to both the Education Society and the church to separate the roles, and to be able to appoint different men, with different gifts, to the two aspects of the work. The College was now established at Stokes Croft, and was developing a life separate from the congregation, since it was now no longer based in the minister's home. The church called Robert Hall to the pastorate, and, although he held a key place in the life of the College, welcoming students both into his home and into the church, he was not interested in being directly involved in the academic life of the College.

The Education Society appointed Thomas Crisp to the newly shaped position of principal. He had been Ryland's assistant at Broadmead, and had already been tutor at the College for seven years, so this was an easy move to make. Crisp remained as assistant at Broadmead church through his time serving the College in this capacity—indeed, he was assistant minister there for fifty years.

Frederick Trestrail, who wrote a memoir of his time at the College was less than complimentary about Crisp's lectures. His recollection was that the lectures themselves were "read out with great deliberation, and with frequent and lengthened pauses" so that students could take their notes, and, as a result, "the lectures appeared dull, and were indeed sometimes wearisome." In the examinations, Crisp did not want the students' own views, but the "exact repetition of what he had said," and failed to see that this was not the most effective means of teaching, being instead an exercise in memory rather "than an incentive to our own powers of thought." A different approach, Trestrail suggested, would have more usefully "secured our progress", and meant Crisp's lectures would have been more appreciated.

However, speaking at his funeral, Dr Edward Steane, who was a student from 1819 until 1821, and later minister at Denmark Place, Camberwell, commented that

> his duties in the lecture room were always discharged with conscientious diligence and fidelity; and his sermons, which the students heard as often as they could, were models of all that was accurate in thought and chaste in language.

Steane also asserted that that he did not know of any of Crisp's former students "who did not look back upon the instruction received from him, as among his most valuable preparations for the ministerial office."

What is certainly clear from his own words is that Crisp had a very high and serious view of the nature of ministry. He described ministers as being those who were "labourers for God"—and we have seen some of his views above as we have considered the defences that were made for the education of ministers. The esteem in which he held ministry is clear in his affirmation that the ministerial office was "the highest eminence to which human nature can be exalted, when God uses us in the holiest cause, and for the greatest purposes in which even his own power has ever been exerted." His concern for his students was not only for their academic development, but that they should exhibit and further develop this kind of identity. He wrote, in *Christian Ministry; An Office of Labour*

> Love to God,—zeal for his glory—firmness to be faithful to the souls of our fellow-creatures—boldness in declaring the whole counsel of God—a determination to do and to bear every thing in which the interests of his kingdom are involved—an understanding enlightened by the Spirit of truth—a conscience

pointing out our duty, and plainly testifying our neglect or constancy in performing it—a heart filled with divine grace, and longing to be an instrument of imparting this grace to others: who does not feel that these are the highest endowments, the richest ornaments of the character?

Whatever the shortcomings or otherwise of his actual teaching, it is clear that he impressed on his students the seriousness of their calling, and took pains to support their growth in it.

New arrangements

The move to Stokes Croft, and the wider cultural context in which the College was now functioning, and for which it was preparing ministers, inspired the Bristol Education Society to reflect anew on the nature of the tutors and of their work. They recognized, as they put it in the Accounts of 1825, that "learning as applied to its sacred uses, among us, is thus stationary, while secular education is in rapid progress."

A subcommittee representing those who were believed to be best placed to ask questions about this put forward some recommendations. The committee recommended that there should be a consistent entry requirement for those who were to come to the College, and that the course should follow a regular curriculum. While there might need to be individual assessment as people applied (since there was nothing like the public examinations with which we are familiar) there were to be common external examinations at the end of the sessions.

They also decided that the College should reduce the number of tutors, but that these tutors should be full-time, and should have distinct areas of specialty in which they could offer the best modern teaching that was available. As well as Crisp as principal, William Anderson was appointed as tutor of classics and mathematics. He was a Scot, whose initial education had been entirely in Sabbath schools, and therefore religious rather than the more broad-based education of the day schools. He supplemented this education with wide reading, and very early showed signs of having a significant intellect. At seventeen, he was accepted into membership of the Independent Church in George's Street, Aberdeen, and it was not long before others were discerning in him the capacity for ministry. However, he had begun to question the nature of infant baptism and began to read and enquire further into the issue. The result was that in 1803, together with three other young men, he was baptized by Mr Edmonds of Cambridge in a branch of the River Don a few miles from Aberdeen.

He moved to London in February 1804, and joined the church at Little Wild Street under Benjamin Coxhead, himself a former student at the Bristol Academy between 1797 and 1800. During this year, Anderson preached "several probationary exercises," and, on 29 August, the church called him to train for the ministry. He entered the Bristol Academy in January 1805, continuing there until the end of 1808. During this time, despite his sketchy initial education, he excelled. In his own time, he read many of the Latin and Greek classics, taught himself French, began to learn Italian, and took lessons in German from a Moravian minister, though he did not continue with the latter two languages. He also read and studied all he could in divinity, biblical criticism, moral science, and history. In the spring of his second year, he was sent to Scotland for health reasons, and when he returned in August his Greek was greatly improved; he had continued his studies, even at a distance. After College, he became pastor in Dunstable and was there for sixteen years, during which time the building was twice enlarged, and during which time he had students with him who were preparing for ministry. After his sixteen years in Dunstable, he moved to Bristol to become tutor at the College and remained in post until a week before his death in 1833.

Anderson was succeeded by one W. Pechey. However, he only served for a year, and then Edgar Huxtable was appointed. He had been educated at Cambridge but had been suspended—quite possibly because he had become a Baptist. He was a Tutor at College for eleven years and during part of that time he was de facto also the first pastor of Fishponds Baptist Church in the city. He stepped back from that role in 1842 and at Crisp's suggestion, the church accepted a student from the Academy, G. B. Thomas, to serve for the summer vacation. He remained as pastor until April 1850.

After eleven years as Tutor, in 1845 Huxtable resigned because he ceased to be Baptist. He gave a statement to the committee setting out how he had significantly changed his views on baptism,

> and also assigning reasons for objecting to the constitution of Dissenting Churches generally, with special reference to the practice of Baptist Churches, and for preferring the Ecclesiastical form of government belonging to the Established Church of England.

This not only disturbed the College Committee in general terms, but raised some anxiety about what Huxtable had been teaching. They considered it wise to make sure that the students were still identifiably Baptists, and were happy to report that that was the case.

Huxtable was readmitted to St John's College, Cambridge, from where he had been suspended because of his Baptist theology, and in 1846 he became a Crosse Scholar and was awarded his Bachelor of Arts degree. In 1847 he was a Tyrwhitt's Hebrew Scholar, and gained his Master of Arts degree two years later. He was ordained as a deacon at Bath and Wells in 1846, as a priest a year later, and in 1848–61 became vice-principal of Wells College, and sub-dean of Wells Cathedral from 1849–61. From 1861–76, he was vicar of Western Zoyland, Somerset, and a Prebendary of Wells Cathedral from 1853 until his death, though he retired to Truro in 1883. After his return to Anglicanism, Huxtable also wrote a number of books. He was clearly an interesting man with an interesting career!

He was succeeded as tutor in classics and mathematics by F. W. Gotch, who had been a student under Crisp. We will say more about Gotch when we come to consider his time as principal, but it is worth noting that when others were critical of Crisp's principalship, he was quite positive.

STUDENTS

College entrants in 1878, during Gotch's principalship. J. S. Whitewright, who was to serve in China later, is among them. (Accession number 14966)

Before we look at Gotch's work in the College, it is worth taking time to examine a little of the stories of some of those who were among Crisp's students. During his time as tutor and then principal, somewhere between two hundred and three hundred students went through the College. As we have seen in Trestrail's comments, Crisp was not perhaps the most electrifying of teachers, and there is a continuing narrative that his time at the College was not one of its golden periods. However, we do know a surprising amount about the day-to-day life of students at several points during his leadership because some have left memoirs.

Trestrail's memoirs

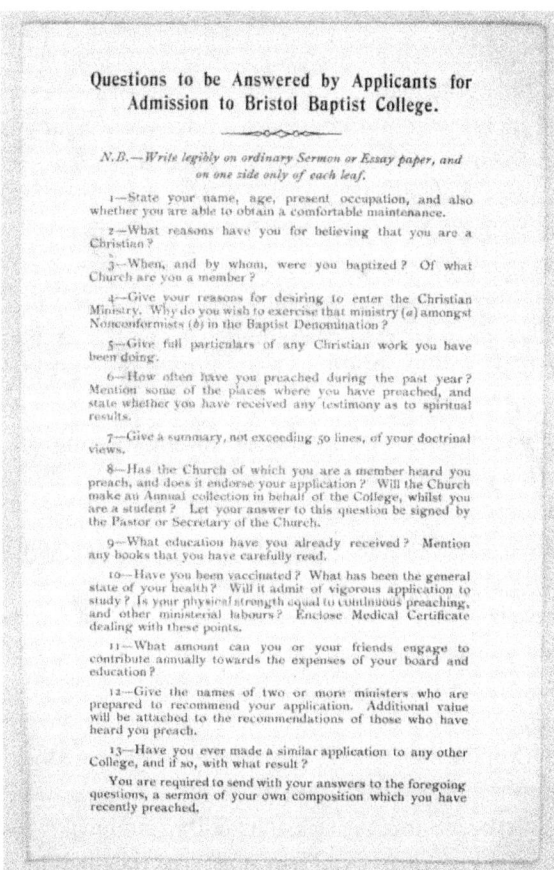

Questions asked of applicants, undated, but apparently in the middle of the nineteenth century. It is interesting to note just how similar application questions remain. (Accession number 19668)

Trestrail, who as we have seen preached at Crisp's funeral, was, despite his strictures, a very keen and long-term supporter of the College. He was a student between 1828 and 1831 and afterwards went first to Little Wild Street in London, and then to Clipstone and to Castlehold, Newport, on the Isle of Wight. Between 1840 and 1844 he toured Ireland to find out about the churches there, and from 1844 to 1849 he was secretary of the Baptist Irish Society. From 1879 until 1901 he was co-secretary (with Edward Underhill) of BMS, with particular responsibility for home affairs, became Baptist Union President in 1880, and returned to pastoral ministry in Castlehold between 1871 and 1890.

He lived from 1803 to 1890, and wrote a biography/memoir called *Short Story of a Long Life*, and also wrote *Reminiscences of College Life*. Much of what we know about life in College at this time comes from his writings. He remained an enthusiastic supporter of the College and on a visit in 1860 he was invited to address the students. He offered insight and advice based on his own ministry and with their future progress in mind. He called on them to take care of certain things that would assist them in their future ministry: their health, their habits and manners, their time, and the connections they formed (by which he meant they should seek to marry, but if they were not yet engaged, they should not seek to change that while students!). He also pointed out that they would now be learning to read the Bible critically as well as devotionally, but he warned them that this should not prevent them from reading it devoutly as well, and he insisted that they should take care of their prayer. They were to seek to become good preachers, for they had not come to the College to become eminent scholars or literary men but preachers, and should cultivate that gift.

He went on to speak of what ministry should look like. First, he told them they should not see their initial pastorate as a stepping-stone to another of greater importance or which would pay more; nor should they seek to make hasty changes. He went on to instruct them that they should work harmoniously with deacons; leave the decision-making in the church's hands; and if, as pastors, they desired either to specialize in one aspect of learning or to equip themselves with a useful general understanding, they should settle upon this quickly. Further, he told them that not only were they take on the office of a pastor, they had to be the pastor, and their goal was to look after their flock, never neglecting the sick and afflicted, and making sure that the church's concerns were their own. They must feed the flock, and to this end they must be students of God's word, which he insisted, required hard work, and this is the pastor's duty. "It is your duty," he said, "to study truth; to illustrate and enforce the doctrines and precepts of Christianity. This cannot be done without continued application and study. No man can preach well who does not prepare well," and this included not leaving preparation to the last moment. And in all this, their aim is to preach Christ "in His person, teachings, sufferings, and death. Christ, in what He has done for man, in dying as a substitutionary sacrifice, and what He is doing now—interceding for all that come unto God by Him." And this is not just preaching the gospel to sinners, but to show all the doctrines relating to Christ's person, work, and death, and declaring these as the great truths of the Bible.

He ended,

> May you, by the grace of God, be worthy and honourable sons of this College, and true successors of those, even the most eminent, who have preceded you. Among the varied and affectionate solicitudes awakened by your presence here to-day, this one rises supreme over all: May you ever be found faithful ministers of the Lord Jesus Christ.

In this address to the students, we see outlined a vision of ministry that reflects an understanding he had developed in the College, and no doubt refined through experience, and so we can see in it something of the concept of ministry that was communicated by Crisp to his students; a vision of ministry well summed up by the adjectives "lively, zealous, able and evangelical."

Trestrail's memoir of his time in College has several aspects that are well worth reflecting on here. He talked about the importance of the friendship made, and the ease with which they were made among the students. Community is an aspect of the Bristol Tradition that continues to be highly valued, and it is notable that it is mentioned so early on in the memories of the students. He also mentioned the way in which students, all of whom would have arrived with a sense of their own specialness as those marked out by their families, friends, and congregations as having a particular call, soon found themselves disabused of this, while they spent time among others equally called—and often more gifted. He wrote of this as being particularly important for himself—with the implication that other students also benefitted from this. In the tradition of Crisp's conviction that ministry was "co-labouring with God", this perception of the minister as "undershepherd" was clearly important.

His own ministry reflected his interest in mission which had started before he began to train. He was a Cornishman, influenced by both Baptists and Wesleyan Methodists in his childhood. His family attended a Baptist church, and he himself was baptized and welcomed into membership by Samuel Green, a student of the Stepney Academy, in 1820.

But the family context was not at all exclusive; his home frequently offered hospitality to visiting preachers from a variety of denominations, and in particular, those who were involved in supporting and advancing the cause of missions, both home and overseas. This breadth of encounter and early encouragement to be involved in the support of mission shaped him profoundly. From his teens he was involved in leading Sunday School and also stepped into the pulpit when somebody was ill, gradually developing from this into an itinerant preacher.

By his mid-twenties, his congregation were discerning a call, and encouraged him to apply to the Academy and he was accepted. He wrote of the welcome and encouragement he received on arriving, and of the development of lifelong friendships.

But he was not starry-eyed. In his memoir, he wrote with appreciation of those who were "the senior men"—the ones in the final year. But he was much less complimentary about those immediately above him. And it is true that at this period in the College's life, there are not many whose names continue in the history. Good, solid, but unspectacular ministries seem to have been the specialty. Faithfulness, steady work among the congregations and commitment to the people were the mark of a Bristol man.

Stanford: an outsider

A grant of permission to present candidates to the University of London for degrees in 1841. It is signed by Queen Victoria. This was during Stanford's time in the College. (Accession number 37049)

Another student of Crisp was Charles Stanford. Stanford is worth noting in our account of the College's life because he was one of those who came to the College with no schooling at all behind him. He was from a poor—and sickly—family, and was entirely self-taught. He had been part of an Independent congregation in Northampton, but had received baptism from Revd Tunley at Zion Chapel in Northampton, not because he wanted to leave the Independent congregation, (indeed, he contemplated training at the Independent College), but because of his reading of Scripture led him to a conviction about believers' baptism. He was a student in Bristol between 1841 and 1844, and it is clear that the fact the College offered to supplement his education, training him not only for "ministry" but grounding him in a more general education, was very important. The importance here of an understanding that ministry did not *depend* on education, but was enhanced by it, is clear. It was and remains an important aspect of the ethos of the College that a calling can be recognized, affirmed, and enabled not because somebody has all the educational qualifications needed to be accepted on a course, but because God has called. The qualifications can then be supplied in a variety of ways.

We will read below of students who left College to serve overseas with BMS—and part of what forms that story is the loss of life that accompanied such service. But death was not only part of the experience of the students who went overseas. During Crisp's time as principal, there were a painful few months in which Anderson, the mathematics and classics tutor, suddenly died, and two other students also died. One of them was Andrew Hall, who arrived at the College in 1831 already not a strong man, and died in the spring of 1833, still, officially, a student.

The other was Richard Hatch who came to the College in January of 1833. It is through his letters, and in particular through a biography written of him that we gain another insight into life in the College some years later than Trestrail.

Richard Hatch, letters and memoir: a life in College

Richard Hatch was only in the College for a few months before his death, but a friend, Samuel Robert Allom, wrote a memoir of him, and through that we have both a picture of one man's struggle to discern a call, and his first impressions of the College community he joined.

The memoir speaks of a deeply pious child who became a young man who had doubts about his faith and his salvation—or rather, about his own worthiness or otherwise for salvation based on his "warmth of feeling," or lack of it.

In his early teens he was apprenticed to a school teacher who was also a minister (and whose name is not given in the memoir), and found great help in his sermons, though again, his engagement appears to have been, at least by his own understanding, intellectual rather than whole-hearted. He was unwilling to call himself a "disciple."

Finishing his apprenticeship he became a private tutor, but again found that he did not settle. But it was while in that position, in about 1831, that he seems to have become "more settled" in his religious position, and more convinced that his faith was sincere and therefore a saving one. His biographer, and it appears many of his friends at the time, were far more convinced of his salvation than he was. His struggles raise an interesting reflection for readers nowadays about the difference of religious sentiment and the new forms and shapes that it can take.

In the early 1830s he was clearly thinking about ministry but feeling unfitted for it. However, he was hoping to be accepted into the Bristol Academy, seeing this as a way forward to train in order "to be useful." He was not actually baptized nor in church membership until October 1832, after he had started speaking about ministry as a possibility, and after he had expressed a hope to start at the College in the following year. He deliberately sought out an open membership church because of the "liberality" of his religious sentiment; this breadth of sympathy and theology was, as we have seen, at this time very typical of the College's identity, and may have been one of the aspects that drew him to it.

A few days after his baptism, he began to preach, and very soon approaches were made to the College about whether he could be admitted. By the end of October, he heard from the College in terms that made him hopeful and in the next month the church agreed to commend him for ministry. Then, in December he heard that he had been admitted to the College.

Over this whole period however, it is also evident in letters from him and from his friends to and about him, that his health was giving cause for concern, and one is inclined to wonder how much of what he (and others) interpreted as spiritual struggle may have had a physical basis.

He came to College in January 1833, and wrote to his parents about what he experienced there—another glimpse into the life of the community at this point. In that letter he described the College building. He wrote that he was given a choice of study as several were empty, so he chose one with "a very pleasant prospect from the window". He described the rooms thus: "like little boxes, they were warmed by hot air, and the bedrooms were about the same size, and equally plain." The Stokes Croft building was "very long and narrow", and "the rooms we occupy are ranged on each side of an arcade that runs the whole length of the fabric, and forms a capital promenade." The studies were about nine by twelve feet, "perfectly simply", without even a curtain for the window, and it was up to the students to make the rooms more comfortable. They had a desk, a small table that was little more than a sideboard or book stand, a backless armchair, a few bookshelves, with "no superfluities, but just what is sufficient for all necessary purposes." Attached to the building was "a large and elegant library and museum, to which we have free access, consisting of several thousand volumes on all subjects," which included some valuable manuscripts and old works, a collection of medals, minerals, natural and man-made curiosities, and relics from all ages and countries.

**P N Bushill's study,
But taken when occupied by
Morley B Simmons**

A room in Stokes Croft—clearly the kind of place described by Hatch to his parents.

He also describes the experience of being a student. Lectures were conducted in the "fine" lecture room, and that is also the place where "we poor fellows have to undergo the fiery ordeal of having our sermons, essays, &c. criticized and cut to pieces." In fact, his experience, noted later in another letter to his parents, was not as bad as he had feared or had been warned. He wrote that he had "undergone the critical ordeal of the lecture-room," and told them that it was less awful than he had anticipated, and was as little agonizing as he could have expected. Anderson had been "tolerably merciful," with his main objection being that Hatch's treatment of "The believer—a friend of Christ" (John 15:14) had been popular and superficial "instead of a more strict and abstracted discussion of it."

This critique is significant in terms of what it indicates about expectations regarding the nature and content of preaching. One wonders if an "abstracted" discussion would be regarded now as something to be commended—though it is be hoped that a superficial sermon would still be criticized.

Also writing to his parents, Hatch outlined a typical day at the Academy.

At 6 a.m., the monitor, an office which students took in turn, rang a large bell to wake the students. At 8 a.m. the bell was rung for family worship, and everyone would assemble with Mr Crisp, his family, and the servants in the large lecture room where students would take it in turn to go into the pulpit to announce a hymn, followed by a reading with exposition, prayer, and then the service was concluded. About ten minutes later they were summoned for breakfast, after which students prepared for classes. Hatch's class usually finished at about 1 p.m., at which point they had some free time. At 2.30 p.m. they would share a meal together which was "plain but always good." This was followed by "some light occupation," during which Hatch and a friend would often read together, or he would study French until 5 p.m. at which time they had tea. Students then would either prepare for the next day, write sermons, or "something of the kind" until 9 p.m. when the bell summoned them for prayer. Crisp would lead this, and afterwards they would have "a supper of bread and cheese or butter," and then study again until bedtime.

RULES.

I. BOOKS.—That every Book taken out of the Lecture-Room be duly entered, with the Title and Number, in the Book appointed for the purpose.

II. That no Book from the Library or Lecture-Room be used as a common Class-book.

III. That every Book taken out of the principal Library be returned to its place within a month.

IV. That all Books be entered afresh every other Thursday, the Monitor to give notice by ringing the bell.

V. That every Exposition taken out of the Lecture-Room be returned within two days.

VI. That the use of Dictionaries and Concordances be restricted to the Lecture-Room and Library.

VII. That if through neglect or improper treatment any Volume, in either of the Libraries, be damaged or lost, such work be replaced by another, or a Fine be paid according to the amount of the injury.

VIII. That if any Periodical work be missing at the end of the year, or be unfit for binding up, such Number be paid for by the Students generally, or by the Student by whom the loss or injury has been occasioned.

IX. That no Book, belonging to the Lecture-Room or the principal Library, be lent by the Students to any one not residing in the House.

X. That no Student leave a Book in any room but his own study.

XI. That in returning Books to the shelves, care be used to replace them in order; and that on every other Thursday, the Monitor for the week, assisted by the Ex-monitor, shall examine and arrange the volumes.

XII. That on the 1st of June and the 1st of December in every year, or on any other more convenient days, every Volume be returned to its place, both in the Library and Lecture-Room; that the Books may be arranged, the labels torn off renewed, and a report made to the Tutor of the state of the Books, and whether any are missing.

XIII. WEEKLY EXERCISES.—That a weekly Sermon and Essay be read from the Desk in regular order, and that all the Students be present on these occasions.

XIV. DAILY LECTURING.—That no Student be absent at the time when his class assemble for Lecture, without permission.

XV. FAMILY WORSHIP.—That the Students be punctual and constant in their attendance at family worship in the morning and evening.

XVI. That if any Student be prevented by visiting, or any other circumstance, from being present at family worship, it be signified to the Tutor by one of the Students after prayer.

XVII. HOUR OF BEING AT HOME AT NIGHT.—That every Student be expected to be home at night by half-after ten, or at the latest by a quarter to eleven. Should any circumstance occasion a deviation from this Rule, information shall be given to the Tutor on the following morning, by the Student himself, or by the Monitor.

XVIII. SMOKING.—That no Student be allowed to smoke in any room but his own study.

XIX. MUSEUM.—That a lighted candle be never taken into the Library.

XX. LIBRARIAN.—That a Librarian be appointed in regular rotation every month; and that it be his office to keep the Library in order, to see that the Books are regularly entered and returned, and to take charge of the periodical works of the month.

XXI. MONITORSHIP.—That every Student, in rotation, serve the office of Monitor for one week, beginning on Thursday.

XXII. That it be the office of the Monitor to ring the bell every morning at Six o'clock, and the bell for the Lecture before breakfast, and to call the Students regularly at Six o'clock, going round a second time after an interval of ten minutes;—to ring the bell for family worship every morning, precisely at Eight o'clock, and in the evening at Nine o'clock: the bell to be rung twice, with an interval of five minutes between the first and second ringing;—to put every thing in order in the Lecture-Room, before and after Family-worship, and before and after Lecturing;—to fix up the detail of business.

XXIII. That it be the office of the Monitor, assisted when necessary by the Ex-monitor, to accompany visitors round the Museum.

XXIV. That in case of Funerals, the first be attended by the Ex-monitor and the second by the Monitor.

Rules for life together. These are undated, but seem to be of the same era as Hatch's memories. (Accession number 19835)

When he first arrived, Hatch was placed in a class with students who had already been there eighteen months, and for a few weeks learned Hebrew on his own under Crisp's tutelage. As for his classical and mathematical courses, Hatch stated that he held Anderson to be "a man of uncommon talent and acquirements." At the time of writing, he was reading Xenophon's *Institutions* and Euripides' *Hecuba* in Greek, with occasional forays into "critical examinations of the Greek Testament," while he was studying Horace and Cicero in Latin. As far as mathematics was concerned, two evenings a week were devoted to it, and his class had reached Euclid's third book, and the binomial theorem in Algebra.

On the practical, ministerial side, Hatch told his parents that he had preached at a little chapel about two miles away, although it had been at short notice and he felt unprepared, though an elderly lady who afterwards gave him some refreshment had thanked him and assured him that the sermon had done her good.

In a later letter, he wrote of how he and some of the other students were planning to start an open-air preaching society. This was not a prospect he looked forward to, but felt he should be more keen, if he were truly devoted to his calling.

However, all his devotion, and his apparent enjoyment of being in the College ended too soon. He developed smallpox in April, and although he recovered from this enough to be back in classes again, it was during the influenza season. Many of the students and tutors were ill, and Hatch, weakened by the smallpox, took the flu badly enough to die at the end of May.

Other students

Hatch and Andrew Smith were not the only losses among the students at this time. Abraham Smith who came from Ross-on-Wye, entered the Academy in September 1827. However, he was taken ill during the 1829 to 1830 session, along with three who had all entered the Academy in January 1827, John Kingdon from Frome, and George Daniell from Bristol, and Charles Bathurst Woodman from London, who was allowed to withdraw so he could pursue a course of private study which his health seemed to require. Both Smith and Kingdon were prevented from completing their final year, and tragically, Smith died, leaving Trestrail to recall how he was "greatly respected for his unaffected piety."

For those men born in the early years of the century, the average life expectancy was somewhere around forty years of age. Of course, all sorts of factors could affect how long somebody might expect to live, nonetheless, to lose two students and a tutor in such a short time was a hard blow to the College. To these losses, were also added the losses of those who served overseas and whose stories are discussed elsewhere. But the impact of such deaths, and the awareness of how easily life could end did, no doubt, add to the urgency both of the evangelistic energy of the community, and of the seriousness with which men addressed their own soul's health, and the nature of their calling.

F. W. Gotch

When Crisp retired, he was succeeded by F. W. Gotch—who had himself been a student at the College, entering in 1833, before going on to study in Dublin. This was followed by a pastorate in Hemel Hempstead. While he was there, he became involved in biblical translation and the controversies with the Bible Society around, in particular, the translation of *baptizo*, a significant ecumenical issue that he maintained also had mission implications. His interest in translation never ceased, and later he was involved in translating *The Revised Version* of the Bible, of which the New Testament appeared in 1881 and the Old Testament in 1885. Gotch was responsible for Genesis to Deuteronomy (other Baptist scholars were also involved: Benjamin Davies, principal of Stepney College had responsibility for Joshua to Malachi, and the New Testament translation included the work of Samuel Gosnell Green who had trained for Baptist ministry at the Stepney College).

In 1841 Gotch was appointed a tutor at Stepney College, and was part of the staff there as the College built and formalized its links with London University. He served as external examiner in Greek for London University—and his links there seem to have been important as the College in Bristol made its own links.

In 1845, as we noted above, Bristol College appointed him tutor of classics and mathematics. On his arrival in Bristol, he did not become part of the congregation at Broadmead as previous tutors had done, but rather joined Old King Street church, and when a group from there formed the new Cotham Hill Church, he was part of that congregation, and served it as a deacon.

As befitted one who was so involved in biblical research and translation, he was clear that he did not fear the rise of modern criticism, but rather saw it as a tool to be used well—nor was he anxious about any so-called conflict between science and faith. Rather, he embraced the new learning, and expected his students to do the same, encouraging open enquiry and expecting his students to be able to take an intelligent part in the debates of the day. This was the contemporary expression of the tradition of lively, able, and zealous ministers and all the aspects were held, Gotch maintained, within the identity of evangelical.

The catholicity of his convictions was present too, not only in the various activities he undertook within the broader reaches of church life but also in the way in which he furthered and secured the connections between the College and the new University of Bristol. From 1872, plans were underway for the University College Bristol, which would be associated with London University—one of the new institutions that was developing as a result, in part, of the removal of the religious bars to attending university. In 1909, the University College Bristol became the University of Bristol.

The connection between the Baptist College and the University College was not taken for granted, but it was something for which Gotch worked and which he achieved, and formal links were put in place. This meant a change in the staff again, as some left so that the teaching could be brought into line with the university. Donald Basset, who had been appointed to succeed Gotch as mathematics and classics tutor resigned, and John G. Greenhough, who had been appointed in 1874 as an assistant theology tutor, also teaching logic and moral philosophy as well as church history, left in 1879 when what he taught become part of the University's responsibility. On leaving the College, he returned to the pastorate in Victoria Road, Leicester. Gotch was very disappointed at his departure, and the College Committee recorded "their conviction that his work and influence in the College were of the highest value."

This broadening of the teaching resource was an important part of broadening the life of the College, and more fully integrating it into the academic life of the city. This is a topic that we will return to, but it is important to note it here as an aspect of Gotch's principalship.

Another 'new' thing that emerged in his time, and again is expressive of the continuation of the Bristol Tradition, was that the first Conference of Former Students was held in 1876—the beginning of what was to be The Brotherhood and then became The Community.

Following this first meeting, the College Conferences began to be held regularly, although at first not every year. These were times for students to meet again and renew friendships, and also times for reflection, theological exploration, and the sharing of knowledge and research. This double aspect was (and remains) important. The Conference was not simply a reunion, but in some ways a continuation of the College's intention to enable lively, zealous, able, and evangelical ministers by increasing zeal through mutual encouragement and deepening understanding, and therefore supporting ability through intellectual stimulation. Worship together and prayer for one another, and those not present were also significant—a key affirmation that the work is God's and the ministers (and tutors) were instruments of that work, dependent on the gracious enabling of the Spirit. It is appropriate to note its beginnings here under Gotch's principalship, at a time when the emphasis on the College body as a community was taking on a particular importance as life developed in Stokes Croft.

Students past and present, gathering in October 1886. (Accession number 29826)

Community as an aspect of life in the College was always important too. We have little in the way of immediate records of day-to-day life for students at this time. But we do know that sport was important. Exercise, team building, links with other institutions; all of these aspects were part of the life together.

The College football team in 1906. (Accession number 29823)

Gotch was sixty years old when he was appointed principal, and by 1881, when he was seventy-three, he asked the committee to appoint a deputy who would in due course become his successor. They approached several people, but it was not until 1882 that James Culross accepted the invitation and was appointed, becoming principal in 1883.

James Culross

James Culross had served as a tutor for a year with the Baptist Union of Scotland Education Committee. In 1870 he was president of the Baptist Union of Scotland. In 1877 he had been president of the Baptist Union of Great Britain and Ireland. He was an evangelical and an activist who got involved in the debates of the day with great energy. He was a friend of Charles Spurgeon and was involved in the Downgrade controversy—as a representative of the Baptist Union. His theology placed him firmly there, and he argued with Spurgeon that this was an evangelical theology. He challenged Spurgeon's demand for a statement of faith or creed and argued instead that the identity and practice of Baptists kept them securely evangelical, namely the practice of believers' baptism, of the Lord's Supper, the call to personal faith in Jesus Christ and trust in the forgiveness of sins through his blood, and a trinitarian theology. In the end, Spurgeon was unconvinced by Culross's argument, though remaining convinced of his evangelical identity. He wrote to Culross, "You are sheltering evil under your wing—though without being aware of it."

Culross, on the other hand, in line with the tradition of teaching at the College argued for Scripture's centrality, and also that there was no necessity for any document to "come between me and Scripture."

In his presidential address for the Baptist Union in the autumn of that year, he also argued for the centrality of Scripture, and for the need to take scholarship seriously. He was convinced that modern scholarship was not incompatible with the truths revealed in the Word, and that far from avoiding or fearing modern research, it was necessary to engage with it and use the tools it provided. He challenged those listening to him to avoid preaching from "random passages," but instead urged them towards "serious and continuous exposition" as an underpinning of faithful interpretation and therefore living. His address was a direct affirmation of an identity that was evangelical and able to engage with contemporary scholarship rather than one that took up what he saw as the backward looking and defensive position of Spurgeon.

This was a challenging time personally for Culross and affected his strength considerably, and the College Committee in a minute of its meeting noted the exceptional service he had given to the denomination through his presidency.

There is not a great deal of material relating directly to his principalship, but we do know that he was a supporter of BMS, and part of his impact in the College was a rise in the numbers of students offering to serve with BMS overseas. He was not blind to the cost of such a service, especially in Africa, but argued that "the result, so to speak, overpay the sufferings." For those who were going to serve overseas he offered teaching on World Religions—an innovative approach, and one which strengthened the capacity of students to work effectively in the new contexts in which they found themselves.

We will consider the story of students serving with BMS as a separate section below.

In 1893, Culross offered his resignation because he was aware of his declining strength, but the committee asked him to stay on, with support from a deputy until such time as a successor could be appointed. He agreed to this, and in 1893, W. J. Henderson was appointed as joint principal. This arrangement continued until 1896, when Culross finally managed to resign because of rapidly failing health. He only lived another three years.

Principals Culross and Henderson in 1895. The joint principalship was an unusual, but very important pattern at this point. (Accession number 29826)

With Culross's resignation, Henderson became sole principal, and he served until 1920, and so is the final principal we will consider in this section of our story.

William Henderson

William Henderson had been appointed to the College after a twenty-one-year ministry in Queen's Road Coventry which was both influential and innovative; his concentration on education as a form of evangelism was new and effective, as was his work with youth groups. He was not a dogmatic preacher, and had little to say about the classical doctrines such as original sin, or the nature of the atonement. He was more concerned with preaching a gospel about transformation and renewal, and was involved in actively exemplifying the results of the gospel in social programmes. He established the church on a firmer footing including both the erection of a new building, and the appointment of a Lady Visitor in 1891, specifically to care for "women and families."

In 1907, he was president of the Baptist Union and was very involved in supporting and furthering J. H. Shakespeare's plans for renewal of the structures to serve a new century.

His involvement in wider Baptist life was also expressed through both BMS and the General Baptist Missionary Society. With Shakespeare, he argued that BMS and the Baptist Union should operate as one organization, and in the centenary year of BMS, he was deeply involved in the publication of its history and in the appeal for new funds.

UNIVERSITY CONNECTIONS

Just before he was appointed to the College, the Congregational College started in 1891 to plan a move to Bristol, which eventually happened in 1901, when the Western College was established. This offered the possibility of a collaboration in teaching, something that Henderson worked to promote. It was also the time at which the area in Stokes Croft was changing rapidly. What had been a quiet country retreat was becoming busy and noisy, and ideas of moving the College began to develop. The possibility of a joint building with the Congregationalists was explored but did not advance. However, as we will see in the discussion of buildings, the loss of that plan did not mean that staying in Stokes Croft was the only option, and before Henderson retired, the College was well established in its new building on Woodland Road.

But though the joint home with the Congregationalists did not transpire, links were still made and teaching was shared. Some subjects were taught at Western College: systematic theology, Hebrew, philosophy, and logic. Others, including denominational history, biblical geography, Greek exegesis, New Testament criticism, homiletics, and elocution were taught at Stokes Croft.

The links with the university were made firmer, and in 1910, both Colleges became associated Colleges of the university. The tutors became university staff members and between them taught "Hebrew, Aramaic, Syriac, Hellenistic Greek, Ecclesiastical History, Patristic Texts, Comparative Religions, The Philosophy of Theism, Biblical and general ethics, and 'anything else the Senate requires'", which seems rather open-ended!

This involvement was to be an important part of the life of the College over the next century and allowed students access to a much broader academic community than had been the case before the university was established in the city. There would have been a time when this was not possible—not only because of the religious tests which prevented non-Anglicans from attending universities, but also because of the suspicion of the universities within the nonconformist communities. This connection and the enrichment that it provided on both sides was a notable achievement and to be celebrated. During his time as principal, and with this developing link with the university, Henderson raised the academic standards of the College, and increased the number of men taking degrees. The debate about the need for and the nature of training had, at least for the time being, found a resolution: the highest standard of education possible, and the recognition that, as Henderson put it, the College did not make ministers, for that was God's task, but enabled those who were ministers to develop their skills to the highest standard possible.

Henderson's theology and teaching

Henderson's theology in his teaching was that of his preaching in Queen's Road. He was not committed to any one system of theology. His concern was to teach that salvation was not through doctrine but in relationship to Jesus, and he argued that "creeds were aids, not cramps." He was convinced that the church was to be a living body, in which all played their part, and so was committed to delegating and enabling, which had been his style of ministry in Coventry, and was the style of his principalship, and the style of ministry in which he trained his students. The idea of one person doing everything and others sitting simply receiving would produce what he called "an organisation" not a church—and was not what ministers were called to be part of.

He was also concerned to insist that he did not make ministers—that was God's task. What he did and what the College was for was to impart knowledge to those whom the Spirit had set apart for the roles of teachers, pastors, and missionaries. Here we see reaffirmed the principle that has been there from the start; the role of the College and of training was not to make people into ministers, but to allow them to become as fully as possible the ministers God had created them.

His time as principal covered many significant events, but three in particular stand out: the move to a new building, the First World War, and the opening of the College to women students.

The move to the new building is discussed elsewhere, but it is very tied up with the First World War, since the actual move was delayed because of the outbreak of war.

IMPACT OF WAR

Beyond the impact on the building project, it is no surprise that the war significantly affected the life of the College. With the outbreak of war, the acceptance of new students was suspended, but those who were already in College continued their courses.

Some of those who finished at the beginning of or during the war itself went into local church pastorates, while others became more directly involved with the war effort. A student called Walter Rose, for example, who started his training in 1912, became a chaplain to the forces, while others—P. B. Pullin, F. E. Thomas, William Ennals, and others—served with the YMCA in France. Four other students served with the army, one with the Royal Army Medical Corp, and one with the non-combatant corps.

Some, naturally, were killed. There were seven Baptist chaplains killed in the war, and three of them had trained at Bristol College: H. W. Wood, who died of influenza, W. H. Spinks, who was killed by a bomb while serving as a chaplain in France, and Arnold Brown, son of Charles Brown of Ferme Park and also a former student, who was killed at the Somme.

As well as the loss of those who were or had been students, the high loss of life during the war meant that there were also deaths of those who might have become students—as with all war, there is a continuing sense of loss of 'what might have been'.

Those who were already students when war broke out continued with their training, and the tutors continued to teach and to write. In addition to the work with ministerial students (and with the diminishing numbers since no others were accepted during the war), other classes were developed for a broader constituency: lectures for lay preachers, and series of interest to laypeople in local churches were developed and delivered. This resulted in the links between the College and the churches being deepened. Those who discovered that they were having to take on roles they had not expected found in the resources and teaching of the College a support for challenging times.

It is broadly accepted that one of the results of the war in terms of social change was the increasing possibility of new roles for women, and it is certainly true that the developing recognition of women as ministers among Baptists has some of its roots in the changes following the war. In 1918, the College Committee agreed that from now on "classes shall be open to women as well as men." There was also a move to appoint women to the committee, and several women, already associated with the life of the College, either as wives or daughters of those who were part of College life, were appointed: Christina Culross, Mrs Stanley Gange, Miss Dorothy Glover, Mrs W. J. Henderson, Mrs Katherine Robinson (nee Gotch). This was a significant number of women to appoint at once and does seem to demonstrate an intention to bring women into the governance of the College in a meaningful way, and not simply as token.

With this decision, the College indicated its willingness to train women for ministry or mission work. However, it was not until 1937 that the first woman student was accepted—Gwenyth Hubble. We will tell more of her story in the next part of the book.

While Henderson was principal, Frank Robinson was appointed to teach church history and Hebrew—and he also became financial secretary and College librarian in 1901. As financial secretary, he was crucial in the management of the new building and the move from Stokes Croft. As librarian, he worked on the reorganization of the library in its new home. He retired in 1937.

THE MOVE TO WOODLAND ROAD

The new building in Woodland Road was formally opened in 1919, after being handed back by the university, who had used it during the war. The opening was a grand occasion, and clearly showed something of the nature of the College's life. Guests included, among others, the President of the Baptist Union, Mr Herbert Marnham, but also local dignitaries from the city, including the Lord Mayor James Thomas Francombe, the pro-chancellor of Bristol University, Mr H. H. Wills, the vice chancellor, Sir Isambard Owen, professors and heads of various faculties in the university, and representatives from other denominations, students of the College, and prominent clergymen and laymen from the denomination.

THE SECOND CENTURY 81

The now aged Principal, W J Henderson, arrives on the arm of Herbert Marnham, President of the Baptist Union, as part of the Procession up the hill from the front of the Main University Building

Card donated by Rev S J Smurthwaite,
Student admitted to the College at Spring exams 1914
First church Spring 1921

The procession that was part of the formal opening of the building in Woodland Road. (Accession number 29816)

There was a public meeting with speeches from various representatives, all expressing good wishes for the future, and Herbert Marnham opened the main entrance doors and formally declared the College open. Then there was a celebration lunch, which was held in the College museum. After this, greetings were shared, and it is clear from the records of what was said that an entire vision for what the College might be was being laid out. For example, Revd H. G. Hoare, BA, from London, who had come to the College from Blagdon, just south of Bristol, to study under first Culross and then Culross and Henderson, spoke of the importance of proximity to the university, which would provide opportunity for developing mutually beneficial social relationships between those studying for the ministry and the mission field with those studying for other careers and holding different aims in life. He was followed by Professor Lloyd Morgan, who expressed the mutual benefit for the university, with its focus on a broad array of subjects, and the Baptist and allied Colleges with their more specialized field of study. Historically, he saw a link between secular study and study that introduced spiritual values, and hoped this relationship would continue for both students and teachers, because it was good to "recognize the solidarity of the search for truth." For instance, he thought it might be an advantage for someone to come to the university convinced in evolution and also to be a believer in the spiritual values which were central to a theological College. If students were helped to see that different points of view exist and that such differences need not be antagonistic then a valuable lesson would have been learned. "After all, evolution might simply be the name for one of God's ways of working in the world. There were physical values, mental values, and spiritual values, and why should they not go together? Why should there be antagonism?"

Others spoke on behalf of Western College, on behalf of the ministers in Bristol, and others brought greetings from individual churches.

After the greetings, the Tyndale window in memory of Dr Gotch was unveiled, and his daughter, Mrs Edward Robinson, remarked on the fittingness of a memorial to one who had studied at the College as a student, tutor, and president, and was one who shared in "maintaining the high traditions" of the College. It was her hope that her father's work might not be forgotten, "and with the hope and belief that the old traditions of the College might not only be upheld but far surpassed." Following the unveiling itself by members of the Robinson family, Principal Henderson spoke on the incidents in Tyndale's life depicted in the window, after which a brief meeting was held in the museum lecture theatre, at which two of Gotch's students spoke.

The day's celebrations culminated at the public meeting held that evening in the Old King Street Chapel, at which the Lord Mayor presided. From his reading of the College's history, he remarked that he "had been impressed by the great things which had sprung from small beginnings," from Terrill, to the over hundred students who had become missionaries, and some fifty who had become presidents and professors in a variety of Colleges, "which only pointed to the spirit of devotion developed in the College and the skill in training men." Others he mentioned were Robert Hall, John Foster, John Ryland, Joshua Marshman, F. W. Gotch, the three former students who had laid down their lives in the war, and continued "that brilliant as was the record of the College, he hoped it would be eclipsed in the future."

Though Dr Henderson and the Revd Ernest Price, the principal of Calabar College, Jamaica, also spoke, the final address outlined in the Western Daily Press was by the Revd F. G. Benskin, the minister of Broadmead from 1908 to 1922 and co-honorary secretary of the College with Charles Brown, who commented on what "a fine denominational asset" the College was, having "sent into the ministry a body of men trained and equipped for the greatest work the world could offer. Bristol had always stood for an educated ministry." Benskin claimed three things for the College: that it had always stood for quality rather than quantity, and that no College had produced such a band of educated men for so little cost; that it had proved to be a benefit to the nation, which was always looking for leadership; and that it had been a worldwide blessing. He believed there was no College in England "where the missionary passion had been more real," and this, he argued, "revealed the power of the College as nothing else."

The opening of the building in Woodland Road showed the way in which the College had become part not just of the religious life the city, but of its civic and academic life as well, and possibly represents something quite distinctive in what we might call 'the confidence' of the College as an institution among institutions. And through all the celebrations and the anticipation of the future ran the conviction that the aim was as it had always been, to enable those whom God had made to be ministers to be the best ministers.

By 1920, Henderson was ready to retire. His wife had been in very poor health for some years (she was to die in 1921) and his own health was declining too. His retirement marks the end of this section of our story—the man who was credited with "bringing a fresh breeze to the life of the College." When he was appointed, he was considerably younger than the previous two principals. He was a man who perhaps brought less in the way of systematic theology, but definitely brought an understanding of churches as communities and of the need for those in ministry to enable that. He brought the College through demanding times—a change of building and a world war with all the alteration to world view and expectation that that brought with it. He was clearly not simply respected but held in great affection. In the College Report for 1920, this tribute was written of him:

[He has brought] the gift of a rare and compelling personality; a mind and heart alive to the greatness of the ministerial office. He has inspired his students with the sense of the sacredness of their work, with lofty ideals, with enthusiasm for preaching and pastoral labour. He has upheld the great traditions of the College and has been a faithful servant of Jesus Christ and his Church through all these years.

When he retired in 1920, he was succeeded by C. D. Whittaker—the only layman who has been principal. And his story will be told in the third century section of the book.

THE COLLEGE AND THE BAPTIST MISSIONARY SOCIETY

As we have seen above, involvement in BMS, and commitment to serving in missions was a marked feature of College life in the second hundred years. From the very beginning, the support of missions, both in serving and in advocating for the work was part of the College's identity. In 1924, a volume of essays was published which brought together a collection of essays and sermons in support of BMS from a variety of contexts. It included sermons by John Ryland, J. G. Greenhough, and James Culross, and also addresses by James Howard Hinton, Edward Steane, Charles Stanford, Richard Glover, and Charles Brown. All these men were involved with College in one way or another. All these men were involved with College in one way or another.

These essays and sermons both demonstrate a commitment to mission at a practical level and also the changing theologies of mission and of Baptists of the Bristol Tradition that grew ever stronger through the nineteenth century.

Several clear themes emerge: the need to "spread the gospel" and an understanding of the call of all to share the good news across cultural and national borders; an involvement with others who were doing this (though this breadth of approach did not include working with Roman Catholics, or even regarding them as fellow Christians); a vision of the work of mission that included a commitment to health care and to education; a recognition of the self-sacrifice involved, and a commitment to supporting it.

The support for mission was not only in encouraging commitment through writing, preaching, and fund raising. There were several students who travelled with BMS and served in various capacities. Their stories are worth knowing in themselves, but also for the way in which their stories were told, focusing on the importance of remembering them as part of the community, as exemplars of the Bristol Tradition as those who were inspirational and to be emulated.

Bristol students served in West Africa, in China, in India, and were involved in the Jamaica mission.

One of the issues that arose for the College as men went to serve in these contexts was to what extent the training being offered was suitable for these forms of service. Thus, for example, George Grenfell, who came to College in 1873 already with a strong call to missionary service found his time studying extremely frustrating and left before the end of his course to go to Cameroon; a practical rather than an academic man, he was impatient with study and wanted to be out doing. His continued relationship with BMS was not without its strains and he resigned at one point in order to concentrate on exploration, surveying and language work—but two years later was involved again with BMS. His focus included workers' rights, and he, along with BMS as an organization were naïve about the colonial rulers' intentions, and the work suffered as a result. But there are other stories as well.

India

Joshua Marshman, principal of Serampore College 1832–37, had trained in Bristol—again, the passing on of an educational heritage and pattern. The College at Serampore had developed directly from the involvement of Marshman, William Carey and William Ward in education. Parents of those educated in the forty-five vernacular schools wanted their children to be able to go on to advanced studies, and this coincided with the missionaries' view that education could play a significant role in Christianizing India, and that the effective evangelization of the country depended on Indian believers.

Each of the Serampore trio had teaching experience before they arrived in India, and were committed to the importance of providing education in mission work, but the Marshman was at the heart of it. The College's goals included "a thorough knowledge of and efficient knowledge of the Sŭngskritŭ language," as well as Arabic, Chinese, Latin, and English, along with European science and information.

The College was for "Native Youths from any part of India," Hindu and Muslim, as well as Christian, on the grounds that those preparing to be missionaries needed to be knowledgeable "of the character, the feelings, and the prejudices of the heathen among whom they were designed to labour, by freely mixing in the general society of a College." Serampore's aim, therefore, was to provide everyone with "an opportunity of acquiring knowledge which might expand his mind, render him eminent in life, and possibly shew him the way to a better, even to life everlasting." However, it is noted that as true Nonconformists, those running the College ensured that the students enjoyed full liberty of conscience, and no one, neither Hindu nor Muslim, was forced to anything as a condition for their being at the College.

The College's acceptance of Hindu and Muslim students in which led to addition to Christian ones proved a cause of contention with the younger missionaries who went out to India and also their supporters on the BMS Committee, calling into question the missionary nature of the College. Carey, Marshman, and Ward, however, were convinced that Christian students would benefit from being in a community which included those of other faiths among whom they were to live and serve.

In 1827, Marshman secured a royal charter from the King of Denmark, Frederick VI, during a trip to Copenhagen, thereby granting the Serampore College powers to award "degrees of rank and honour according to their proficiency in as ample a manner as any other such College." Serampore was, thereby, the first College in Asia to be able to grant its own degrees. In June 1833, Carey prepared regulations for the College which were signed by Marshman and John Clark Marshman, who, along with Carey, were the first members of the College's council, Ward having died in 1823.

By the end of 1827, the total number of students supported by College funds was fifty-eight. Of these, seven were European, and were receiving instruction in order to become missionaries, while the goal of the native class was to educate Indian Christians, some of whom were expected to take their faith into whatever occupations they would enter, while others would become ministers. With the exception of a brief period of time, the College had had only one theological professor, Dr Carey, who lectured twice weekly. With the money Ward raised in Europe and America, a fund to support native tutors was set up, but not immediately drawn upon. Dr Marshman returned from Europe in June 1829, and new stations began to be opened. However, in 1830 cuts in funding started, such that the only people able to contribute to the funds were Carey, Marshman, and his son, J. C. Marshman, and Carey's ability to continue doing so was soon severely curtailed by declining health. Carey died in 1834, with Marshman following three years later. But Marshman was just the first of many Bristol-trained tutors at the Serampore College.

Some confusion surrounds whether another Bristol-educated missionary served as a tutor at Serampore College. However, William Yates was certainly a student at Bristol, and a key missionary in India in the early years of the Mission. Yates was a young shoemaker from Loughborough, Leicestershire, was baptized aged thirteen and received into membership of the General Baptist church at Woodgate Chapel, at the time under the ministry of the Revd James Brand who was soon followed by the Revd Thomas Stevenson, under whose ministry Yates learnt much.

He was keen to study, but also needed to earn. His friends made it possible for him to attend the Revd Shaw's classical school for two hours in the mornings and two hours in the afternoons, with the result that in a very short time he could read the Greek Testament fluently and had an advanced knowledge of Latin. This was soon followed by his securing the position of an usher in a school, but he found this unsatisfying and even a hindrance to his own daily studies in spite of its ample remuneration. He was now determined to enter the Christian ministry and believed all his activities had to serve that goal.

In 1812, he entered the Bristol Academy, and W. H. Carey believed that much of what he learned was self-taught, even though he was regarded as a very capable student, pursuing the learning of languages. At this time, he had not thought of becoming a missionary, but the achievements of the missionaries were attracting widespread attention back in Britain, with the accounts of conversions, the formation of new churches, and especially the translation of the scriptures. But just as he was leaving Loughborough for Bristol, news of the fire at Serampore on 11 March 1812 causing damage to the amount of £10,000 became known. Dr Ryland's updates of fundraising progress across the country kept the missionary cause alive for the students. Renewal of the East India Company's charter quickly followed, whereby a religious establishment in India would not guarantee protection for Dissenters. News also came that William Hopkins Pearce, Samuel Pearce's son and a printer trained at the Clarendon Press in Oxford, had offered his skills to the Serampore Press. The combined effect of these three things hastened Yates's desire for mission work, but his family did all they could to dissuade him. However, he won them round. He was initially drawn to Abyssinia in Africa, and he had duly learned Amharic and Arabic, however rather than becoming involved in opening a new mission field, the BMS steered him towards Serampore, where it was felt that his talents would be best suited.

So, after two years at the Academy, Yates was engaged by the BMS for service in India, to where he was expected to sail soon after the annual meeting of the Bristol Education Society, held in early August 1814. His designation service was held at Harvey Lane, Leicester, on 31 August, with Dr Ryland, Robert Hall, and Andrew Fuller all participating. He arrived in Madras on 2 April 1815, then two weeks later was in Calcutta, where he was met by J. C. Marshman and Eustace Carey. They went together to

Serampore, where he also met the veteran Indian missionary, John Chamberlain, who had trained at Bristol from 1799 to 1802.

During the voyage Yates read a chapter of the New Testament in Greek before breakfast, and then studied Bengali until dinner, reading the Gospel of John and William Carey's Colloquies (1801) in both English and Bengali, to help with the acquisition of the language, as well as two chapters from the Old Testament. In the afternoons he studied Greek, reading Homer's *Odyssey* and much of Plato's dialogues, while the evenings would be occupied by general reading, and he devoted Saturdays to sermon preparation. Once he had settled in Serampore he continued mastering Oriental languages, continued his reading of Greek and Latin classics, on top of which he continued his Hebrew and Greek biblical reading and studies.

William Carey asked him to study Sanskrit, which he did and promptly commenced work on a Munipore grammar, as well as the study of Khasi, and a Sanskrit grammar. He also became pastor of a congregation at Barrackpore, and during this period he finally completed his own translation of Job from the Hebrew. However, in 1817, a year before the Serampore College opened, he separated from the Serampore Mission together with others of the younger missionaries, and remaining with BMS established the Calcutta Missionary Union, which founded a school and built chapels and other religious institutions in and around the city.

The first, undisputed Bristol-trained tutor arrived four years after Yates's departure. Born in Edinburgh, John Mack originally planned to enter the Church of Scotland ministry, though he studied natural and physical sciences at Edinburgh University. When he finished this, he attended a course on chemistry at Guy's Hospital, as well as lectures on surgery. Having completed a number of classes at Edinburgh, he was advised to spend some time south of the border on account of his being too young for the ministry, and his need to improve his diction. A place was found for him in Gloucestershire at "a classical and respectable school" run by a Quaker where he would be an usher. Nearby there was "a very intelligent Baptist minister," who, in the course of years, had drawn around him a "pious and enlightened circle." The minister was the Revd William Winterbotham, and the church was Shortwood, in Gloucestershire.

While in Scotland, Mack had never encountered the baptismal controversy. However, getting to know Quakers, he discovered those who denied water-baptism altogether, and his Baptist friends denied infant baptism. For a time, "he was sorely perplexed," but once he had studied the controversy for himself, he adopted Baptist convictions, "and his putting on Christ by immersion in the face of a congregation of a thousand people." This step distressed his family back in Scotland, especially his mother, who at first wrote to him and told him she never wanted to see him again in this life. However, in due course she relented, and before his setting sail for India joyfully welcomed him home, giving him "the most ample credit for having, in all that he had done, acted according to his convictions of what he believed to have been truth and duty."

Now that the ministry of the Church of Scotland was no longer a possibility for him, Mack turned his thoughts to the Baptist ministry, and "it was deemed advisable [. . .] that he should reside for a time in their College at Bristol." So, with the recommendation of the Shortwood church, he entered the Academy at Christmas 1818.

Every Sunday morning, between six and eight students would meet very early in the morning in one of their studies "for the purpose of praying together, and chiefly of mentioning to each other our several experiences in religious things during the past week." Mack and his friend Andrew Leslie, who later wrote a memoir of Mack, from which we learn most of this, were among this group. On one such occasion, Mack told the others "that of all his recent religious exercises, prayer had been to him the most appalling, and so appalling that he had felt as if he could hardly engage in it at all." He did not expand on this,

> but this was not needed. We could all, without any explanation, sufficiently understand him; and perhaps, too, we could all, or at least the most of us, sympathize with him, being ourselves bound in fetters formed out of the same kind of materials with his, or perhaps of even worse than his. We were not all, however, equally open with him, nor all equally disposed to display our imperfections to each other's eyes as he. But concealment was no part of his nature; nothing having been more abhorrent to his mind than hypocrisy on the one hand, or feigned humility on the other. When he spoke, he uttered his heart; and when he told his experience, all knew that the truth flowed from his lips.

Leslie also wrote that

> though his [Mack's] interest in all missionary proceedings was uncommonly great, he, reading with avidity everything that came in his way, and listening with the most fixed attention to everything that was said in his presence on the subject, yet I know not that he ever once anticipated going himself as a missionary to the heathen.

In retrospect, Leslie saw that the designs of his friends and those of God "were somewhat different," for while his family and friends were preparing him for the home ministry, God, "by so occupying his mind with the missionary field, was evidently preparing him for work abroad; and the sequel shows who succeeded, God or the relatives of the strangely pondering boy."

It was not long before "his lot and his calling in the world" were "finally determined." At some unspecified date, William Ward visited the Bristol Academy, but it must have been in the first half of 1819 because of the comment in the Report that six months later Mack returned to Edinburgh. The occasion was vividly depicted by Leslie, who remembered "this devoted servant of his Master coming amongst us, seating himself in the midst of us at our fireside in our long dining room, and conversing with us on various topics of a religious kind."

Leslie admitted that most of the students there did not realize "that the excellent missionary was even then at work for India, being in reality at that time in search of a suitable person for the College at Serampore." But "his eye fastened itself on John Mack," and Leslie speculated that he had been prompted by Dr Ryland, "who well knew the different capacities and acquirements of his students. The call was altogether unexpected by Mr. Mack; but so obviously did it appear, both to himself and even to those friends who had been so desirous of keeping him at home, the call of God, that not only did he almost immediately yield himself up to it, but they encouraged him to proceed in this way."

After just six months, as the 1820 College report states, Mack went back to Edinburgh University to study "chemistry, and other branches of natural philosophy—things which at that time it was intended that he should teach in India." At the end of this period in Edinburgh, he returned to the Bristol area "in order to be set apart as a missionary to the heathen." Leslie and some of the other students attended Mack's ordination in 1821 at the chapel in which he had been baptized, Shortwood.

Along with Ward and Hannah Marshman, "and other missionary friends and passengers," Mack arrived at Serampore on 20 October 1821, having, as noted above, learned Bengali during the voyage. Once there he was made professor of science. For fourteen years he also directed the students' studies, was particularly involved in the training of young men for missionaries in India, and quickly developed "a strong attachment to Dr. Carey." Three years later, the Serampore Press published his *Principles of Chemistry* in both English and Bengali, the first book on modern science in an Indian language, as well as the first map of India in Bengali. The Press continued to publish other books and articles on science in its journal *Dig-Durshun*, founded in 1818. At the College, Mack also taught mathematics and the natural sciences, as well as Greek and Latin, and along with

Marshman, he edited the periodical *The Friend of India* between 1835 and 1876, while also teaching chemistry in Calcutta.

In June 1832, Mack was ordained co-pastor of the Baptist church at Serampore alongside Carey and Marshman, and then succeeded Carey as principal in 1837, remaining in post until his death in 1845. When he had to return to England in 1836 to recuperate from a fever, Mack signed the Act of Reunion of the Serampore Mission with the BMS, healing the breech that had divided them for so many years. Following Marshman's death in 1837, Mack took charge of the seminary on his return to India in 1839, significantly raising its reputation, and establishing it as the first private education institution in India.

Though a member of the church at Shortwood, Mack was financially supported by Charlotte Baptist Church, Edinburgh, under the ministry of Christopher Anderson, himself a graduate from the College in Bristol, and was one of many missionaries from the church sent out over the years. It likely that it was during his second period of study at Edinburgh that Mack developed his relationship with the Charlotte Chapel.

Mack's loss, J. C. Marshman knew, would be most difficult to replace. In times of trouble and difficulty, people had turned to him, certain to receive "the most affectionate sympathy, and the soundest advice." Marshman called Mack "the last of those great and good men, whose public labours, during the last forty-five years, have so powerfully attracted the affections of the Christian world to the Serampore mission." In conclusion, Marshman hoped that "some one [sic] be found speedily to occupy the post of this esteemed labourer, who shall carry forward the work in which he was engaged with great efficiency and success!"

The successor J. C. Marshman had prayed for never came in one person, but in a series of people, continuing the link with Bristol, and with Charlotte Chapel in Edinburgh. The first was Thomas Swan whose parents were Scottish but living, at the time of his birth, in Manchester. Aged six, his family returned to Edinburgh, and he was baptized by Anderson at Richmond Court in October 1817 and in 1821, Anderson and the Charlotte Chapel church sent him to Bristol, where he commenced his studies on Lady Day, 25 March. When he left in 1824, he went to Edinburgh University to prepare for his position as divinity tutor at Serampore. However, he served at Serampore for only two years from 1825 until 1827, leaving when the Serampore Mission withdrew from the BMS, a decision he did not accept. He returned to England via America, where he encountered first-hand the horrors of slavery. This turned him into an ardent and vocal abolitionist. In 1829 he accepted the pastorate at Cannon Street, Birmingham, remaining there until his death. During his ministry there he was one of the secretaries of the Birmingham Auxiliary of the BMS from 1829 to his death, and in 1839 served as President of the Baptist Union.

Another Scotsman, born in the west of Scotland, was John Leechman who came the College from Glasgow, and left in 1829. He then went to Glasgow University, from where he earned his master's degree. He was ordained at Charlotte Chapel on 3 July 1832 and arrived in India in November. He began preaching to the Indians, often going from door to door, and also served as a tutor at Serampore College, remaining there until 1837. When Carey died on 9 June 1834, Leechman became co-pastor with Joshua Marshman and John Mack at the Serampore church, and this was soon followed by a revival in the church. He was a specialist in logic and wrote *Science and the Art of Reasoning*, published by the Serampore Press in 1836. On his return to Britain, a second enlarged and revised edition appeared in 1845, and a fourth edition in 1864, which no doubt contributed towards Glasgow University awarding him an honorary Doctor of Divinity in 1859 in recognition of his scholarship.

By 1837 his wife's health had deteriorated in the Indian climate so much that they had to return to Britain, where he became involved in deputation work for the Serampore Mission, and he was also involved in the negotiations with John Mack, who was, at this time, back in Brtain and which led to the reunion of the Serampore Mission with the BMS.

The next Bristol student to arrive at Serampore was John Trafford, who came in 1853, and remained in post until 1879. In 1860, he was joined by William Sampson who had entered the College in 1850 from King Street, Bristol. He arrived in India during 1855, and was soon appointed a tutor at Serampore College. For nearly ten years, 1856–66, he taught in the College, and also preached in both English and the vernacular. Sadly, his time in India was cut short by a disease, which prevented his return to the mission field, so in 1867 he settled into the church at Folkestone. His health sufficiently improved for him and the Revd John Aldis to go out to the north-west provinces of India on behalf of the BMS in order to deal with certain unspecified circumstances which required both his "judgment and tact," as Swaine puts it. In 1880, he accepted the invitation to become joint Secretary of the Baptist Union and the British and Irish Home Mission, the former in succession to Samuel Harris Booth. However, the pressures took their toll, and he died in 1882. In tribute to Sampson, the Baptist Union spoke of "the zeal, the courtesy, and the ability" with which he had conducted his duties.

Sampson was followed a few years later by Joshua W. Thomas also from King Street, Bristol, who entered the College in 1862, and in 1866, after matriculating from London University, received a year's extension to his studies. While his application to the BMS was initially deferred in 1867, the probability that he would be accepted for service in India was noted, and this, in fact, is what happened. His time of service at Serampore College was in two phases, 1868–80, and 1905–7, during both of which he officiated as principal.

China mission

The involvement in China was never easy or straightforward, and the story of H. H. Rowley, who studied in Bristol, gives a good example of some of the complexities and struggles that were part of the China Mission in the nineteenth century.

H. H. Rowley

H. H. Rowley was born in 1890 in Leicester and was part of the Baptist church at Melbourne Hall from the beginning of his life. Mission was part of the regular teaching in the congregation, and the place of BMS was often highlighted. The preaching often focused on a call to serve with BMS, and from an early age, this was Rowley's sense of where he was headed. When he eventually applied, he said that he had wanted to be a missionary—and indeed, a missionary to China—since he was about nine or ten years old. He was not physically strong or robust, and in fact was not expected to live long. When he left school, he went to train as a teacher as a first step. By 1909, he was also pursuing academic study through the University of London with a view to serving overseas, while also recognizing that he would need theological training as well. He was convinced that this was not best done by correspondence course after a full day at work, and that attending College was important. However, he did not have the financial means to do so.

He wrote to the *Missionary Herald* pointing out that although there were regular appeals to support the missions, there was very little encouragement for *people* and querying whether this was because there were no means available to support would-be applications, or that the possible means were not well known to those who might benefit from them. Nevertheless, he believed he was now ready to pursue his desire to service in China and so he applied to BMS in 1910. It was recommended that he attend the Bristol College and also worked to gain more experience in preaching. He was still only nineteen years old, and his experience was very limited, but he knew what he wanted to do, and he knew what he needed to do in order to achieve his goal. In his application to the College, he made the most of the reading he had been able to do and argued that he was ready to do more. He was also required to give a summary of his faith, which he did, in terms that would look remarkably familiar to anybody writing such a statement today. It is noticeable that by now, we have moved into a theological landscape that seems to be much more closely related to that of the early twenty-first century, and where the disputes that had shaped much of the eighteenth and nineteenth centuries have faded into the background, at least as far as making personal statements are concerned.

Rowley was accepted into the College and started in September 1910. He was clear that his intention in studying was to prepare himself as fully as he could in order to serve in China, and so he specifically took courses in comparative religion and in languages. There were times in the College when he was unable to study because of weakness in his eyes, but he continued in the attempt. In fact, during his time in Bristol, his health gave enough cause for concern to call into question his capacity to serve overseas, but he continued to hope that it would be possible. He went on to gain a Bachelor of Arts degree from Bristol and a Bachelor of Divinity degree from London both in 1912, and then to follow these up, thanks to scholarships which he won, with further qualifications in Hebrew and Aramaic from London. He planned to go to Germany for further study, but the war was to stop that. Instead, he pursued further study in Oxford, and in 1915, he reopened the possibility of service with BMS overseas. However, the scholarship he had been awarded meant that some of the committee at least felt he ought to remain in the British Isles. His health was also clearly a concern for some, and all this together meant that he withdrew at this time from applying for overseas service. He did go to Egypt with the YMCA, but was so unwell, he had to come home. He was then called to the pastorate in Wells, to a united Baptist and Congregational church.

In 1921, there was a further appeal for workers to go to China and he tried again. His health appeared to be much more robust, and he was now married and he and his wife had two daughters—a situation he clearly believed was helpful in his application. He made formal application to be considered by BMS, and again, as part of this gave a statement of faith, one that shows him to be well formed within the Bristol Tradition of evangelical theology. This was a very necessary reassurance to BMS at a point when many Baptists who were also scholars, in particular biblical scholars, were regarded as suspect. The impact of modern scholarship, and the way in which people did or did not embrace it, had become one of the fault lines that divided so many denominations.

By the end of 1921 he had been accepted by BMS for service in China, with the expectation that he would be doing educational work. However, by 1922, not long after the family arrived, anti-foreign and specifically anti-Christian attitudes were growing stronger, especially in universities, and schools and Colleges with Christian links came under particular attack as agents of western imperialism. By the middle of 1925, this was becoming violent. At the university at which Rowley was now teaching, Shandong Christian University, students went on strike in sympathy with the anti-foreign demonstrations. The Senate of the university expressed sympathy with them, and rearranged the exams that had been disrupted. Rowley was horrified at what he saw as a capitulation on basic principles and resigned, although he later withdrew his resignation when the Senate cautioned students that they should not disrupt the work of the institution.

However, in the next two years, Christian education came under repeated attack; it was abolished in primary schools and made a matter of choice in other institutions. Many students, as a sign of their commitment to their national identity, opted out of the Christian aspect of education, arguing that it was a foreign imposition. In 1927, the Shandong University removed any Christian objectives from the formal statements of the institution, and at this point, Rowley finally resigned. He eventually left China in 1929, and took a post in Cardiff.

His story is one example of the ways in which life-long and passionate intentions to serve in a particular way can be frustrated by circumstances beyond anybody's control. But the contribution that he went on to make in biblical studies within and far beyond the denomination are also a reminder that what we and what others might think is the best way for us to serve, might not be the only way. Rowley's writings on various aspects of Old Testament studies were to enrich the wider church for several generations.

There were others who served in China, some for many years. E. W. Burt entered the College in 1886, and spent forty years with BMS in China, between 1892 and 1932. He wrote *After Sixty Years*, "a masterly survey" of the BMS work in China, and he died in Worthing, Sussex, in the year that the missionaries were finally expelled from China, 1951.

The work in China has a particular form of reciprocity about it. The mission work from 1870 onwards was dominated by Timothy Richards, who was supported by, among others, students from Bristol. As part of the mutuality, Richards donated books to the Bristol College library—and in turn, several more students went from Bristol to serve in China.

Othe China Missionaries

In 1899 came the Boxer Uprising, with its rejection of Christianity, in which some from Bristol died. The College Report of 1901 told the story of the Underwoods who were visiting and who, the Report stated, "were called to lay down their lives for Christ", along with six others in the party. Thomas J. Underwood, a member of the Manvers Street Church in Bath, had entered the College in 1892, and sailed for China in in 1896 to serve with BMS. His sacrifice and that of the others was commemorated in a plaque that was in the chapel in the building in Woodland Road. The impact of those who died in service became an inspiration to others to serve, and the commitment to the work in China continued.

The work in China involved not only students from the College going to serve, but the setting up of a College to train local workers, under the principalship of James Whitewright, a former student of Bristol College, which used a curriculum very similar to that of the Bristol College. This raises interesting questions of course about cultural suitability and appropriateness, but nonetheless, it is another demonstration of the practical connections to mission work in so many forms that emerged from the life of the College community at this time.

John Sutherland Whitewright in China (accession number 14968). His adoption of Chinese dress indicates the way in which he followed the pattern of Timothy Richards.

Another aspect of the impact of the Bristol College on the mission in China was the founding of a museum. The College in Stokes Croft included a room for a museum, as did the building in Woodlands Road—often a source of amusement to later students. The use of a museum as a way of furthering education and interest in the wider world, as well as holding a directly apologetic aim, was an important part of the Bristol experiment. And it was one that Whitewright also explored in China; Whitewright's goal for the museum had been to open the minds and widen the outlook of his students and other Chinese, who quickly flocked to visit it, and in this he succeeded. In 1905, the museum was transferred to Jinan, and in 1917, the Jinan (Tsinan) Institute was incorporated into Shandong Christian University as its Extension Department and then later became part of Cheeloo University.

Jamaica

This pattern of founding schools and Colleges, and training men for ministry as part of the missionary enterprise also occurred near Rio Bueno, Trelawny, Jamaica, with the founding of Calabar College, the fruit of work begun by William Knibb, Thomas Burchell, and James Mursell Phillippo. Following their independence from the BMS in 1842, the Jamaican Baptists founded their own Jamaica Baptist Missionary Society and, in 1843, established a theological College, the Calabar Institution.

As its funds became increasingly stretched, the BMS began to urge the missionaries in Jamaica to follow the example of their colleagues in India and develop the island's own indigenous ministry. However, the missionaries had already been quietly working to this end.

From as early as 1831, while in England, Burchell had urged the BMS Committee to establish a school in Montego Bay in the conviction that schools were an essential part of the missionaries' work, both for evangelism and also in preparing slaves for full citizenship once emancipation had been won. In 1835, he began training teachers in the county of Cornwall, which would enable him to double the work he had to date achieved through Sunday School work. He wrote,

> Already I have two young men under instruction, for masters; one of whom is sent by brother Knibb, designed for a school he contemplates at Falmouth. Other persons are making application for instruction and situations; but it is impossible for me as an individual to undertake more than I have done. I have now above one thousand children under instruction, chiefly in

Sunday schools, at Montego Bay, and at some of my out-stations; at the rest I am about to commence schools; and I could enlarge at all, had I the means. The same cause prevents my establishing day schools at most of my stations, which lie situated in an important district of country. I feel intensely anxious for the welfare of the rising generation, now growing up to be a free people. At present, I have strength, and I think I have at least an equal disposition, to work: all I need is help, pecuniary help. Let me but have this in sufficient measure, and I will pledge myself to establish schools, so as to have at least a thousand children of apprentices under instruction.

In early June 1836, Burchell's "British school" in Montego Bay was "in a pleasing state" with 160 day-scholars "whose progress is satisfactory." Three months previously he had also begun an infants' school, which had already enrolled fifty children. At Mount Carey, he was setting up another British school which would open on 1 August and accommodate two hundred children. A teacher for this school was already being trained by Burchell at the Borough Road institution. At Montego Bay he was also training a young man for work at Gurney's Mount. As well as all the work going into setting up and staffing schools, Burchell's educational concerns extended to training church leaders; he had the intention that the schools and the churches would develop their own lives.

Plans were made, but support was hard to generate. At a meeting of ministers in 1839, the three British missionaries moved a resolution that a Jamaican ministerial College should be established, and in 1842 Knibb travelled back to England to raise support from the BMS. They finally agreed bought the land on which the mission house belonging to Rio Bueno Baptist Church already stood. When the Jubilee of the BMS was celebrated by the churches of the Baptist Western Union there were three days of celebration. The first day saw people gather for the preaching event, which celebrated translations and freedom. The event took place in a tent, the entrance of which was decorated by a large banner depicting two angels, "one with a trumpet, designed to represent the preaching of the everlasting gospel among all the nations of the earth, the other with an open book, representing the bible, on which was written, 'Translated into forty languages,'"; this was about the number of languages and dialects into which Scripture had been translated by in the East Indies by missionaries. In front of the banner was a tablet under which was written "Africa shall be free," and above it, "Slavery abolished August 1, 1838." The text of Leviticus 25:9 was also displayed, "Then shalt thou cause the trumpet of the jubilee to sound," as well as the BMS's motto, "Expect great things from God, attempt great things for God." The service was led by Knibb and Burchell, and there were five sermons.

On the third day of the Jubilee, fifteen hundred people met for the morning prayer meeting at 7.00 a.m., followed by the Great Jubilee Meeting at 11.00 a.m., at which Knibb read Psalm 72. Burchell chaired the business meeting at which six resolutions were proposed and adopted. The third motion called "upon the church of God, and especially upon that portion of it in Jamaica, not only fully to support their own missionaries, but by enlarged liberality and zealous exertion to assist in carrying on the great work of evangelizing the world," and in particular those "openings which present themselves for the formation of new stations in the destitute districts of this colony, and new missions to the surrounding islands," as well as to Western and Central Africa.

This provided the context for the following motion which welcomed

> with delight the establishment [. . .] of the Jamaica Baptist Theological Institution for the training of young men for the Christian ministry; and, believing that it will, under God, prove the means of raising up a class of educated native agents, who shall in this island and on the continent of Africa, proclaim the unsearchable riches of Christ, we cordially recommend it to the sympathies, the support, and the prayers of our churches.

The desire for the churches to be indigenous, and independent was a guiding principle for another Bristol student who went to Jamaica, and who was part of the Calabar College. Joshua Tinson came from the same church as Burchell, Shortwood in Gloucestershire. From there he was sent to study with Joseph Kinghorn at Norwich in 1817, before entering the Bristol College in 1818 under John Ryland. His studies were funded by the BMS, and in 1821, he requested a year's extension, finally being set apart as a missionary in Jamaica in 1822, sailing in May that year. Most of his work on the island was at Hanover Street, St Thomas Parish, where he remained till his death. Following a home furlough, he was also appointed the first president of Calabar College in October 1843 with eight students.

Tinson believed that European missionaries had no place on the mission field as he was unaware of one which had been successful under European control. For him, "the religion of the Bible, like all the productions of the Deity, has its seed in itself," and that the gospel needed to be spread by national converts. He also believed that personal and national morality came from self-respect, which was derived only when people and nations were self-sufficient, free from foreign control.

It would be over half a century before another Bristol student went to Calabar College. Ernest Price's early Christian influences came from The Salvation Army, acting as secretary to one of the Booth family. However, in 1894, aged twenty, he became a Baptist by conviction, and entered the Bristol College from the church at Poplar. He matriculated in the First Division for the London University degree in June 1896, the year he was also granted a Dr Ward Scholarship. The following year he passed his London Intermediate exam, and finally graduated with a Bachelor of Divinity from London University in Mental and Moral Science. In 1910, along with eight other former students, Price was conferred an honorary Bachelor of Arts by Bristol University, and in the same year he accepted the post of president of Calabar College, "for which he is admirably fitted."

On Price's arrival in Jamaica in 1910, he found that the College was at a low ebb, but over the next few years things improved. Though people back home sought to dissuade him, with the help of his colleague, Australian born David Davis, who had gained his first degree from Adelaide University, South Australia, and second from the University of London, which he studied for in Bristol College, Price founded Calabar High School in 1912 to provide education for the sons of ministers, and he remained its headmaster until 1937. The school grew quickly and became one of the leading education establishments in Jamaica. In addition to his work as principal and headmaster, Price preached regularly in small churches across the island. Davis was a tutor at the College and the deputy at the high school. However, the demands on his time at the school were so great that Davis left the College in 1942 in order to give all his time to the school.

Sadly, the latter part of Price's principalship proved controversial, as he fell out with key leaders of the Jamaica Baptist Union, in particular with the English minister at East Queen Street in Kingston, Cowell Lloyd. The whole issue revolved around the control of the management and finances of the College. The College's trust deed set out that a general committee was in charge of the institution but under the BMS's guidance. The vagaries of this arrangement meant that in practice every minister on the island was eligible for membership of this committee, and a clash was inevitable between the ministers and Price as the principal, who understood himself to be answerable to the BMS. In the late 1920s and early 1930s relationships became unsustainable, despite BMS's attempt to propose a solution. In 1934, the general committee refused to work with Price, and ministers and churches ceased their financial support of the College. In 1937, Price resigned and left the island. (What Davis did is not known.)

During their time, however, one Jamaican student, Keith Preston, was in Bristol for a year. When he was back in Jamaica, he undertook the pastorate of a group of churches in Thompson Town between 1924 and 1926. Then he moved to Cotessey in Norfolk, and then in 1928 he became minister of Sherborne in Dorset, and in the following year he was accepted onto the accredited list of the Baptist Union.

Links in the other direction were restored in 1948, when Keith Tucker was appointed principal of Calabar College and the BMS representative. He had been a probationary student in 1924 at Bristol College and was awarded a Bachelor of Arts in 1929. He was also one who benefitted from the developing links with Regent's Park College and studied for two postgraduate years there. He served in three pastorates in England before his move to Calabar—an appointment the Bristol College report celebrated as "continuing the long and honourable association with Calabar" working backwards from Ernest Price and David Davis through John Rowe, Joshua Tinson and eventually to "the illustrious Thomas Burchell."

Trinidad

The links with Jamaica were not the only ones in that part of the world. In 1906, B. E. Horlick who was the minister of St John's Baptist church in Port of Spain, Trinidad, approached BMS to ask if they could help him find a young assistant from one of the British Colleges, and James Poole was appointed. He had started at the Bristol College in 1904, and on completing his course in 1907 had applied to serve with BMS in China, though he was turned down on health grounds. However, he was able to accept the call to Trinidad, and served there for three years, with oversight of a small group of churches in the south of the island. There were financial problems and in 1909 he and his wife came to England where he became pastor at Sidcup. However, in 1911, he returned to Trinidad and succeeded Horlick as minister of St John's. He was recognized by BMS, but was not regarded as a missionary, but as the minister of the local church; this was the local church which paid his stipend. He served there (with an interim of three years in the 1920s in which he worked for the YMCA in the Bahamas) until he retired in 1946. Retirement actually meant that he went to the Bahamas and served in a church in Nassau, for six years, and then returned to England where he was minister of Great Samford Baptist church. In 1961 he when back to St John's for a further nine years of ministry. Brian Stanley in his history of the BMS, says that Poole "more than any other individual" was responsible for "keeping the weak Baptist cause in Trinidad from extinction and eventually, for persuading the BMS to recommence work on the island in 1946."

Several students came from Trinidad to study in Bristol. Among them, S. E. E. Payne who having completed his course was accepted by BMS to serve in India. He was in Orissa from 1940 to 1960 and then went back to Trinidad where he and his wife worked as missionaries for five more years. Rudolf Cross came from Port of Spain in 1946, and when he left in 1950 went to Jamaica to undertake pastoral work. Among other things, he lectured at Calabar College. As part of an American mission, he was appointed Superintendent of the Lott-Crey Mission Convention in Haiti until he died in a fishing accident in 1955.

With the opening of a College, St Andrew's Hall, specifically to meet the needs of those training for service overseas, the number of those who went from Bristol to serve with BMS changed, though there were still those who, having trained in the College, went on to work with BMS—right up until the present day.

There have also been those who came from elsewhere to Bristol under the auspices of BMS. In the 1990s, Ah Li Yang came from Myanmar to do a degree and then a doctorate. Ah Li, on her return took up a post in the Lisu Theological Seminary in Myanmar, and became Principal there. Her contacts with her fellow Bristol students from those days remain, and benefit ministers here and the seminary there.

There were also opportunities for students to make trips with BMS, and spend some time, usually during a summer break, with BMS workers and understand something of the work. Thus, for example,in the 1990s, Rachel Haig, visited Thailand in her time as a student. These were very significant trips for the individuals concerned and served to keep alive links between College and mission agency.

As we will see below, since 2008, this has been developed even further, serving to deepen ties with BMS, and broadening an understanding of cross-cultural mission (which is important not just for those who will serve overseas but also for those working in UK towns and cities), as well as giving a significant context for theological reflection on issues of poverty, injustice, and interfaith work. Again, the importance of the Bristol Tradition can be glimpsed: lively, zealous, able, and evangelical preachers of the gospel are not only shaped and trained within a well-known context, but they can be deepened, broadened, and opened up as they discover a wider world. Those who have been on such trips talk of how life changing it has been, challenging their view of ministry and of themselves. This kind of stretching of what is possible and where comfort zones might be is part of what it means to develop ability, and to increase a sense of zeal. Additionally, these trips have encouraged students to reflect on the nature of the gospel and the way in which culture shapes perception of the gospel, and to challenge a western-centric understanding of what Christian faith might look like.

As we have seen in all the involvement between the College and BMS, this awareness of mission and ministry beyond the immediate and known context has always been important. From involvement in the struggles against slavery in Jamaica through to discovering diverse ways of being a church in today's Mozambique or the liberating presence of the gospel among sex workers in Thailand, the re-creative powers of the gospel that is the heart of evangelicalism has been nurtured through the College's links with BMS. And in being those shaped by the tradition, students from the College have brought something to the overseas service of the denomination.

As BMS became less and less an agency with which people served all their ministry, and more opportunity was available for short-term service, so others from the College have served overseas. Some, however, have continued to offer for long-term service. Peter Lynch, for example, a student at the College in the early part of the 2000s now serves with his wife Louise in Bangladesh.

CONNECTIONS WITH OTHER COLLEGES

The influence on theological education through BMS was not the only way that Bristol was part of a developing pattern of theological education. As one of the oldest Colleges, and the survivor of the early seminaries, its impact on the new theological Colleges in the nineteenth century is also important.

Horton

So, for example, when the Northern Baptist Education Society was formed, centred at Horton, it was a Bristol-trained man who was eventually appointed as principal, William Steadman. He was soon joined by Bristol-educated Jonathan Edwards Ryland, son of John Ryland Jr. Steadman was succeeded by another Bristol man, James Acworth, who served as principal from 1835–63, and oversaw the move to new premises in Rawdon in 1859.

A third Baptist graduate to serve as a tutor at Horton was Francis Clowes who came to Bristol College in 1827 from Heacham in Norfolk. He was one of Crisp's students. He was allowed to leave before Christmas 1830 so that he could be on trial at the church at Thrissell Street, off Stapleton Road, Bristol, where he remained until 1836.

In 1837, Clowes, who at some point had earned a Master of Arts degree from Aberdeen, became the classics and mathematics tutor at Horton

Academy alongside James Acworth, a post he held for thirteen years. While a "truly good, and able, and learned man," he was reckoned not to be in the same mould as his notable predecessors, largely due to his diffidence and retiring manner, but also because his voice was weak, and delivery seemingly unacceptable to congregations. In the classroom, however, "he was a power, and a power for good," possessing "fine gifts" as a teacher, who "won the warm gratitude" of his students.

He was also greatly concerned about the social issues of the day, and at a meeting of the Lancashire and Yorkshire Baptists in Bradford he asserted that while God should be given his rights, so, too, should other people. He was particularly involved in the questions around legislation that might threaten religious liberties, and was part of the Association committee which attended to such issues. One threat had been detected in the Conservative Prime Minister Sir Robert Peel's proposal to endow new churches, which would be Anglican, and the committee feared this would lead to legislative hostility and a curbing of freedoms. Clowes was concerned that people whom he feared would limit the freedom of education that had been gained would also

> not hesitate soon to invade the ministry of the word and the freedom of the press. Baptist churches are, in God's providence, the chosen nurseries of freedom. They emancipated the negro— they have been the core of the liberal cause. Baptists are the only body, who, as a body, care neither for the traditions of the elders, nor the adherence of wealthy trimmers. Our denomination must, then, gird itself to its duty. If we lose a few wealthy, we shall gain the many. We shall be the body to convince them that the Bible is the book of the people, and, however the interested of all parties may scorn, that Bible Christians contend equally and honestly for the rights of all.

He is notable for introducing Aramaic and Syriac into the course at Horton. After student numbers peaked in 1842 with thirty, the course became more demanding, and in 1843 was extended to five years when Syriac and Chaldee were added. In 1844, Clowes had co-edited *The Church*, a Baptist penny magazine, and was later an assistant editor of *The Freeman*, a Baptist newspaper, and these roles perhaps paved the way, following his retirement in 1851 due to poor health, to his becoming editor of *The Sun* newspaper.

He was followed at Horton by Charles Daniell, who had started at the Bristol College in January 1825, and studied under Ryland, Crisp, James, and Anderson until 1828. When he was awarded a Dr Ward's Scholarship, he was allowed to leave Bristol in June 1828 so that he could continue his studies for the next session in Edinburgh.

Thus, the impact of the Bristol pattern of education and of the Bristol Tradition was offered to a new College as it was getting itself established in the first half of the nineteenth century. But those were not the only connections.

Wales

The links with Wales that we saw in the first century of the College's history continued in the second. The funding of Colleges in Wales had a chequered history. The first principal of the Abergavenny College was Micah Thomas, another of John Ryland's students. In 1820 Micah Thomas was joined by another Bristol-trained man, George Thomas, who served as tutor from 1841 to 1870. The later and complex history of this College is not a matter for this book but reflects well on the commitment to education that Thomas carried till the end of his life.

Two more Welsh students who studied at Bristol went on to become principals in Welsh Colleges. Dr Thomas Davies became principal of the Haverfordwest College from 1856 to 1894, while Gethin Davies, who had studied under Gotch, went on to become tutor of classics (1872), and then principal of Llangollen College (Yr Athrofa; The Institute) from 1883 to 1896, overseeing its move to Bangor, Gwynedd, in 1892.

Stepney

In 1813, one of Ryland's students from Bristol, Solomon Young became tutor of classics at Stepney College, then succeeded William Newman as president in 1827 until his death that same year. Another Bristol graduate, Benjamin Davies, served as president from 1844 to 1847, then returned to the College as classical and oriental tutor from 1857 to 1875 once it had relocated to Regent's Park. After his time as a student at Bristol from 1830, Davies studied in Dublin, Edinburgh, and Germany, gaining his doctorate from Leipzig, and a Doctor of Laws from Dublin. He was an expert in Hebrew and cognate languages, including Syriac, and among his students were future leaders of the denomination.

The next Bristol-trained tutor at Stepney was Joshua Taylor Gray, the fifth son of the Revd William Gray, himself a Bristol-trained man, who was pastor of the church at College Street, Northampton. Gray was at the Stepney College from 1841 to 1845 as tutor of classics. He had entered Bristol College in 1827 and was a student for nearly four years. Crisp remembered him to be "a diligent and successful student," and that his studies were marked by "accuracy and power." He was proficient in Hebrew, "and stood high in classical attainments." James Cowles Prichard, MD, who regularly attended the College's annual examinations, made the same assessment of his achievements and his accuracy in classical subjects. During his student years, Gray sat under Robert Hall's ministry and was often invited to his home which "furnished to him sources of improvement and enjoyment which he readily appreciated." This, he said later, "combined to render his time at College more than ordinarily valuable, and to place its reminiscences among the happiest of his life." He also preached in the vestry at Broadmead, and, following one such occasion, Hall commented, "The passage from which our friend has spoken has been so correctly expounded that there is really nothing left for me to say."

General Baptists

The breadth of the life and theology in the College is demonstrated by the fact that several future General Baptist tutors were also educated at there: Stephen Freeman and John Evans, for example.

Freeman had studied at the Bristol Academy between 1783 and 1787, under Caleb Evans, James Newton, and Robert Hall, and among his fellow students was his future successor at the General Baptist Academy, John Evans. The General Baptist Assembly of the Old General Baptists turned to Stephen Freeman when it met on 30 May 1792 at Worship Street, Bishopsgate Street, London, and resolved to establish their own academy. He agreed to teach students in his home at Ponders End, but this only continued for two years from 1792 until 1794, and he only had one student, Benjamin Austen, who went on to minister at Smarden.

John Evans took over as the General Baptists' tutor in 1795 and served until 1818. During that time, Evans trained twenty-one men, first at Hoxton Square, and then at his home in Islington, where two, or a maximum of three boarded with him throughout the duration of their course. One reason that lay behind Evans's support for the General Baptists' provision of theological training for their own ministers was a concern he had about what he called John Ryland's narrowing of "the terms of admission on account of religious sentiment." This possibly means a lack of sympathy for Arminianism or that Ryland had detected a wavering of Evans's Calvinistic convictions, whereas Caleb Evans had been, in John Evans's opinion a more "worthy and liberal president."

CHANGES, CHALLENGES, AND CONTROVERSIES

This century of the College's life was not, of course, simply marked by success and applause. There were challenges within and without the churches which made demands on the College and on occasions led it into controversy and dispute.

Theological shifts

To start with, theology was shifting significantly, in general and in particular for our story, among Baptists. Broadly during the nineteenth century, there were several movements that asked questions of theology and shaped theological thinking both in content and in style. While the impact of Darwin's theories has, in later times, been over-emphasized in its impact on believers, more broadly, it is true to say that scientific developments, archaeology, cosmology, and indeed, biology, did at the very least raise questions, and for some provoked serious doubts about the witness of Scripture and therefore of the whole basis of faith.

It is probably more true to say that such scientific challenges added to questioning that was already going on around such topics as the impact of new forms of research into the Scriptures, with the development of form criticism and historical research, the challenge raised as people considered certain moral questions around the nature of eternal punishment (can a good God inflict infinite punishment for finite sin—is this not disproportionate?), the questions raised by the new philosophies, and in particular, questions about providence and intervention that were posed by the Lisbon earthquake on All Saints Day in 1755, when many were at worship, and thousands were killed. In all sorts of ways, the theology that had been developed in and had sustained the community of Baptists and other evangelicals was being tested, stretched, and, in some cases, broken. Several broad reactions can be seen within the whole community. There could be a shoring up of boundaries, an insistence on the supposed "old ways," on drawing the lines more firmly (we might for example, classify the writings of Spurgeon that eventually provoked the Downgrade Controversy in this category). Another reaction was the complete rejection of the old ways and a move into what was classified a "fully rational" position—which may or may not have space for God, and faith to be expressed. Another possibility was the move into a less systematically defined theology, with room for the new learning, and even an appreciation for what was now on offer.

As mentioned above, Culross, for example, was less a dogmatic preacher than one who was concerned with exploring experience, and provoking action among believers.

Social and political shifts

The particular legal status of Nonconformists was also changing significantly through this century. The formal removal of most of the legal disabilities for Nonconformists meant the opening up of attendance at universities, participation in the professions and the possibility of taking part in the political system of the day. This set free not only a significant amount of energy, but also brought Nonconformists in from being secluded and self-contained communities to a much broader engagement with society as a whole. This, together with an increase in numbers (it is estimated that by the end of the nineteenth century roughly half the population of England would identify as a Nonconformist of one sort or another), changed the self-perception and the aspirations of those involved in the dissenting churches—and in the Dissenting academies.

Such a move is seen, for example, in the changing style of architecture of the churches of Baptists and other Dissenters in the middle of the nineteenth century, moving from cottage style buildings to buildings that were recognizable as churches, reflecting the growing interest in neo-Gothic architecture.

Such a move also had its impact in what was expected of ministers—and as such, increased the debate about the nature of ministerial training. As congregations became more educated, and more involved in the affairs of the day, there was a need for their ministers to make the same moves, academically and socially. But was this to move ministerial training away from the emphasis on spirituality and service to the Kingdom and more into an academic qualification and social advancement?

The affiliation with London and then with Bristol University was part of the move towards respectability in the academic world, as was the increasing emphasis on taking a degree. This change was also reflected in an openness to the new learning—the nineteenth century was a time of rapid advancement in knowledge and change in approach. The developments in archaeology, in scientific research, in historical studies, all of which had roots in the eighteenth century were becoming mainstream in the nineteenth century and needed to be at least noticed in theological training. The question remained however, whether such notice was to be in order to refute the new learning, or whether it was possible to embrace it and remain orthodoxly Christian.

As we have seen above, those who were on the staff of the academy in Bristol by and large, and often much more enthusiastically than that, embraced the new learning, seeing it as part of the ongoing discovery of the life of faith, and expecting their students also to engage with it. The College had long had a commitment to freedom of thought for all, and the expectation that all truth will ultimately lead to God, and so there was little fear of science and what it might be offering.

However, such a position did lead to changes in the nature of the training on offer. As well as the changing academic standards as a result of being involved with the universities, there was a change within the kind of theology that was taught, and the uses to which it was put.

There was, or at least, there was perceived to be much less emphasis on the kind of evangelism, particularly among the unlearned, that had previously been the pattern. The academic emphasis of the training took attention away from the direct appeal to the hearts of men and women, and concentrated more on the academic apologetic, engaging with the issues raised by science and by biblical criticism in particular. It was argued that this was no less evangelism, but a different sort of evangelism, more directed towards the realities that people lived with. But it was perceived, including by some of the Colleges' supporters, to be a change not for the better. Language of "spiritual depression" began to appear when people spoke of the Colleges, and a widening gap between the Colleges and churches began to be noticeable. There was a fear that academic theology, far from deepening and enabling faith, actually undermined it, and led people away from the kind of religious identity that had been the mark of previous generations. The studies that students now undertook—largely literary and classical, as required by the university degree curriculum—were seen as not calculated to heighten religious ardour, but rather to "puff up with knowledge."

The tension that we have noticed about whether Colleges were necessary was heightened during this second century of the College's life. In some cases, notably for example with Hinton, this was increased by a tension over the need for an ordained ministry at all. The rise of the Oxford Movement in the second part of the nineteenth century served to fuel Nonconformist, and in particular Baptist, wariness of "priestcraft" and suspicion of anything that looked like clericalism. Hinton argued that every convert should be a preacher and also that having a professional ministry allowed others in the church to be lazy, since they could leave certain things to the minister. The proper role of each member of the congregation was an aim he upheld, and as such, he remained ambivalent about the role and place—and the need for educating—ministers. However, he did argue that if there were going to be ministers, then they should be well educated because they needed to be able to think well about the significant issues of the day. This therefore implied a need for study, and the resources to do it.

Not everybody accepted this position of the need for study. There were those who maintained that an uneducated ministry was a virtue. It led to people who were not distracted by "book learning" but concentrated solely on Scripture, on the care of the congregation, and the call of evangelism. For those who argued so, the Colleges were a liability and indeed a hindrance to the work of the Kingdom, since they used resources that might otherwise be available for churches and for mission.

This was not an argument that was easily resolved. It was clear, for example, that with the opening up of Oxford and Cambridge, there were young Nonconformist men who began to study there and who subsequently left the chapels of their youth, either to become Anglicans, or in many cases to cease any church connection at all. Even those who did not go to study were moving out of the orbit of the chapels; the move from the countryside to the cities increased in this century, and such a move in search of work, often led to a severing of ties with the churches.

The need for evangelism therefore was still seen to be of a high priority. But Evangelicalism, and therefore evangelism, was changing. And it was necessary for the Colleges, if they were to continue to serve the churches at all, to change along with them. There was a need to recognize the place of knowledge, and likewise the ability to communicate with those who were sophisticated, university educated, and who took the new approach to knowledge for granted, and the Colleges were attempting to meet this need.

However, all the Nonconformist Colleges, and in particular for our story, all the Baptist Colleges were small, even when they were connected with other Colleges or with universities. They were chronically understaffed and had little in the way of financial resources. One of the results of this was that those among the wider community who were academically gifted had to combine their academic work with work as pastors, and sometimes in other areas of employment as well, since many churches were not able to support a minister unless the minister also had access to other income. There were clearly strengths in such a position. A minister working in such a situation was well grounded in the life and concerns of a local congregation, for example.

But there were also disadvantages. There was little time to pursue the kind of intense academic theology that marks the Anglican church at this period for example. This led to a thinness of theology and a lack of resource to meet some of the challenges of the new thinking that became particularly significant towards the last decades of the nineteenth century.

Resources

The lack of resources also raised the question of the number of Colleges. In 1846, the second Conference of the Former Students was held. They considered the issues around training, particularly its content, and also the question of the number and size of the Colleges. The question about the need for prior learning was discussed in depth; there was a recognition that in order to benefit from studying theology, and to be of use to the churches in this new situation, a broader education was needed. Many of those applying did not have the necessary background. Because of this, a significant part of the time at College was being taken up filling in such gaps and there was less time and resources for specifically ministerial training. There was a suggestion therefore that the four Colleges should work together: two should be preparatory Colleges, providing a good solid general education for those who did not otherwise have access to it, and the other two should concentrate on specifically theological and ministerial training.

These ideas, though floated, did not develop, since the Colleges could not agree on which would adopt which position—and thus started a discussion that still continues: how do we as a whole community make best use of limited resources, and yet offer the breadth and variety of training that is important within a community as diverse as ours? This is a topic to which we shall return.

CONCLUSION

This second century of the College's life saw many changes—socially, politically, theologically. The world of 1921 was very different from the world of 1825. The world had passed through a war the like of which had never been seen. Technology had changed the way people communicated, travelled, and lit their homes. The franchise had spread from being limited to wealthy landowners to all men over twenty-one years of age and all women over thirty. The Baptist Union had not only been established, but it had also survived a major crisis over The Downgrade.

Mission overseas had grown in parallel with—sometimes in unity with, sometimes in opposition to—the British Empire. Mission at home was becoming ever more important, in particular as the twentieth century progressed, and numbers attending churches began to decline noticeably.

Conceptions of ministry had changed—there were new situations to deal with, new social positions to negotiate, new intellectual challenges to meet. The long-term effect of the war (and the subsequent flu pandemic) was only just beginning to be understood.

5

PHYSICAL HOMES OF THE COLLEGE

In the three hundred years of its history, the College has 'lived' in a variety of places. Each of these homes has been shaped by an understanding of what training should be, but also by other matters. Finances have always been important, the number of students to be accommodated has mattered, as has the age and life-stage of the students. Links with other institutions have played their part, together with the role of theological Colleges in the wider life of the city and the country. The building(s) in which the College exists at any point is both determined by and determines the way in which the community functions and the way in which training happens.

NORTH STREET

The Academy started based in the manse of the Broadmead Church minister. In common with other forms of dissenting ministerial training at the time, the model was of living in a home and learning alongside a practitioner. That the learning, under the terms of Terrill's deed of gift, was rather more structured, and in particular that the finance was more organized, did not on the whole change the pattern of living in household. The Broadmead manse at this point was in North Street and was a big house and at first, this was where everybody lived. The model of learning was of household life: living and praying together with and indeed as a family, with time for reading, discussion, and mutual encouragement provided. However, by the early 1770s, the number of students was nearly twenty and the house was not large enough. Another house on North Street was bought to house the principal and his family, so that the original manse could become the lecture room, dining room, and library, as well as provide living space for some of the students.

There was provision for students to live in lodgings nearby as well, at times when there were more than could be accommodated in the manse, and a 'rent' was paid for the use of space in the manse. Thus, in 1803, for example, the Bristol Education Society accounts show that Ryland received twenty-five guineas for each student.

By 1803, perhaps as a result of the need to pay rent, plans were beginning to emerge to move from this home-based model into something built for the purpose of a being a College. The records around the early stages of the discussion are missing, and so we do not know exactly what prompted the intention to move, but it is clear that numbers were increasing, and were expected to increase more, and this was presumably a significant reason for the desired move.

THE MOVE TO STOKES CROFT

As well as numbers actually increasing, such records as we have suggest that there was an intention to seek to increase the numbers in order to ensure that the College would remain viable. This also seems to have been part of the perceived necessity of a new building; such a resource would be more attractive for students than moving into the manse or living in lodgings. In 1804, an agreement with Broadmead Church was reached to move the College out of the manse, and to begin to build up the fund rather more independently of the church. At this time, land in Stokes Croft became available. Until the middle of the nineteenth century and the coming of the trams, Stokes Croft was an area of open fields and small hamlets. It was within reach of the city, but separate from it, quiet and secure; an ideal place for a seminary. By the end of 1804, the decision was taken to go ahead and buy the land in the hope of being able to refurbish an existing building already there.

In order to do this, of course, money was needed, and the raising of the money took a longer time than people had hoped. Part of the method of fundraising was by trips beyond the Bristol Baptist community and churches to broaden the base of supporters. The campaign to raise funds also involved arguments to this wider constituency to justify ministerial training and in particular, training of the sort that the College was committed to.

THE Baptist Academy in Bristol, for the Education of young Ministers, is an Institution of long standing; first set on foot, on a small scale, by the Liberality of an ancient member of the church in Broadmead; and considerably enlarged, by the establishment of the Education Society, formed in the year 1770, by the special exertions of the late excellent Dr. Caleb Evans; who was then united with his venerable Father Mr. Hugh Evans, in superintending this Seminary.

It's usefulness and importance having since been confirmed, by the experience of above thirty years, in which period many of our churches have been from thence supplied with able and evangelical ministers; it will not appear arrogant to solicit, from the friends of Religion, particularly of the Baptist Denomination, their assistance towards its farther enlargement. It has hitherto been almost the only Institution of the kind, among Christians of our persuasion; while numerous Academies have been established by our pædobaptist brethren, to some of which many Baptists have afforded the friendly aid, it well became them to impart. But while we rejoice that other protestant Dissenters are educating a number of young men, under very respectable Tutors, at *Hoxton, Homerton, Hackney, Gosport, Rotherham, Wymondley, Axminster, Wrexham* and *Carmarthen*, shall the Baptists, who in England and Wales have nearly 500 Churches, be able to afford literary advantages, to only seventeen or eighteen students at a time? Yet this number has scarcely ever been exceeded, and seldom equalled at Bristol. Nor can it be increased, unless we can obtain a situation for a larger building than that which we now occupy.

Such an opportunity is offered at this time, if the Zeal of our own Denomination, and the friendly Assistance of our fellow Christians of other Persuasions, will but enable us to pursue it.

The Patrons of the Institution in Bristol are ready to exert themselves, on so important an occasion; but they are strongly persuaded that their brethren would not wish them to serve alone, in a case which greatly concerns the whole denomination. Members of the remotest churches have often been received for education, into this Academy; and from thence have congregations, at a great distance, been furnished with faithful pastors.

Must not then the distant Friends of this Seminary, and of the blessed Cause it is intended to promote, unite with us in wishing it to be enlarged, suitably to the exigencies of the times? Our Churches are more numerous than ever, while death is continually removing those who were best qualified to defend the truth as it is in Jesus. Literature is so attentively cultivated in this kingdom, and good taste so generally diffused, that the want of literary accomplishments, in those who sustain the character of ministers, must be more sensibly felt than at any former period. Though we ever wish to keep in view the far superior importance of an experimental* acquaintance

* See on this subject, Mr. Dore's excellent Sermon at our last annual Meeting, entitled *Religious Experience essential to a Christian Minister*.

A page of the appeal leaflet (Accession number 317756)

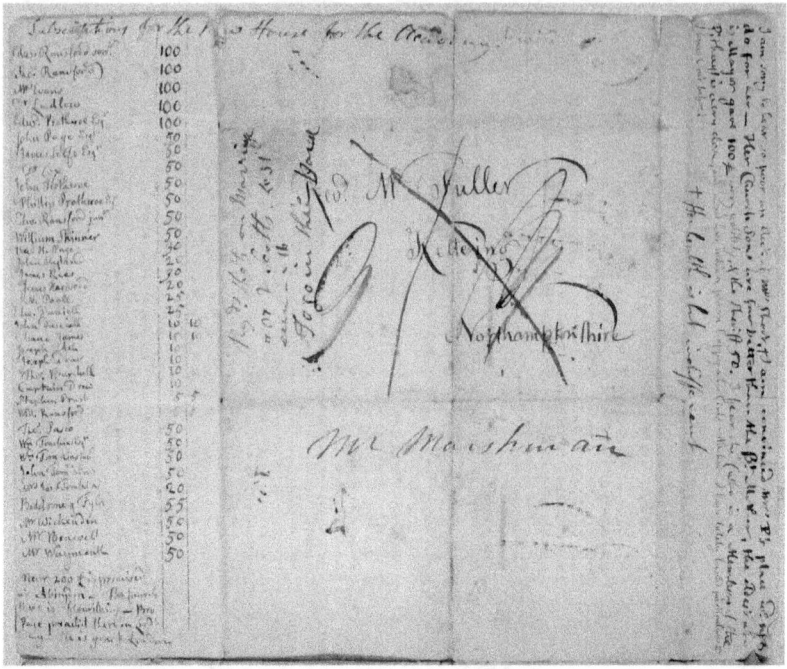

A list of some of the subscribers (Accession number 317560)

By the AGM in the August of 1805, £4,130 had been raised, and £900 was still needed. The hope was that the new College home might be brought into being without debt. Such minutes as we have show that sketches of buildings and developments were looked at and Trustees for the new organization were elected.

However, it became clear that the existing buildings on the site were not suitable for renovation, and that a new building was going to be necessary. This both increased the time and the cost. Discussions and fund raising (including selling off material from the building that could not be renovated) continued throughout 1806. In the middle of the year, sufficient funds were considered to be in hand to start the building, and the AGM that year included a stone-laying ceremony. However, by the AGM of 1807, reports were not encouraging (they will be recognized by anybody who has ever been involved in a building project). The costs were higher than anticipated, and though the ground floor had been built, another £5000—of which about £2000 was already available—was needed. The committee wanted to know where the money was going to come from before they committed the Education Society to the contracts. Various plans for fund raising through subscriptions and loans were undertaken, as well as seeking other tenders that might be cheaper. By February 1808 things were beginning to move again. However, the minutes show that the AGM in 1810 is still concerned with the building project, and how to get it moving. This meeting resolved that the treasurer should circulate the list of all those who had expressed interest and willingness to support a new building, with notes about who had contributed and about what was still needed, in the hope that more money would be forthcoming. The new building was completed by 1811, at a cost of £12,862.17.1. The fund was formally closed in 1813, though some loans remained to be repaid.

The new premises were regarded as being situated in a healthy location and highly suitable for student life. The building comprised a sitting room, a dining room, a lecture room, a museum, and a library on the ground floor. The first floor had thirty studies, and the second floor, thirty bedrooms.

The lecture room in Stokes Croft. (Accession number 29816)

The study corridor. (Accession number 29816)

Life in Stokes Croft

Frederick Trestrail, whose writings give us so much insight into life as a student in this period, describes (though incidentally) something of the life in the new building. Now that all the students were living in one place, rather than some in the manse and some in lodgings, there was a growth in what Trestrail calls "family feeling" and "the constant friction of mind on mind." This community among the students as a context in which part at least of the learning and formation took place was best supported when more senior students took their role seriously.

And it was not only academic. Trestrail points out that there was now a "real dining room" for which the students were expected to dress appropriately, and within the context of which they learned "how to conduct themselves in society," especially as the president and the matron would dine with the students.

The Dining Hall

The dining room in Stokes Croft—possibly an intimidating space for some?

This social polishing was as important a part of formation as the academic development, for it allowed Baptist ministers to move easily among a wide range of people in a social context in which manners and 'politeness' were becoming ever more important. The gradual raising of the social standing of Baptists may be a missiological issue that we still have to wrestle with, but this period in the early and mid-nineteenth century certainly sees a move for Baptists, in terms of both the congregation and minister, away from the working class towards a more middle-class position, which had implications for both assumptions and behaviour.

Academic studies, eating together and spending time together—and worship together. This too formed part of the life of the community in Stokes Croft, according to Trestrail. Prayers, morning and evening each day, and a prayer meeting (social prayer) on a Saturday evening were all a regular part of life together, and not to be present was to raise anxiety about one's well-being, physical and spiritual.

The new building at Stokes Croft allowed for the life of the College to develop in new ways; the benefit of being together with others of similar but not the same views and intentions, and time to think, talk, read, and argue, was a very real one. Here men were not just taught but learned together. Eating together, worshipping together, sharing a building, and negotiating all the complexities that come with living in any community was part of the formation that took place both formally and informally and fitted them (or attempted to) for ministry in a changing context.

However, Stokes Croft did not continue to be the healthful and quiet retreat that it was in the first half of the nineteenth century. In the middle of the century, a major tramline was established which ran through the district, and its character changed rapidly. Shops and businesses were opened, houses were built, and, above all, the noise increased. By 1897, the Education Society was beginning to talk about the possibility of another move.

On the move again

The change in the district was part of the driver, but there were two other factors as well. One was the links being built between the College and the new University of Bristol. The idea of being closer to the university site was appealing, both from the point of view of convenience and of prestige. The other was the possibility of a joint building with the Western College, the Congregational Seminary, which was also looking to settle near the university. Part of this desire was shaped by the recognition that, despite the hopes of the early 1800s, the numbers of students had not increased sufficiently to sustain the Stokes Croft building indefinitely, and a shared building would not only enable shared teaching and common life, but also cut, or share, the costs of the building itself.

In 1901, a joint site was identified, but it did not in the end work out, and so a new idea of a separate building close to both the university and the Western College began to be developed and by 1903 a site had been found in Woodland Road, opposite University College Bristol and near the Western College. This was a much quieter position than Stokes Croft had now become, and was to move into a more salubrious area. The decision was taken to move and consequently to raise the money that would be needed to buy a new home. However, in 1904, the Church Extension Fund became a priority for the wider Baptist community, and so fund-raising for the new building was postponed, although a loan was taken out to bridge the finances until the old site was sold.

On top of the money raised by selling the Stokes Croft site, which had now increased significantly in value, £15,000 was still needed. An appeal was launched across the denomination, based on "200 years of service." By 1907, £7,481.6.11 had been raised. At the same time the sale of the Stokes Croft was postponed because the market had become depressed. The appeal was still continuing in 1909, and in 1910 a big push was instigated with a view to bringing things to an end. In 1911, architects' plans were drawn up, and there was a search for those who would lend money so that things could be progressed. But the Stokes Croft site remained unsold. New plans were drawn up to try to reduce the costs, though there was still a sense that the College needed a "fitting home," and a desire not to lose what the move was intended to gain. The new plans were approved in 1912, and in fact did not actually achieve much in the way of savings, but in 1913, even though there was still a shortfall in the funds, a tender was accepted and the stone laying ceremony took place in November of that year.

WOODLAND ROAD

A competition for a design was held in 1905 (judged in 1906), and the winning entry was by Oatley & Lawrence of Bristol. It proved too expensive to build so the design was altered—and even then, the committee recognized that running costs would be greater than at Stokes Croft! But it was a self-confident moment, making a splash on a prestigious site beside the university.

This was the initial proposed design for the building in Woodland Rd. The actual building was modified to save money. (Accession number 18835)

The building in Woodland Rd at its opening. (Accession number 29816)

The building was completed in 1916, and the opening is discussed above. But since at that point war dominated, and no new students were being accepted, life in the new building did not immediately commence as planned.

The work of the College went on, as we have seen above. But with the finishing of the building, it was lent to the university for its arts courses, and served as part of the university Arts Faculty for the next three-and-a-half years. As well as consolidating the relationship with the university (and perhaps ensuring that, for the rest of the century, the university continued to covet the building; see below), it also meant that the new building was not commandeered by the army, which was a matter of great satisfaction to the Education Society.

The final cost of the building in Woodlands Road was £28,926. £22,996 was raised by subscribers and gifts, while the Stokes Croft site eventually raised £5000. The remaining debt was cleared within a year of the building being finished. This building comprised lecture rooms, dining room, library, common room, and study bedrooms. Also, in the grounds, there was a house for the principal.

By the late 1950s, this building was beginning to be too small for the number of students, which was now in the thirties, and so some rebuilding and remodeling was decided on. What had been the principal's house was now taken over and refurbished so that there could be another twelve rooms for students on the first floor, and some more rooms for use in various ways on the ground floor. A new, and rather smaller house was built for the principal in the grounds, and the new enlarged building was opened in 1961.

As well as more room on the ground floor for a common room and for teaching rooms, one of the significant changes was the transformation of the museum into a College chapel. The place of communal prayer in the life of the College community has always been noted, but this provision of a space for the community to meet to worship was an indication of a particular shift in the theology and the practice of community life at this time. As we will see below, in the report of a Baptist Union commission in 1958, there was some anxiety about the spiritual formation of students, and of the spiritual depth of the denomination as a whole. In the creation of a chapel in the remodelled building, there was a very definite statement of and commitment to prayer and worship as a community being at the centre of the College's life.

The other statement that this building made was, of course, about the academic identity of the College as an institution. By being placed in the centre of the university buildings there was a clear statement that the College teaching was to be in the mainstream academically and that the "new learning" that had so divided the churches in the nineteenth century was to be embraced and included, rather than avoided. In terms of the ongoing debate about the nature of training men (and, in this building, eventually, women) for ministry, the place of a wider academic context and the engagement beyond narrow denominational limits, with the proximity of the Western College, was literally set in stone.

ANOTHER MOVE IS NECESSARY

By the end of the twentieth century, this building was in its turn becoming inappropriate for the way that College life was developing and so the third move took place, right to the edge of The Downs, to The Promenade in Clifton. With this move, the major transition was away from a residential model of training.

The move from Woodlands Road to the eventual new home on The Promenade was one that took several years to work out. The Woodlands Road building was created for a model of ministerial training and formation that was no longer meeting the needs of presenting students nor of the churches whom the College was serving. There was a move away from expecting people to start training for ministry in their early twenties. Indeed, those who were advising possible candidates were often deliberately discouraging men and women of that age from going to College immediately;

instead, people were encouraged to spend some time in other forms of work first, in order to increase experience and broaden their involvement in society beyond church. This was at least in part in response to churches who wanted their ministers to have shared something of the delights and struggles of 'normal' life, and not simply to have moved from school to College to ministry. There were financial constraints too; those who came into ministry training and then ministry from another sphere of work would often have some resources behind them which would allow for the financing of their training, and this had become a real consideration as many churches were finding it harder and harder to fund students, and grants and other forms of support were becoming less available.

One of the consequences of people coming into College later was that by the mid-1990s, the overwhelming majority of those approaching the College were married and many had children; living in a community building designed for single people was no longer an option.

Another major change that was happening was the increase in what came to be called church-based training. There had long been some who combined service in a local congregation with attendance at College classes, but again, by this time, this had become the dominant path. Finance also played its part here; church-based training provided a student and family with a manse, and often some income. And, again, this was a development which was a reaction to the expressed needs of the churches. Many churches found themselves unable to sustain full-time ministry any longer, as churches became smaller and income fell. Such churches often still had a manse available and some finance to enable them to offer a smaller stipend in recognition of 'part-time' work. Thus, rather than completely losing a minister, this became a creative way of enabling some pattern of continuity and sustained presence, without over-stretching resources. And it enabled people to become part of a College community without, in some cases at least, uprooting children from school or disrupting a partner's career for a short number of years, which made later moves once College studies were finished less disruptive. We will discuss this new pattern more below, but here, what is important to note is the impact that this too had on the form of building which the College needed as a home.

A changing pattern of training

Residential training in one form or another of the pattern that had been the norm since the early days, was now something that had to be structured differently. The community, which in the Bristol Tradition was so much a part of the formation that the College offered, could no longer depend simply on physical proximity. Again, we will discuss this below. But there is no doubt that for those who had valued the experience of living together, the loss of the building on Woodland Road was deeply felt. It was not a decision that the College Committee took lightly. If I may be personal for a moment, as one who was part of the discussion process, I can bear witness to the hours of conversation, debate and consideration that took place over at least three years before the move to The Promenade took place.

Various plans were investigated, including sharing accommodation with the Methodist Wesley College, a partner in the Bristol Federation for Theology which had developed in the mid-1990s. The building in which Wesley College was housed was very much larger than their student body required and a possible building share was investigated. However, it become clear that this would not solve the problems that were at issue. The question that Wesley College was seeking to solve in looking at sharing their building with the Baptist College was that they had a surplus of accommodation for single students on site. Since this was exactly the problem that the Baptist College also had, this was clearly not a way forward.

The possibility of a new build in the grounds of the Anglican Trinity College was investigated. Much of the teaching was already taking place in the existing building, since the lecture rooms there were large enough to hold the combined numbers of Baptist, Anglican and Methodist students that made up the classes. There was also a large dining room, in which Baptist students were already sometimes sharing lunch, as the communities grew together.

A new block which would allow for the housing of the Baptist College library, staff rooms for the Baptist College lecturers and a common room in which Baptist students could gather, as well as spaces for dedicated denominational teaching looked like a possibility for a while. The memory of what had been planned in a previous generation of a combined space with the Western College, shared space and separate space all on one site, fed into these plans as they were investigated for a new time. However, cost proved prohibitive, and there was also considerable resistance from the larger community of former students, as represented both on the College Committee and in views canvassed at the times of College Reunion. There was a fear that the identity of Bristol Baptist College would disappear if there was no longer, as it were, a separate address.

Since it had been clear from the beginning of considering a move that the university was interested in buying the Woodland Road building (indeed, one of the university staff was known to refer to it as Naboth's Vineyard) there was some investigation of a swap; of giving the building to the university and of receiving from them another one of equal value that would suit the needs of the College better. However, although several buildings were considered, none of them were suitable; sometimes the question was one of location, sometimes of the kind of premises—and sometimes because the state of repair of the possible swap was even worse than of the building at Woodland Road.

THE PROMENADE

When the site on The Promenade on Clifton Down came on the market, it looked at first as if it would not be suitable either, because it was part of a larger 'lot' and the complete site would have been too large and would have required too much work to be done on it to make it viable. But then, unexpectedly, things changed, and the College was offered The Promenade site at a cost and in a form that was possible, and the decision was taken to move. In that year, as part of the College Community day, there was a presentation of information about the new building, and about the developments that would be part of the move. The conversation with former students that took place on that community day was an important part of the way in which life in the building took shape; questions about access were raised, about the provision of facilities for those who were not physically able, about where the library would be and how students would be able to use it outside of times when the building was formally open. For those who were planning the move, this discussion with the Community was an important and fruitful part of the decisions that were made.

Those who made the move possible were numerous: from staff in the College, such as the Bursar, Pearl Woolnough, whose tireless visiting of buildings and drawing up specifications was a gift to all concerned, through to voluntary members of the various committees, who undertook site visits, managed finances, and spent long meetings reflecting on what a newly shaped College, which was no longer primarily residential, would look like.

Leaving the previous building was a solemn moment. There were various 'leave-taking' events, and one of the most memorable was when the then community of staff and students shared together in an act of worship on the final evening, which ended with walking together out of the main door of the building and closing it for the final time.

This was then matched with an act of worship in the chapel of the new building which recognized that the ongoing life of the College as held in the hands of God was now to be housed in a different place and so would develop in new forms. The emphasis on what Roger Hayden called "Continuity and Change" in his discussion of College life in the nineteenth century was well picked up in the leaving and the arriving, and reflected the depth of the Bristol Tradition in the College's identity—the renewing aspects of the Tradition, setting us free from the dangers of stifling traditionalism, which carries the risk of idolizing one way of doing things, and so of failing to meet the needs of the world which the College is called to serve.

The public side of the move was different from that of the move into Woodland Road. Rather than processions and opening events in the new building, there was a large service and meeting in the Bristol Council House on College Green, at which members of the wider College community, members of local churches and friends and colleagues from the university and the other theological Colleges were present. There was prayer, reflection, and a telling of the story of what had been, as well as an expression of hopes of what might be. As well as the new building, the new shape of the course, the new links with Trinity College in particular and therefore the new opportunities of training were presented and dedicated.

Life within this new home was inevitably different, and we will discuss it below in the chapter on the third century. But as a building it presented both delight and challenge, and over the years that the College has lived there, there have been significant changes. Some of these changes have been required because of a new community sharing the building, as the Centre for Youth Ministry also made its home there, and some were to do with meeting the ongoing needs of the College itself—reshaping rooms, removing a heavy door which had belonged to the safe of the bank who had owned the building previously, redeveloping the safe as a place where the historic collections are housed. There is also now a quiet room to allow space for withdrawal in a building that can become very busy and buzzy. The library has expanded from one space to several, and the accommodation of staff has had to be flexible as staff numbers and needs have changed.

The maintenance of the building has not always been easy; students who have been part of the community in the years since the College has been in this building will tell stories of the lift that live in memory for a long time! The garden, which it was hoped would provide social space, has not been as well used for that as it might have been. And although there is a car park, the increased numbers attending the building on some days has meant that parking can be challenging. The steps to the front door mean that disabled access needs to be round the side and that is not ideal.

In addition, there has been a continued need for some kind of accommodation, and houses to meet the varying needs at varying times have been bought—and sold. The flexibility allowed by a changing portfolio of properties has meant that families have been housed at times, that single students shared a house (and indeed, gave a home to this tutor and her husband when their own home was uninhabitable for a time, in a granny flat that was part of that house), students from overseas could be accommodated and sabbatical students were able to stay for short periods, while at the same time at least trying to avoid the demands of empty spaces. It has not always been easy, but it has proved possible.

6

THE LIBRARY

Wherever the College has 'lived', there has always been, at its heart, a library. From the very beginning it was necessary that there should be a useful and workable library available to students, especially those who could not afford to buy books. The original College library belonged to Broadmead Church and in 1722 consisted of 198 volumes, and there were another nine available that belonged to Bernard Foskett personally.

In 1772, there was an appeal to fund the development of the library and Caleb Evans, the then principal travelled around to raise money from both churches and individuals. The appeal was successful enough that eventually a library building was put up in the garden. Andrew Gifford, who had been a tutor of the College in the mid-1720s gave £100 to the initial appeal, and then, in his will, he left his own extensive library of 3,500 theology books, together with manuscripts and other collectables to the College, including what was then believed to be the only surviving complete copy of Tyndale's English New Testament.

In the same year as the Gifford Bequest made such an impact on the library, two other bequests were made: Thomas Llewelyn bequeathed a Classical Library (valued at about 2,000 guineas) and Frederick Bull, one of those who was a Founder Member of the Education Society left a money legacy of 1,000 guineas. In 1784, acknowledging all three legacies, the College Report stated, "this institution is able to boast of a library equal if not superior to that of any private academy in the Kingdom."

In 1795, a printed catalogue was published. This included The Gifford bequest, the Llewellyn bequest, and a further donation in 1790 by James Newton, a part-time tutor, who gave three hundred volumes of practical divinity.

The Gifford Bequest was of course not only books, and formed not simply the centrepiece of the library, but also the beginning of the museum, the collection of treasures that kept the College in touch with a deeper and wider life. When the College moved to the new home on Stokes Croft, not only was a library space provided, but there was also a museum space. This connection to the wider world of study and understanding the world remained very important, and, as we saw above in examining the influence of the College model around the world, was part of the model that was exported and developed in different contexts.

When the Woodland Road building was remodelled, the cost of the building works, some £20,500, was met by selling three of the books left by Gifford, three books printed by Caxton. The British Library bought the most valuable, rather as it bought the Tyndale New Testament in the early 1990s. It seems fitting that these books from the Gifford Bequest should end up at the British Library, part of the British Museum, since Gifford was a sub-librarian there for many years.

Other books were sold at the same time, from the Gifford collection, to various universities around the country; books outside the normal range of a theological library, covering subjects as diverse as astronomy, Gaelic, and medicine. It was believed that this would make the books more available to those who actually needed to see them, and money was released to be invested in teaching.

A fund was established by Katherine Gotch Robinson, Frederick Gotch's daughter, in memory of Gotch, to help the College to continue to buy current publications. And when the Western College closed, the K. L. Parry Collection, which it had held, of books about hymns and of hymns came to the College. With the move to The Promenade, there was a need to slim the library down, and with the access that students now had to the library at Trinity College and at Bristol University, it was a suitable time to bring the library up to date. Following that move, several special collections were brought into the library.

When The Centre for Youth Ministry arrived to share the building, their library was housed in the existing library and the collections merged, giving CYM students access to a wide range of theological resources, and ministerial students the chance to find specialist material on youth and children's work.

When Tony Peck was pastoral studies tutor, the short-lived Thomas Helwys Institute brought together a collection focused around issues of human rights and religious freedom. Later, when the Centre of Anabaptist Studies was started in 2014, the library that had been previously housed at the Mennonite House in London was brought to Bristol and enriched with other Anabaptist sources from around the country.

As a relatively small institution, the College can perhaps no longer boast of "a library equal if not superior to that of any private academy in the Kingdom." But it does have a library that is well resourced and provides significant access to specialized material that makes it an important collection.

Librarians

Generations of students have cause to be grateful to those whose skill, patience and presence has made the library a resource that has been accessible. Here, because of gaps in the research, and with regret, I need to ask former students to fill in the names of those who have filled this post. It is a significant gap in a history of this type not to be able to include not just names, but also accounts of those who have cared for the library, built it up, and helped students and staff to use it to its fullest. No matter how well resourced a library is, if it is not cared for and curated well, it is not a full library. Over the years, the College has been immensely well served in those who have undertaken this role.

7

THREE HUNDRED YEARS, NOT OUT

INTRODUCTION

As we move into the third century of the College's life, we will once more trace the chronology through the various principals and take time to reflect on some of the themes that emerge and shape the story.

We saw major changes socially, politically, and theologically in the second hundred years of the College's life; this did not change in the third century. Again, a world war dominated for six years, and its aftermath shaped life for at least another decade. Among the churches, the predominant story has been one of decline, with the diminution of numbers that was starting after 1906 rapidly increasing so that by the end of this period we are living in a context which those in the second century of the College's life would barely recognize.

Alongside these changes there have been dramatic changes in the social composition of our nation. From the point of view of theological thinking in particular, issues of living and working beside and with those of other faiths has become a significant factor, though not the only question that has arisen. Questions of war and peace, and in particular of issues to do with atomic warfare have been matters of concern. With the increase in communication and globalization, what mission actually is has come under question, and issues of justice, especially in questions of food and water, as we have become aware of endemic famines, and latterly, of ecological issues have required serious theological reflection and engagement.

In addition, churches, and those who are training for ministry within them have had to grapple with questions over gender roles, over deindustrialization, the Cold War and the ending of the Cold War, the new tensions around the impact of international terrorism, and issues that seem to be particularly important to believers, understanding the questions of the Middle East and in particular relationships between Israel and the Palestinians.

Within this period, in addition to a second world war, we have passed through the social and political upheavals of the 1960s, the issues raised first by the war in Vietnam, and then by wars in Syria and Afghanistan and the involvement of the UK in the latter ones. Britain has seen a significant shift in her position internationally—the formal ending of Empire, joining the Common Market and then leaving the European Union, the depression of the 1930s and the economic chaos of the 1970s.

As a world, we have seen technological change that has been breathless. Powered flight had just started ten years before the period we are considering—and in the hundred years since then, we have put people on the moon, the International Space Station has become so much a part of life that we barely notice it now, and we have landed exploratory craft on Mars, as well as sending spacecraft out beyond the edges of our solar system. Medical science has developed beyond anything we could have imagined during the influenza pandemic following the First World War, so that we now treat transplants as routine, assisted conception as a right, and need to have significant discussion about assisted death, since keeping people alive in extremis is now possible.

The information revolution has been as life changing as the industrial revolution. It has happened much more quickly, and its impact on training and teaching has been incalculable. But its impact on the life of congregations is also beyond measuring, as we can now access communities other than those we gather with, physically (and the last two years, as this book has itself been written has served to move this even further!), and the impact of this on what it means to be gathered congregations is something we are still working to understand.

Theologically, the rise of Pentecostalism around the world has had a major impact on how the church has existed, as has the rapid growth of Christian communities in the Global South, changing the dominant locus for theological thinking; again, a difference we are still trying, in the western world, to come to terms with. The impact of Pentecostalism, both theology and practice has perhaps been most noticeable among Baptists in terms of the charismatic movement and its influence on worship styles, and on participation, even when the whole theology of supernatural gifting has not been adopted.

Other major theological strands in the UK in particular have been the development and embedding of ecumenism in a variety of institutional and more informal ways. The Great Reversal—the move away from a concern to change the world through activism, and a concern specifically for ameliorating the situation of those caught in poverty dominated Evangelicalism in the first part of the twentieth century and was itself reversed after the Second World War, gathering speed and depth during the 1960s, so that involvement in agencies and expectations of reflecting Kingdom values can now be taken for granted.

Among Baptists, there have been several reorganizations of the Baptist Union, some of which we will reflect on as we tell the story of the College, and there have been significant changes in the understanding and expectation of ministry and therefore of training which will form a major part of this strand of our story.

It is also, perhaps, at this point in the history that we become aware of this as 'our' story. As we move into the twentieth century, we are coming into the period that some of those who read this book at the time of its first publishing will remember. As we do so, I note, that Dr West, having been invited to write a history and memoir of his time involved in Baptist life eventually decided not to. This decision was precisely because he was aware of the challenges of writing *as* history that which *is* memory and I reflect that he was wiser than perhaps I have been.

Over this period, we have six principals including three who served for short periods. Dr Whittaker became principal in 1921 and resigned in 1923. He was succeeded by Dr Dakin, who served until 1953, and was followed by Dr Champion, whose tenure lasted from 1953 until 1972. Dr West then assumed the role and was principal until 1987. Dr John Morgan-Wynne was principal after this, until 1993, and was followed by another relatively short tenure, that of Brian Haymes, who was principal from 1994 until 2000, when he moved into a pastorate. His successor, Dr Chris Ellis, having started in 2000, also moved back to local pastorate in 2006, and was succeeded by Dr Steve Finamore, who is currently principal.

As we noted at the very beginning of this book, we have been writing this history under very particular circumstances, and they play a particular part in writing this chapter. Because of the pandemic of 2020 to 2021, which closed down the possibilities of travel, and of access to both archives and people, the research for this chapter has been severely limited. Only materials that were freely available, such as printed reports could be consulted; minutes and other records that would explain much could not be consulted. People have been generous in their time in giving interviews over the phone and via video calls, but travel, and tracing those who were not personally known, has not been possible. In addition, Dr Cross's illness meant, in the end, that the research on which this chapter was based was significantly incomplete, and this will become very obvious to the reader; there is much concentration on the lives and work of the principals, and much less than in previous chapters on the stories and experiences of students. Every work of history should include the indication of further work to be done. Such indications will be very clear on the way through!

DR CHARLES WHITTAKER

The first principal to take us into the third century is also the first—and so far only—principal who was not a minister.

With the retirement of Dr Henderson, the appointment of a successor was something of a problem, and the College Report for 1921 refers to the appointment subcommittee spending "months of anxious thought and prayer" before they came to the College Committee with a proposal. The man whose name they brought was Dr Charles Whittaker, who at this point was headmaster of Taunton School. He had grown up in the Baptist church in Harlow, been educated at the Nonconformist Grammar School in Bishop's Stortford and then in Sidney Sussex College in Cambridge. He also had law degrees from London and Cambridge Universities. He went into teaching (as well as serving as a Justice of the Peace) and taught in the school he had attended. He was head there for fourteen years and left to become headmaster at Taunton School—which, at the time he arrived, was in serious financial trouble. He arrived just as the whole organization of the school was being restructured, and he took it into its new form, and made a success of it. In the twenty-two years that he was headmaster, the school grew from seventy-nine to 736 pupils, with an extensive scheme of scholarships and bursaries, and a much-improved building. It had, just as significantly, also gained in status and reputation.

The achievement that meant the most to him personally at the school was the opening of a chapel, which he set out to make the centre of the school's life. He preached himself, and also invited local ministers, preachers, visiting missionaries and other members of staff to preach. He maintained the school's identity as a nonconformist institution, but not narrowly so. He was deeply shaped by being a Baptist, but was also influenced by Congregational ministers, and was on friendly terms with the local parish clergy. His guest list for those to address the school was not in any way narrowly denominational, and this practical ecumenism was one of the marks that was appreciated when people spoke of his time as headmaster. It is clear that he deeply loved the school, and when he moved to Bristol in 1922, he continued with his involvement by becoming part of the School Council as one of those representing the Bristol City Council. One wonders how his successor took to that!

However, his reason for moving to Bristol was not primarily to become part of the School Council but to become principal of Bristol Baptist College, which he did in autumn of 1922. The commendation of him to the College by the appointment committee spoke of his administrative capacity, his gracious personality and his wisdom, generosity and his "gifts as a Christian teacher."

The College Report for the following year spoke in warm terms of Dr Whittaker's first year, with good reports of students. One of his innovations was the work that was being developed to enable non-collegiate ministers to be recognized by the Baptist Union. The Report noted that Dr Whittaker lacked church-based experience and outlined steps that had been taken to address that by bringing in others to teach on "the minister and his work," "the conduct of public worship," and "preaching." Numbers of students were increasing and the financial situation was therefore improving. All looked fair.

It came as a shock to everybody, then, when, at the beginning of the autumn term in 1923, Dr Whittaker became so ill that, on medical advice, he resigned. Early in 1924, he moved to North Wales for specialist treatment and there seemed to be some improvement. However, he died towards the end of 1925, aged sixty-three. It is clear that the last few years at the Taunton School had been deeply traumatic. These years had covered the deaths among his former pupils in the First World War, and the loss of life in the subsequent flu pandemic, as well as a local tragedy in which one of his pupils drowned trying to rescue another boy who had got into difficulties. In those last years at the school, it was noted that he aged visibly. It is to be supposed that this at least in part led to his illness and early death. Indeed, for all the good things said "in public" of Dr Whittaker's work, in the reports and speeches at the occasion to mark his retirement, H. Harry Pewtress, one of the students of the time, had a different description. He said of these years that they were

> rather unhappy ones, both for the man chosen—oh so unwisely- [. . .] and for the men in the College who were lately left like sheep without a shepherd [. . .]. Against his [Whittaker's] inclination he had accepted the invitation, and although outstanding as the headmaster of a boys' school, he had no training at all for the Baptist ministry. And he was already unwell. It was soon evident a mistake had been made [. . .] he was a very unhappy man glad to give up his task, who in his personal dealings with us students could not have been more of an elder brother and who was to everybody an all too generous friend.

Great hopes had evidently been placed in Dr Whittaker, and one can only guess at what was desired, at what his hopes were and at what, in the end, appears to have gone wrong. It is noticeable that the College Report that was published after his death made no mention of it, and he is not even always mentioned in the published histories. While it is tempting to make deductions, and even seek lessons from this event, we simply do not have enough material to draw even tentative conclusions.

What is reassuring is that, even given the glimpse we have that things were not happy, it is still obvious that there was also good work going on. It appears that the senior student, one H. E. Stickler, together with the Chair of the Council R. C. Griffin, a member of the Horfield congregation, were skilled enough to keep things on course, and maintain something like an effective collegiate life.

Life under Dr Whittaker

What also undoubtedly helped was the ongoing teaching structure. We have seen that some of the shortcomings, which were acknowledged in appointing somebody with no experience of local church ministry, were met by bringing in local ministers to speak from their experience. In addition, students were taking classes at Bristol University and there was shared teaching with Western College, and another full-time staff member at the Baptist College, Frank Robinson.

We may not know much of the life in the time of Dr Whittaker's principalship, but it is clear that students graduated with Bristol degrees and with London degrees. Some progressed far enough to take the matriculation exams for London, others passed intermediate exams in Bristol University, while two graduated with Bachelor of Arts degrees from Birmingham University.

Students also did summer placements in churches in Bridgnorth, Boroughbridge, the Scilly Isles, Street, and Malmesbury, and appear to have been appreciated by the congregations. Students who finished their time in College settled in Birmingham, and in Beckington, while others went to serve overseas with BMS—two students are recorded as going to The Congo.

In the time when Dr Whittaker was ill, and before the appointment of the next principal, Frank Robinson sustained the life of the College, with help from a Mr Lawrence, about whom we know very little, but given the way he is addressed was presumably not a minister, who took the matriculation classes, and Revd Charles Brown, minister of Ferme Park in London, who travelled in to give "an exceedingly helpful series of lectures" on homiletics and on pastoral theology. The minister of Cotham Grove Baptist church also came into offer reflection and criticism in sermon class. There was too the continuing link with Western College (although during this period, one of their long-term members of staff also had to retire through ill health).

In addition, according to the published reports, the College numbers were increasing, and the finances were good. The increase in numbers actually meant that the possibility of external accommodation for some students was being considered—an unexpected development.

Overseas links

Those who were coming into College were not all UK based. There is mention in the reports of students from Estonia and from Latvia.

The student from Estonia, Johannes Wuhner, came on the recommendation of J. H. Rushbrooke. Although he passed his BA Intermediate exam, his health broke down. He did benefit from treatment, but it was decided that it would be best for him to return home and so he did, with everybody's good wishes.

A year later, Rudolf Eksteins arrived from Latvia, having already been studying in Rochester Divinity School in the USA. He was in Bristol for two years and was clearly a very successful student. He returned to Riga for further ministerial training and to serve as minister of the Baptist church in that city. Following the Second World War he was among those who were displaced persons and was detained in a camp in Lubeck. Dr Dakin, Dr Rushbrooke, and others tried to enable his emigration to the UK or the USA, but it was a slow and ultimately unsuccessful process which took its toll on Eksteins and his family. They were finally able to go to Canada, and he became pastor of the Latvian Baptist church in Toronto.

In 1936, following Rushbrooke's recommendation and "in conformity with previous practice" the College Committee agreed to accept another Estonian, Artur Proos. He did well academically, and in 1939 took the BA Intermediate exam. However, he went home for the summer that year and while there, received a letter from Dr Dakin suggesting that "in view of the outbreak of war" he should not return, and we have no further record of him.

DR ARTHUR DAKIN

The overseas links were not all one way, and in the College's next principal, the benefits of exploring another culture, studying in another context, and being in touch with a broader theological stream were to be represented by his background. Dr Dakin, who succeeded Dr Whittaker, entered Rawdon College in 1904, and went on to study in Halle and then Heidelberg, where he was awarded a Doctor of Theology in 1910.

In Halle, he studied with Prof. Friedrich Loofs who was known as a pastor engaged with political and social issues—and later at Heidelberg, he studied with Ernst Troeltsch. His specialty was medieval church history and his dissertation was on the relationship between John Wycliff and the Lollards—in which he engaged deeply with scriptural teaching, and also with social and political arguments. This remained important to him, influencing his convictions about what it was to be a church: engaged with, but not identified with the powers-that-be, and deeply rooted in Scripture.

Quite apart from the topic, and the impact of studying on the Continent, what is noteworthy about Dr Dakin's doctorate is that he is the first of the principals to earn the degree, rather than be honoured with one. In this, he opens a new tradition in the College's life, that of the scholar principal. The place of academic study in the formation of ministers continued to be an issue of contention, and this enshrining of academic excellence in the identity of the College is significant in placing the College in that debate.

Unlike his predecessor, Dr Dakin had significant pastoral experience when he arrived at the College. He served first in Waterbarn in Rossendale and then in Queen's Road in Coventry where he was known for "vigorous preaching" combined with "clear thinking and conviction." He arrived there as war broke out and led the church as it found ways to serve those who were in the forces, both men and women. He was also their pastor as the deaths mounted. By 1918, he was wondering about whether ministers should join the armed forces, and spoke with church meeting about it. The church was involved with support for the YWCA caring for women workers in France, and in May 1918, Dr Dakin went to spend some time working with the YWCA in France.

Soon after he came back, he received an invitation to move to Ferme Park and Campsbourne in London. This was clearly an exercise in succession planning, since he was to be co-pastor with Dr Brown, with a view to succeeding him when he retired. Thus, he moved to London in 1919, to a large church, and one deeply traumatized by the war. His ministry there was much appreciated and his preaching in particular was "appealing to the young." However, Dr Brown showed no signs of retiring, and though Dakin had a successful time there, it was not a situation that was sustainable long-term. Thus, when the invitation to move to Bristol and succeed Dr Whittaker came in 1924, he seems to have been very pleased to accept it.

The church in Queen's Road grew under his ministry and the involvement in life beyond the immediate neighbourhood was important; not just in the support for YWCA, but through all his years there, in support for BMS, and in sending people to serve overseas. This was a deliberate policy of Dr Dakin, following his time overseas, and even more following the war. With his convictions about the need for the church to be engaged in changing the world, he was very clear that the Christian Faith was a way of uniting a world that was otherwise irreparably divided: "Mission is not mere philanthropy; it is world politics" he announced in a sermon. He looked widely, and he looked to home. In the same sermon he argued, "we cannot sentimentalise about African babies and be indifferent to the squalor of our own courts. Our very support of missions leads to all the social applications of the Gospel in every part of the world."

Emphases in Dr Dakin's teaching

He served as principal for twenty-nine years, retiring in 1953, and this was the context and the emphasis that he brought with him. As we reflect on the Bristol Tradition, we can see clear connections; he himself was lively, able, evangelical, zealous. Preaching was particularly important to him, and something in which he was broad, or catholic in his sympathies—he had a proven track record as a preacher both in terms of sermons and in the wider sense of enabling people to encounter the good news in all its aspects.

Preaching

Preaching was something at which he clearly excelled. Walter Bottoms, who was a student in the College under his principalship, commented that

> [. . .] his own preaching genius often flowed into his lecturing, so that, sometimes men forgot to take notes until, with a sudden realization of what was happening, he would tell them to "get it down".

He continued, "To many of his students, his lectures on preaching were among his best." There was disappointment that these were never published. Indeed, none of his lectures were published, and so we glean what was important in his teaching from the reminiscences of students, and from his occasional writings.

He was not only a preacher who took the craft very seriously as a skill to be worked at and developed in himself, he was an advocate for the importance of preaching in a ministry. He argued, in *The Baptist View of the Church and the Ministry* (which we will consider in greater detail below), that the place of the pulpit as the focal point in a Baptist church reflected the one indispensable for Baptist worship to take place: the presence of the Scriptures. He continued that preaching was at the heart of the gathering to worship.

> It is fundamentally the proclamation of the gospel, having precisely the same end as the reading of the Scriptures. In fact, it is only an extension of the reading of the Scriptures, seeking to expound, explain and apply them. Nor should the word ever be divorced even in thought from the reading (as they easily tend to be, for example, when a lectern is provided for the one and a pulpit for the other). Nor is it right to think of the preaching and the worship as though these were separate activities. [. . .] The whole service is indeed a unity, every single part moving to one end, name the proclaiming of the gospel, that its Author may be known and praised and the hearers of it strengthened and blessed.

In his appreciation of Dr Dakin (the principal while he was a student) his successor Leonard Champion said, "The preacher and the teacher was always . . . the man of integrity".

Ecumenical links

Within the Bristol Tradition, it is not simply to be a preacher that matters, but to be an able, lively, zealous, and evangelical one, and as we have seen, also to be wide in sympathy. That is clearly the model that Dr Dakin embodied and taught. The breadth of his sympathies is clear in his reaction to the proposals that emerged during this time about church unity. J. H. Shakespeare, the general secretary of the Baptist Union at this period brought forward possibilities and proposals which explored what a United Church of England would look like. Even before he came to the College, Dakin was involved in considering and responding to such suggestions. Along with most other Baptists at the time, he was not interested in the full unity that Shakespeare was discussing. But he was, with many others, interested in exploring a Free Church Federation. These ideas came to nothing at the time, but when in 1940, the Free Church Federal Council was formed, there were new possibilities regarding mutual recognition of ministries, sharing Communion and transfer between churches (mutual recognition of Baptism was not yet something to be considered). The Second World War slowed down the reflective consideration of the issues raised, but in 1950 a report, *Church Relations in England,* appeared. This ecumenically prepared document, sought to work out some of the questions posed by issues of episcopacy and mutual recognition between episcopal and non-episcopal churches. The next year, the Baptist Union Council appointed a committee to consider this, and Dakin was appointed to chair. The report from the committee makes it clear that the question of required episcopal ordination in order to preside at the Communion Table was clearly a sticking point for the Baptists. The report also pointed out that intercommunion between Baptists could not always be taken for granted, and thus, the plans offered by the ecumenical report were not such that Baptists could take part.

But the ecumenism that mattered to Dakin had a very practical place in his principalship. The link with the Congregational Western College was already well established, and in his first year, Dakin put an existing informal arrangement with the Moravian College in the city on a more formal footing, so that now students from all three Colleges shared in collaborative training (the Moravian College disappears from mention in College documents after 1938, so presumably the relationship ended for some reason).

Other links and relationships were also started and developed in Dakin's time. The pattern of students doing an undergraduate degree in Bristol, and then moving to Regent's Park College for postgraduate study was developed by Dakin and Frank Robinson, starting early in the 1930s. This link also helped to open up overseas study to some students. For example, Morris West, having an undergraduate degree from Bristol went to Regents Park, then after a year there, he went to Zurich to complete his doctorate. This was to be an established pattern over many years, especially the move from Bristol to Oxford. This was one of the new things that Dr Dakin helped to bring into being: a commitment to enabling students with particular academic ability, without being defensive about it, as it were, or 'hoarding' able students in Bristol. The reciprocal arrangement was that those who were not yet prepared to start their studies at Regent's Park College could do their preparatory work in Bristol. (This is close to the pattern suggested by the College Community Meeting some years before.) In 1936, this arrangement was formalized by an agreement between the Colleges, to run for five years at first. Two students from Regent's Park came to Bristol and by the end of the year both had passed the Bristol University Supplementary Matriculation examination, and both went on to pass the intermediate examination for the Bristol Bachelor of Arts in the next year. Others followed, and at the same time, several went from Bristol to Oxford for two years further study. This configuration continued for many years, with appropriate variations as the examinations and patterns for both the College and university altered.

With changes in the validation of degrees, the provision of postgraduate study in Bristol developed in the later part of the twentieth century, and so the felt need for this precise kind of connection diminished, but the ongoing links between the Colleges developed in various other ways.

Understanding of ministry

In the year that he retired from the College, Dakin wrote concerning *The Training of the Minister*. As well as covering the need for training and the history of the way in which such training had been approached, he described the actual course of study as he knew it, and this gives us an interesting insight into what students did in this generation.

He started with Biblical and theological studies, in order to "mak[e] the student wise concerning the Bible and in how to develop his thoughts starting from the Biblical material." He noted,

> There is [. . .] a preoccupation with the Bible throughout the whole College course and this interest in the Bible is the thing that links all the subjects into a unity.

He delineated the different areas, although he insisted that they "occur and proceed together." [BL1–5]

- A knowledge of the contents of the Bible.
- Knowing how to read the Bible so that they can understand its right meaning, which is done in English, Hebrew, and Greek, through use of commentaries and biblical criticism.
- Close and meticulous study of two books from each Testament in order to inculcate skills and habits.
- Scripture interprets Scripture, thus the study of doctrine—what the church over the years has made of the Bible, including the writings of Origen, Aquinas, and Calvin, examining one or two doctrines in detail.
- This then was grounded and illuminated by the study of church history: "The same errors crop up in the same conditions and some of the outcrops of our own time are easily recognised by the man who knows the history of the Christian Church."

Other things might be added, he acknowledged, but insisted that these essentials must remain. They form the irreducible minimum of a theological course [...] making life-long students of the Word with all the advantages to personality that such a study brings.

From this course list, Dr Dakin taught Church History and New Testament—and he also taught courses in homiletics and in pastoral psychology, together with a sermon class and seminars in Christian Ethics.

In addition to teaching in the College, Dakin lectured in the university, and in particular in what was called university extension work—that is, courses for those who were not attending as full-time students, and who were not seeking a qualification. Specifically, he taught a course on "The History of Christianity." He also lectured to Bristol teachers and the Bristol Young Baptists, and after the war he was a recognized teacher in Religious Knowledge for the university.

The "woman question"

Among those who became students in Dr Dakin's time was the first woman to train at Bristol. The College had agreed in 1919 to accept women as students, but it was not until 1937 that the first woman applied. This was Gwyneth Hubble. When she arrived, she already had a Bachelor of Arts degree and a teaching diploma, she had been Educational Secretary of the Girls' Auxiliary and had then become personal assistant to Eleanor Bowser, who was Women's Secretary at BMS headquarters. Her presence in the College records however is rather anomalous; she never quite appears in the lists in the way that the other (male) students did. She was listed first as an "external student," possibly because living in the building would have been inappropriate, but is not listed as becoming a full student in the way that those who started with her are. In 1939 she gained her Bachelor of Divinity. The other student who was also listed as "external" has his degree noted, and his future work described, but nothing is said of Miss Hubble.

Nonetheless, in 1939 she was appointed as assistant secretary of the Student Christian Movement and ordained to this post by Dakin. (The term "ordained" was the one that Dr Payne used in his article about her later.)

Gwyneth Hubble was to go on to have a distinguished and influential ministry training women for overseas service and as deaconesses, and to serve with the World Council of Churches. She also regularly and forcefully asked the wider denomination to take seriously the issue of women as ministers and challenged Baptists in particular to think about the place of deaconesses and the questions that raised about the shape and form of ministry, and the training that was necessary.

After the war, the next woman appears in the records: Joan Cole from Waterlooville was sent by BMS to study in Bristol and she was awarded her Bachelor of Arts degree in 1947–48, going on to teach in Melksham. There is further study to be done here about the women who went to Bristol, and to other Colleges, and then began to take their place as ministers. In particular, the whole transition from deaconesses to ministers needs further examination, as do the processes by which women were recruited, interviewed, and settled. It is however, one of the areas in which the research for this current work has been derailed by circumstances.

Legacy

By the time he retired, somewhere in the region of 130 students had passed through the College in his time. Seven became principals and tutors in Colleges, three had become secretaries or assistant secretaries of BMS, both at home and abroad, one was an area superintendent, twenty had become missionaries, and seventy-five were in pastoral ministry. Four left the denomination, one at least to become an Anglican.

That the majority of his students had become local pastoral ministers was a delight to Dr Dakin. For of course, what he is best known for in the canon of Baptist history is espousing a particular view of the connection between ministry and the local church. And it is to this controversy that we need to turn.

The Baptist view of the church and the ministry

By the nature of the role, and the place that such a role holds within the denomination, principals have, over the years, been involved in a variety of controversies, reflecting the current discussions in the wider community, and we have seen these in several ways so far. The controversy for which Dakin is best known is the difference in views between him and Ernest Payne and others about the nature of ministry in relation to the local and the wider church. It emerged from a recognized need for the Colleges to contribute to the denomination's thinking about the nature of ministry and forms of church.

In 1942 the Conference of Principals agreed that it would be helpful to have a small book setting out the denomination's view of church and of ministry, and they decided that one person should write it to preserve a consistent voice. Dr Dakin was selected, and in 1944 *The Baptist View of the Church and the Ministry* was published "with the commendation of the College principals." However, the commendation also pointed out that this did not necessarily imply "their concurrence on at all points," and made it clear that the hope in writing this was that the book would provoke further discussion. This is the first sign that what Dr Dakin had written was about to become controversial.

As we have already seen, there is no doubt that Dakin was committed to an ecumenical view of the church. He did not locate the meaning of church *only* in the local congregation. In *The Baptist View of the Church*, he affirmed that "the Church of God is the whole completed company of the people of God and this is the one true Church, holy and catholic." It is seen, he argues, in three forms: "the local church where sincere Christians are met together in the name of the Lord"; "each denomination in its corporate witness"; and thirdly "the great body of Christians through the world realizing in any degree their unity and acting on it." He understood the tendency to over-emphasize independence among Baptists as not only a weakness but a theological mistake:

> [I]n their independency and democratic rights to the extent of living entirely alone without reference to other churches of the Baptist body as a whole [congregations are mistaken]. It need hardly be said that this this is neither sound Baptist doctrine nor good Christianity.

However, it was in his presentation of the understanding of ministry that the differences with some others were to become obvious. He asserted that "there are several kinds of recognized ministry," citing local preachers, lay pastors, deaconesses and ministers of local churches. He acknowledged that in theory any member of a Baptist church could preside over any of the church's functions, from presiding at the Table through to carrying out the administration. But he argued that only those who had been discerned to possess the gifting and had been appointed by the church should undertake any of these roles. The gifting of the Spirit was the significant feature in his argument: "All spiritual endowment is open to all," that is, God can gift whoever God chooses. Thus, there is no "special order" set apart by a particular conferral of grace at ordination. So while a minister might be recognized as having a particular role, the role is one of office, rather than by "special grace or holiness." The call of God is absolutely central. We hear echoes of the continuing affirmation within the College and in the wider denomination from the earliest days that ministers are "made" by God—anything else, such as training, and in this discussion, a service of ordination, is dependent on that and cannot, in and of itself, make a person a minister.

Dakin then continued,

> Here it must be emphasised for the sake of clarity that the term Baptist minister implies a Baptist church [. . .] a Baptist minister is one who is closely related to one Baptist church which has given him an invitation and over which he presides. He is a Baptist minister (with the emphasis on the word "Baptist") partly in virtue of that relationship and if that relationship were entirely to cease, leaving him with no church over which to preside he would for the time being cease to be a Baptist minister, just as a deacon ceases to be a Baptist deacon when he gives up the office. There is no sense in which a man can claim to be a Baptist minister when he is not head of a Baptist church. [. . .] There is actually no minister without ministering.

Dakin did make a distinction between "being" a minister and being "qualified to exercise the office" and recognized that, while not being in local pastorate somebody could remain on the list of those "regarded as qualified"—but, he said, "that is a different thing."

This position, he argued, was not to say that a call to preach was therefore invalidated. So it remained possible for such a person to preach and preside, just as a local preacher did. But his central point remained that among Baptists, ministry was

> designated primarily in terms of the local community and not in terms of a central authority or of an ideal whole [. . .] A union of churches is not, and cannot be a Baptist Church, nor can the Union of Great Britain and Ireland be regarded as *the* Baptist Church.

He went on to discuss issues around those who were exercising different forms of ministry, such as tutors, chaplains, and others. He acknowledged that the New Testament described different kinds of ministers, but he put his argument in these terms:

> A College principal is a College principal, a superintendent a superintendent—all sufficiently honourable titles and the title of each clearly defines his position in the denomination [. . .] for missionaries the correct designation is missionary, again a sufficiently honourable title and one which carries with it both the idea of the call of God and assent of a representative part of his Church.

In view of his ecumenical convictions, this clearly raised an issue. How was the position of a Baptist minister in regard to the universal church to be understood? He maintained that there was no difficulty: "Baptists believe that every true Baptist Church is an expression and part of the Church of God [and so] every minister of a Baptist church is ipso facto a minister of the Church of God." But local was not as a *result* of the universal, it was the *root* of the universal.

We cannot imagine that the other principals who asked Dakin to write the book were unaware of what he was going to write. However, once written, there was a drawing back by others and the subsequent controversy is one that generates "more heat than light," and that does not reflect well on all those involved. The pain that was caused between those who were friends and colleagues can only be surmised, as can the reasons for the intensity of the controversy. What is clear is that the disagreement provoked writings on each side—and the representation of the "opposite" view was not always as full as it could be. The setting up of straw men in order to bring them down is evident in the way the discussion developed. The main riposte was from Ernest Payne, then a tutor at Regent's Park College, who—rapidly—wrote *The Fellowship of Believers*, which presented a very different view, though in the version that was eventually published it has clearly been toned down from being a direct answer and attack on Dakin's position, and is a more general presentation of an alternative position.

> We must not be misled by what is after all a comparatively minor matter, i.e. who has the right to the title of "Baptist Minister" and ignore the important conception which Dr Dakin will present [. . .] that ministry is not an order separated from others in the church, but is a mode of serving the church.

Another response was given by one of Dakin's own students, Leonard Champion, in a review in the *Baptist Quarterly*, in which he deliberately set out to address what he believed to be the important points around ecclesiology, remarking in the review that

> [t]his book deals with problems which are in the forefront of Christian thinking today. The widespread feeling that Christian organisations are on the whole outmoded and irrelevant compels Christians to give thought to the nature and function of the church. Changes are occurring within many Christian organisations and the shaping of these changes calls for an understanding of the principles which have made the organisations; as Dr. Dakin remarks . . . ". . . the problem of Baptist statesmanship at the moment is to adapt our organisation to the new conditions

in such a way that by adaptation our essential principles will be, not negated, but further elucidated and advanced.

The Baptist View of the Church was not the only book that Dakin published, and reading his other works gives a broader view of his position. *The Growth of Brotherhood*, his first book, is an argument for the development of what he calls "the complete reorganization of human society to the satisfying of man's deep-seated sense of justice." He surveyed the medieval church, and its eventual capacity for domination, and therefore the need for reform. In this, his commitment to the balance between community and individual is very clearly set out, and challenges any idea that he was as deeply individualist as some of those who disagreed with him suggest.

His role in the denomination was not hampered by this controversy. He was elected vice president of the Baptist Union in 1944. He also served as president of the Western Association in 1932 and was its chair for many years. He served on the Baptist Historical Society committee and was part of Baptist Union Council. He wrote a booklet about Carey for the BMS Ter-Jubilee. He shared in the Baptist World Alliance congresses several times and addressed the 1923 Congress on "Organization and Work of Young Baptists of the World," as part of his commitment to his conviction that Christianity was about binding people together across geography and culture for the good of the whole world.

World War Two

Just as Dakin's ministry in Coventry had been shaped by the war of 1914 to 1918, so his time as principal encompassed the Second World War. Although we have discussed the impact of the controversy with Payne during this time, because it holds a dominant place in Baptist historiography (and it is important therefore to understand the nuances), this was hardly the dominant theme of these years. What people were most concerned about was living through the war and doing it as well and as faithfully as possible.

In 1939, the College Committee noted that the government had decided that churches should remain open for the duration, and that those who were already in training for ministry should complete their training and proceed in the service of congregations. They decided therefore that the College should continue to operate, while recognizing that there would be students who wished to offer for National Service, and that therefore appropriate arrangements should be in place to suspend their training until they returned.

In 1940, two students were accepted for National Service while continuing their training: F. D. Batten who served with the Home Guard, and C. C. Morgan who became an Air Raid Warden with the ARP.

E. I. J. Morrish, who had progressed to Oxford, enlisted to serve in in the Armed Forces, while a student from Spurgeon's, A. C. Elder, who was living in Bristol during the war completed his London Bachelor of Divinity degree and then went with BMS to China, until the missionaries expelled in 1951. He and his wife then served with BMS in Brazil.

In 1941, Bristol suffered greatly from air raids and there was a great deal of destruction and many deaths. The College Committee noted with thankfulness that the building had undamaged, and that nobody from the College suffered in the bombing. Indeed, the College was able to offer a temporary home to a printing and packaging company, Robinsons Ltd, whose headquarters was destroyed by fire in 1940.

Several US Army officers were also billeted in the College in 1943–44 and the College report described this as "an interesting event" which it was hoped formed "a slight contribution to the great cause of Anglo-American unity so important for the future welfare of mankind." No doubt this was also furthered by Dr Dakin's lecture to US Army chaplains.

Day-to-day life in the College continued fairly normally, and students continued to achieve academic success and to serve the churches. Churches continued to invite students to preach, and the College asked if churches would be willing to increase these invitations since such preaching was "one of the most important ways in which the Churches can collaborate with the College in training men for their future work as ministers of the Gospel, for in this as in all other service, practice makes for efficiency." It was also hoped that a wide variety of churches would be willing to hold a "Student Sunday" at least once a year.

Several also became involved in various ministries of service. The Dakins collected and dispatched bundles of clothing to victims of the bombings in the East End of London, and several students became involved in helping the West Ham Central Mission in caring for those in Barking who were homeless because of the air raids.

Students were also involved in fire watching in the city and acted as air raid wardens (in the vacations, the Dakin family *en masse* took on this role). An allotment in Westbury-on-Trym, under the care of Henton Davies, who was a tutor at the time, was tended by students and provided food for the College.

Significantly, the support of the churches—even at times when they themselves were under great strain—continued and this was both of material benefit and great encouragement to the College.

By 1943, three of the students were in the military: F. D. Batten, who had originally been in the Home Guard, R. H. Browell, and L. Whitney. Dr Dakin wrote to them regularly, and their letters to him helped the College to maintain a sense of what was happening beyond the city.

Several former students also served as chaplains during this war. One, Revd Levi Gethin Hughes had been a chaplain in the First World War and was appointed assistant Chaplain General and finally Honorary Chaplain to the King and Deputy Chaplain General, War Office. Another, Revd Osborn Wiles had also served in the First World War and had been awarded the Military Cross. He trained at Bristol following this war and served at Wycliffe in Birmingham where the church grew rapidly in his ministry. He moved to Ipswich in 1928 and when the Second World War broke out, he immediately volunteered and left the congregation in the care of his wife. In 1943 he was appointed Assistant Deputy Chaplain General and in 1946 was awarded the DSO for bravery on the Normandy Beaches. In 1948, he was appointed Deputy General Secretary of the Baptist Union and served in that capacity until 1960.

A third also served as a chaplain during both wars, David Merrick Walker who was a Navy Chaplain in the First World War. However, his actual service in the Second World War is not known, simply that he was a Forces chaplain.

Some students, while not yet finished at the College, served churches in a variety of ways around the country: R. H. Robinson was in Queen's Road, Coventry during the worst of the air raids on that city, and was said to have been of great help. When he returned to Bristol his place was taken by John Harper. Paul Rigden Green served as temporary pastor in Aylesbury during the summer in 1940 (and at the beginning of the new term was another who followed the path to Oxford).

At the end of the 1943 to 1944 academic year, seven students settled in local pastorates, and several who were currently serving in the forces were applying to come to the College when the war was over, in addition to those who would return from their war service. The College Committee believed that, although things were difficult, it was important to keep the doors of the College open, since there would be a need for ministers after the war.

By the time the war ended, the College Report was able to rejoice that the College had stayed open and, although now reduced, was ready for the reception of fresh students. Among those who applied in the closing months of the war, with the intention of starting in the new session was one W. M. S. West, who would later follow the pattern of a principal being selected from among the former students, and we will return to his story below.

Reconnecting overseas

Among those whom the College welcomed after the war were students from overseas, continuing the welcome that had been offered to students from Latvia and Estonia before the war.

The first to arrive was Mikko Kolomainen, who was born in the Soviet Union and through the 1930s was living in Finland. In 1946 he came to Bristol under the patronage of the BWA's Baptist Continental Fund. He finished his course in 1949, and eventually returned to serve in Finland with the "encouragement" of the president of the Finnish Baptist Union, who told him that this was his duty, since it was the Finnish Baptist Union who had provided his three-year scholarship to study in Bristol. He served as rector of the Finnish Baptist Union's Bible school which opened in 1949.

Over the next years, students from the Soviet Union were also to come and share in the College's life. In 1956 Ilya Orlov from Moscow and Matthew Mullnik from Kyiv were part of the College, both returning home in 1958, taking back with them "many volumes of Spurgeon's sermons."

Not all the College's overseas links were with European visitors. We have seen something of the connections developed through BMS. There were also links with Australia through emigration and family connections.

In 1914, for example, Thomas Ruth, who had been at the College between 1897 and 1901 emigrated after serving in two churches in England, to become the minister of Collins Street Baptist Church in Melbourne. He stayed there until 1922 when he started an itinerant ministry around cities—and in 1923 he was preaching regularly on a Sunday evening in Pitt Street Congregational Church in Sydney. These services grew to be very large and in 1925 he accepted the call to be the minister there. He had a growing reputation, writing books on theology and social issues. However, the Great Depression of 1929 affected the support for his work, and numbers also began to drop. He retired in 1938, though he "did a remarkable work in the pulpit and among the people" in Flinders Street Church in Adelaide when they had a pastoral vacancy. His continuing commitment to the College was demonstrated in a gift, shortly before he died in 1956, of £20.

The involvement went the other way too: in 1907, David Davis came from Adelaide, having already complete his Bachelor of Arts degree there, to study in Bristol, He did well, winning various prizes and scholarships and served first at the church in Street, Somerset when he finished College, and later going to Calabar in Jamaica as we have seen.

Five years later, A. H. Bell also from Adelaide came to Bristol. He too did well and won the Anderson-Pratten Prize for advanced Hebrew studies. After a pastorate in South Australia, he stayed in the state, becoming a tutor at Parkin College, the Congregational institution where Baptists also went to train. Their training there was supplemented by additional lectures from various Baptist ministers. Eventually Bell became a Congregational minister.

The next to come was E. C. Burleigh, from Tasmania who arrived in 1924, and graduated in 1928 (and later, in 1950, completed an MA from Bristol). He was eventually to become professor of Old Testament studies and church history at the Baptist College in Victoria (later Whitley College), and finally the founding principal of the South Australian Theological College in Adelaide, where he remained until he retired in 1968.

During the war, it is worth noting Edward Roberts-Thomson, who came to Bristol in 1937, already having trained and served in a pastorate. He returned home having completed his Bristol Bachelor of Arts degree in 1940, and later attained a Bachelor of Divinity at Melbourne. His preaching, in Hobart Baptist Tabernacle was highly regarded and he made a significant impact on the life of that congregation. He was also deeply part of a very lively ecumenical scene in Hobart. He left there in 1949 to move to Brunswick, Victoria and while he was there his Bristol Master of Arts dissertation was published. In 1953, he moved to New Zealand to become principal of the New Zealand Baptist College following a period of significant tensions and the very public resignation of the previous principal, who made claims of a "witch-hunt." Roberts-Thomson proved to be the man for the task in healing the divisions and steering a steady course of recovery over the next eight years. In 1961, he moved to be principal of the Baptist College of New South Wales in Sydney. This was not such a happy time, and he was pressured into resigning in 1964 because of his ecumenical convictions, and he eventually became a minister of the Presbyterian Church in Australia. This was not an uncommon action for those Baptists who became disillusioned with the anti-ecumenical position of Baptists in Australia at the time.

Over the years, many men came to Bristol from Australia, and it is fitting that a full discussion of their story has been written by one of them, Ken Manley, in an article in the festschrift that was published in 1997 for Dr Champion, entitled *Bible, History and Ministry*. In this article, Manley tells the stories of men who came to study in England. To start with, most came to Rawdon College, but as Manley points out, Bristol also produced a number of "able, evangelical, lively and zealous ministers of the Gospel." He identifies twenty-four such men, some of whom we have mentioned above. Others whom he lists from the twentieth century include W. D. Jackson, who succeeded T. Ruth at Collins Street in Melbourne, and later Ted Woods who came to Bristol in 1971, and went on to teach Old Testament at the Bible College in Victoria; Graeme Chatfield who came in 1989, and returned first to be a pastor in French's Forest and then to teach history in Morling College, in New South Wales; and of course there was Manley himself, and his comment at the end of the essay perhaps sums up something important about the story. He draws his essay to a close with the following:

> I would like to conclude on a more personal note, and record my own deep debt to Bristol College. I was given practical help with tuition fees, was welcomed and accepted by both staff and students. Lifelong friendships were formed. It is a happy privilege, to have this small part in honouring Dr Champion, to whom this study is dedicated with respect and affection. I find it difficult to specify what I owe to Bristol but it certainly includes gratitude for a model of scholarship and genuine pastoral concern which I like to think has shaped my life and ministry.

We have strayed beyond the end of Dr Dakin's time now, and into the principalship of his successor, Leonard Champion; though there is a link. One of the other candidates for the position of principal of the College in New Zealand, where Edward Roberts-Thomson served, was Leonard Champion.

Before we move into that period, it is worth noting the "appreciation" of the College Committee at the twenty-fifth anniversary of Dakin's appointment.

In the appreciation that the Committee wrote at the end of his quarter-century, they stated,

> The College has been splendidly served by an able leader, preacher and teacher. We are thankful for his buoyant cheerfulness, his radiant vigour, the voice like a trumpet that rouses the dreamer, the zeal that "upraises the humble good from the ground". He is careful of adjectives, suspicious of superlatives, "chary of praise, prodigal in counsel" critical but not cynical. He has "held the target high" for himself as well as for others.

Coming in at a time when the College had been bruised and shaken by the shorter than expected and apparently less than happy principalship of Dr Whittaker, Dakin served for twenty-seven years, and put his own mark on the life of the community. Continuing the commitment to the training of lively, zealous, able, and evangelical preachers of the gospel in a broadly ecumenical context, he had built links, developed connections, and above all taught and inspired generations of men (and a sprinkling of women) with his deep commitment, plain speech, and desire to communicate the good news.

LEONARD CHAMPION

Dr Dakin was, reportedly, delighted that his successor was one of his own students, Leonard Champion. He had been appointed as a tutor in the College when Henton Davies left to be Chair of Old Testament Studies at Durham University, and in 1953, when Dakin retired, the General Meeting of the Society unanimously appointed him as the next principal. He was also appointed to lecture on religious knowledge at Bristol University. He served as principal until 1972, and as many before him, he served the College through times of profound change.

He came as a former student, deeply imbued with the College Tradition, and with both a ministry in Minehead and Rugby, and a deeply formative time studying in Germany as part of his heritage.

His period in Germany was particularly important in his thinking, and after the war, he went back to visit and was an important player in helping Baptists in the UK stay in touch with Baptists in Germany—of whom he was not uncritical. This breadth of connection, and capacity to be a critical friend was a significant feature of what he brought to the principalship.

At the heart of his thinking was an ecclesiology which determined his understanding of the nature of ministry and therefore of how ministers should be trained and formed. He also brought a deep commitment to what we might call public theology; he argued that theology was a communal practice, and that the denomination needed to take its theology seriously and find ways of reflecting together on the call of God. He understood that the Colleges had a particular, but not an exclusive, role in this activity, and continually called for the whole community, from local churches through to national gatherings to think theologically.

As principal throughout the 1950s and particularly the 1960s, he faced leading the College through a time when the nature of church and in particular of ministry went through significant rethinking. That of course, required the Colleges to think carefully about what training and formation was to look like. During the 1960s, the numbers leaving the ministry increased significantly, and most who did, did so within five years of leaving College. But the sense of problems around the ministry were not something that only emerged in the 1960s. In 1958 the Baptist Union produced a report on ministry, and Leonard Champion was part of the commission that wrote it. He had been impressed at the sense of vocation among those who were applying to the Colleges, and was deeply disturbed by a *Baptist Times* report of the commission's findings that there was a "grave decline in quality and numbers entering ministry."

Champion argued that the issue was with the churches, who had a fixed view of what ministry should be and were limiting their ministers' capacity to reimagine life for a new age. The editor of the *Baptist Times*, Walter Bottoms, argued that part of the issue was the rise in the number of unaccredited ministers—and certainly there seems to have been a rise in those who may well have been theologically trained, but who were not aware of and immersed in Baptist life and identity. This context is important in understanding some of the energy which Dr Champion brought to his consideration and teaching of Baptist distinctives and practices. When he was pastor in Rugby, he took part in a series of lectures, in which he argued his case of Baptist identity and the need for theological seriousness about the church and its role. This was to remain a significant feature of his practice.

He came to the principalship, bringing with him, therefore, a strong sense not only of a Christocentric ecclesiology, but the need to communicate that, and the implications of such a position for the nature of ministry.

Champion's thinking on ministry

A couple of years after starting as principal, Champion wrote a piece called *The Minister and the Application for the Ministry*. He started from the assumption that those who would be exploring a call would be "young" (and also, despite the fact that there were several women already in ministry, that they would be male) and said that such a one would need "wise counsel and guidance" in the first instance, from their minister. The minister had an important discerning role, since it was not unknown for somebody to be attracted to the work who was not called. Champion was clear that this was damaging both for the individual and even more for the churches, since much harm could be done.

A call therefore was to be "probed and examined [. . .] encouraged [. . .] without haste." Whether the appropriate gifts were present was to be explored, and such gifts were to be given a context for development; we can assume from this that he expected candidates to be given a chance to preach, but also perhaps to be involved in other tasks of leadership, administration, pastoral care, and also to be encouraged to share in the wider life of the churches.

The next stage was to be "some kind of training," which Dr Champion expressed as "a period of study and reflection in which the mind may grow, knowledge be acquired and the personality disciplined." Here is a theme that has emerged regularly in our story—that ministerial training is as much about personhood and growth in depth as it is about the acquiring of knowledge, or as previous generations put it, "parts." Champion's expectation was that such a training would normally take place in one of the Baptist Colleges and that a candidate's minister could help in three ways: by encouraging somebody to think of College, obtaining information about the College and the entry requirements, and helping the applicant to apply and to gain the entry requirements. Again, this is a pattern we will recognize, in particular, the encouragement to attend College and the support in doing the necessary preliminary work.

The next considerations are practical, namely, how is the training to be funded. There was a long tradition, which Champion acknowledged with gratitude, of the Colleges taking students "on the basis of what each man could pay," and so financial questions were to be considered after application and acceptance and not to be a criterion for application or acceptance. Support from home churches, and local education grants were to be sought, but they were not to be the basis of a decision either. Nor was previous educational attainment. A good education was an advantage, but not essential, and as long as applicants were willing to learn, the assumption appears to have been that educational deficiencies could be made up in the College.

Then there was the consideration of personal circumstances. Champion argued that an appropriate age was twenty or twenty-one years old; old enough to have been "out in the world," and not straight from school, but still young. Younger candidates could be considered if they were mature enough, and older candidates, if they were willing to undertake the course of study required. Alongside this was a hope that there would be some life-experience. Completing two years National Service was a good grounding (National Service was not discontinued until 1960), and it was preferable if students were unmarried, and that they remained so during the course. Married men were considered, and not ruled out simply because they were married, but their particular circumstances required especial consideration. In line with the general assumption of the time, it appears that if any women were to be considered, it was assumed they were, and would remain, unmarried. This was the model of the deaconesses, who left their role if they married. (The marriage bar, as it was called, in teaching and in the Civil Service was only beginning to be lifted gradually after the second war.)

It is worth noting however, that by the time Dr Champion was considering retirement, in the early 1970s, the age range and the marital status of students had become much broader. More students were applying to College after some time in various careers, several already with degrees in other subjects, and a growing number were not only married but had children. The development of what was later to become known as church-based training (and which was at this time known as "student pastorates") become rooted in the College life during these years. The reflective practice made possible by pastoring and studying at the same time came to be understood to be very valuable, as was the setting of habits of study alongside the practice of ministry. This is a model that has since been adopted by the denomination as a whole for the whole of a ministerial life. That it was very hard work was also noted, and the cost to family life was recognized and acknowledged as being something that needed to be taken into account in considering a candidate for such a mode of study.

The final aspect to be considered was the support of those who knew the candidate; this could not simply be a personal sense of being called, nor even one that a minister agreed with. There was to be a testing of the call and a commendation on that basis from a local church, and then from an Association (this was the pattern that was required for accreditation by the Baptist Union).

There is a strong continuity here, as we have seen, with previous patterns and expectations, but there are also differences. The involvement of the Association which may have been assumed before, is now much more clearly required. This dates from earlier in the century and the organizing and developing of the accredited list, and reflects a growing sense that ministry belonged not just to the individual church but also in some sense to the denomination. In light of the debates in which Dakin had been involved, this development is significant. That Champion was not unhappy with a local congregation having a stronger sense of belonging to wider body is clear in his writings on ecclesiology. Indeed, he was quite explicit about it, interestingly, as he discusses ministry and ecumenical recognition. In *The Doctrine of the Church*, as he discusses why high Anglicans might find Baptist ordination "invalid," he spends some time arguing that there seems to be no good reason why Baptists should accept episcopacy (the "condition" on which unity was being suggested at the time), and he goes on to comment that Baptists would "in time, drop the plural churches which step Paul took, and speak of the Church." He also argued that Baptists should not be anxious about the consequences "which sometimes follow from a stressing of unity which involves a strengthening of the Baptist Union as an organisational necessity." He goes on to suggest that such an organization would operate as part of the Body of Christ and be held accountable by the members of the Body.

The strength of his ecclesiology, and his willingness to follow where the scholarship led was a mark of the understanding of ministry that shaped him, and which he brought to the training that the College offered.

Champion had more to say about ministry and about churches than we have noted here, but that will be discussed elsewhere. As we tell the story of the College, it is not simply the story of the principals. There were those who worked alongside them, as we have seen. Working with Leonard Champion were Norman Moon and Harry Mowvley.

Tutors

Norman Moon was another of Dakin's students, who came to Bristol in the mid-1930s. One of those who, in another time would have taken his studies further by going to one of the Continental universities (in his case, Zurich) he was prevented from this by the outbreak of the Second World War. He settled in pastorate and continued his studies alongside that work, earning his Master of Theology from London University. On coming back to the College as a tutor in 1953, when Champion moved from being tutor to being principal, he took on the teaching of church history and part of the Old Testament course, while Dr Champion taught New Testament and Greek and was also responsible for the pastoral theology training. In 1960, Norman Moon was also appointed librarian of the College.

Beyond College, he was involved ecumenically. He served for many years as secretary of the Bristol Free Churches, and in 1967 was elected their president.

Over the next few years, the numbers of students increased, and more capacity among teaching staff was needed. Financially, it was not possible to employ another full-time member of staff and in 1959, an arrangement was made with the Cotham Grove Baptist Church that when they called a new minister (who would be part-time since the church could not afford a full-time stipend) there would be a job-share. Another former student, Harry Mowvley, was called to Cotham Grove and to the College in 1960 and for three years he combined the two posts. His specialty was Hebrew and the Old Testament course. In 1964 he became a full-time tutor at the College. In 1949 he had gained his Bristol Bachelor of Arts degree with distinction (a rare accolade) and had then gone on to Regent's Park in Oxford. He was followed there shortly by three other Bristol students, including Morris West, with whom he forged a lifelong friendship.

His commitment to ecumenism was also significant in his ministry outside College. During his ministry in Cotham Grove, the membership at the church grew, and good relationships were developed in the neighbourhood. Ecumenical experiments took place, which led to the church calling the Revd Keith Forecast from Arley Congregational Church in 1964, and within two years the church had become an ecumenical fellowship between Baptists, Congregationalists, and Methodists, with Mowvley and the

Methodist minister, Revd Raymond Morris, drafting a constitution for the new church. He also attended the World Council of Churches' International Consultation on Practical Theology at Bossey, Switzerland, in 1967.

One of the reasons for the need to increase the teaching staff was the extension of the qualifications on offer; as well as the Bristol University degree, it had long been possible for students to attend the university classes, but be examined by the College itself and be awarded a College Diploma. In 1957, for the first time, these students were set to sit the External Diploma in Theology from London University, and this proved successful. However, it also challenged the teaching, since the curriculum of the two awarding bodies was not the same. Hence the need to expand the teaching staff.

Teaching patterns

Another effect on the College of this new pattern was to further separate the groups of students; some spent most of their time in university classes, while those doing the Diploma in Theology were almost fully within College classes, shared between the Baptist College and Western College. The link with Western College continued to be an important part of the teaching life of the community, with shared classes and combined resources of teaching faculty, until 1968. At that point, Western College had become so small that it was no longer viable, and it combined with several other Congregational Colleges and was centred in Manchester. The loss of that link further strained the resources and energy of the teaching staff.

The links with Bristol University were further developed, as the university teaching changed. In 1964 a Department of Theology was established in the university, with Kenneth Graystone from the Methodist College being appointed professor. Along with straightforward full-time university appointments, the department also decided to appoint members of the faculties of the theological Colleges as part-time lecturers for specialist subjects. Dr Champion was the special lecturer in New Testament, Harry Mowvley the equivalent for Hebrew and Old Testament. Dr Mowvley was a recognized teacher for a specialized course in seventeenth-century Dissent.

Dr Champion's Impact

One of the ways in which a principal's impact can be seen is in how those educated under his care go on to have an impact on the denomination. For Leonard Champion, with his deep determination and commitment to think about the nature of the church and the shape of the denominational community, one of the lasting legacies can be seen in the coming together of a significant group of pastor-theologians in direct response to a call that Champion gave in the Annual Lecture of the Baptist Historical Society at the meetings of the Baptist Union, which was subsequently printed in the *Baptist Quarterly*. In his paper "Evangelical Calvinism" in 1979, he spoke of

> a fresh theological formulation of profound spiritual experience bringing people together in a mutually responsive and trusting fellowship [which]provided the means whereby the Spirit of God brought into being new structures of church life for communicating the gospel.

And he asked, "Is the Spirit seeking such means today?"

In response, Keith Clements, then a tutor at Bristol, Richard Kidd, minister in Botley in Oxford, Paul Fiddes, tutor at Regent's Park, Roger Hayden, minister at Haven Green, Ealing, and Brian Haymes, a former Bristol student under Champion, and at this point minister of Mansfield Rd, Nottingham, started to meet and finally produced the collection *A Call to Mind*. In this, they discussed what they recognized as basic questions, not in order to define final answers, but to outline resources from which "a renewed theology might emerge."

In this writing, and others that followed it, this group of ministers, which shifted in membership slightly over the years, sought to provide what Champion himself had been seeking all through his own ministry and in particular in his work as principal and which he identified in the 1979 paper, namely a theological foundation and context for the church in the world (and incidentally, and consequently, for ministry). Their intention, just as Champion's, was to be Christocentric; to start from the conviction that God is as God is known in Jesus—and to follow this through in thinking about church and Christian identity.

The connection to the Bristol College was not accidental or fleeting. Emerging from a call issued by a former principal, one of the first members of the group was a tutor in the College, one of the members was to be superintendent of the area and to be deeply committed to the College's ongoing life, and one was to become, in due course, another principal of the College. The link with the Bristol Tradition is there in Champion's paper—the evangelical Calvinism which we have seen early in the story, and its impact on the denomination in one generation as a resource and call to seek a similar resource for another generation.

Dr Champion's influence in the College and the denomination did not cease with his retirement from the principalship in 1972, but we will leave his story here, since we are concerned less with the broader story of the denomination and more with the ongoing life of the community of the College. When he announced in 1970 that he would retire in 1972, after due deliberation and "consideration of a wide range of ages and theological positions," the unanimous recommendation of the committee was that W. M. S. West should be appointed as co-principal for a year prior to becoming the principal when Dr Champion retired.

DR MORRIS WEST

Morris West was, as we have noted a former student of the College who entered immediately after the Second World War. In studying in Bristol, he was following in a family tradition: his father had been a student, entering in 1899, and taking the London Bachelor of Divinity. In 1905, West's father became minister at Zion Baptist Church in Bradford-on-Avon, and in 1911 moved to Kingsgate Chapel in Holborn, London. This was in the time before any kind of superintendency or settlement board, and Dr West spoke later of the difficulties in being able to move, unless one had contacts. In 1913, West's father moved to Lower Edmonton, north London, and during the First World War, served with the YMCA in France, then after the war went to Old King St in Bristol, returned to Lower Edmonton in 1925, and stayed there until he retired in 1943.

Morris West himself started school in Edmonton in 1928, and then in 1931, he was sent to school in Taunton. He entered the sixth form in 1937, intending to go on to university. Then the Second World War came. In 1940, when he was preparing to sit his examinations, his father had a conversation with a deacon of the Lower Edmonton church who owned a small arms factory in Enfield. He was anxious about the pressure they were facing because of the loss of arms when equipment had had to be abandoned at Dunkirk. The factories, including that owned by the deacon, were working day and night, seven days a week, and were short of workers. West Senior suggested his son as at least a temporary worker, since he was training in science (he intended to be an engineer), and when he spoke to his son about it, Morris West agreed to go. In the event, he accepted a post as a chemist, testing steel. He left school immediately he finished his Higher School Certificate, and starting at the factory the very next week. He was there for five years, serving in London during the Blitz, where he was also a fire watcher, and then was moved to what he always called "an establishment" in Poole, in Dorset and was able to watch the D Day invasion force set off in June 1944.

We tell this story in some detail because it shaped his life; many of his age served overseas and did not come home. For the rest of his time, he was aware that his years of life were a gift not to be taken for granted. In June 1945, he applied to Bristol Baptist College for ministerial training, having become convinced of a call through these months. Later he was to explain that his call was formed in the "context of war" and went on to explain,

> That is why my attitudes in ministry have been what they are—they have been shaped by the need for compassion, individual concern for everybody, reconciliation and community building.

He was a student in Bristol for four years, since he needed to do a first year to cover what he had missed in the School Certificate because of his war work, and having completed his Bachelor of Arts degree, he won a two-year Baptist Union scholarship. He went with several others to Regent's Park College in Oxford, in the pattern we have seen, in order to do post-graduate study. This was not a foregone conclusion; he had in fact been invited to take up the pastorate at Alveston in the Lake District, following a preaching visit there in the summer of 1948. However, when he talked to Dr Dakin about this, he later reported that his principal's reaction had been

> Rubbish! You [. . .] are going to Oxford to take the Oxford degree. Let me hear no more about you trying to settle before you have been to Oxford for two years.

Dr West, in writing about this commented, "this was Dakin's way of doing things. And more often than not he was right. Certainly he was in my case."

So, to Oxford he went—causing no small consternation because he was already married to Freda, whom he had met at the BMS Summer School in 1946. Since Oxford did not accept married students, Freda remained in Yorkshire for the following two years.

When he completed his two years there and received a second-class honours degree from the university, they went—together—to Zurich where he studied, in particular history, and eventually was awarded his Doctor of Theology from the University of Zurich. While there he was invited to become the junior tutor and bursar of Regent's Park College, and when he returned from Zurich this was where he went. His commissioning service was held in September of 1953, and was referred to as a "commissioning and ordination."

He remained in Oxford until 1959, calling it later "a fascinating time," but he was strongly convinced of a call to local pastorate, and in 1959, he was inducted as minister of Dagnall Street in St Albans. He was there for twelve years, and over that period, was regularly approached by academic institutions to serve with them—and regularly refused. However, when he was approached by Bristol Baptist College, he was ready to move to a new sphere.

He was already involved in the life of the College, and particularly in the efforts to think about the future.

College Policy Committee

In 1968, the College Committee had set up a College Policy Committee. Apart from Dr West, all the members of the committee were members of the College Committee or members of the teaching staff. Later in the year, in his message from the principal, Dr. Champion explained the context and purpose. Western College had closed, bringing to an end a long relationship and breadth of teaching resources, the Methodists had brought together several of their Colleges and centred the new institution, Wesley College, in Bristol, and three Anglican Colleges had amalgamated into one, Trinity College. Dr Champion pointed out that these changes were "sharp reminders of the many changes occurring in theological education and in concepts of ministry." While Bristol College was not declining in numbers, it was important to be aware of the changing situation and the need to "discern more clearly what the policy of the College should be during the next decade or two."

The committee "examined [. . .] the witness and work of our churches in the present challenging and confusing situation," and then wondered together, "What can and ought the College to do?" The report that they produced outlined four areas of development of the College's activities:

- To continue to train men and women for full-time ministry in the UK and overseas, and to provide training for those who would work in other forms of Christian service.
- To provide special courses for ministers and probationary ministers to meet "the exacting demands of ministry today."
- Training in education courses for both young and retired men and women for Christian service.
- Lay education and training led by Tutors either in College, or in local churches.

The committee recommended an appeal for £20000 to support these plans.

This fund, and the work that it was to enable, form the bridge between Dr Champion and Dr West as principals. Numbers of students were continuing to grow, and by 1976 there were more than forty, and the appointment of another tutor became necessary. This was especially important with the commitment to what now came to be called "open option" students. These were those who were referred to in terms of the first aim listed above: people who were seeking to serve in some form of Christian work, but not necessarily in full-time ministry, in the UK or overseas. As Dr West was to make clear later in his reflection in 'Autobiographical Material', this offer of training to people who were not intending to be ministers or missionaries was actually nothing new. It had been part of the College's practice from very early on. However, in making it such a fundamental part of the core purposes of the College, there was a shift.

Changing circumstances

Or was there? One of the realities which the Policy Committee was grappling with, along with every other group throughout the denomination, and indeed, the whole of the church in the UK in the late 1960s and early 1970s, was what the committee referred to as a "challenging and confusing situation." While it was demonstrably the case that Baptist congregations had rarely been powerful and central to society in the way that parishes of the Established Church had been, it was nonetheless true that all the churches were aware of and trying to come to terms with what could be viewed as a catastrophic loss of numbers and presence. Of course, it did not begin in the 1960s (we might look, for example, to the beginnings of decline that can be dated to 1906), but it is nevertheless true that those living through the 1960s and 70s were very aware of declining life. While writing with thanksgiving of the year 1970, the College secretary G. W. Byrt remarked in his report that "our students have to pursue their studies and training well aware of the secularised, indifferent society by which they are surrounded, and into which they will go as ambassadors of Christ." They could no longer expect or look forward to preaching to chapels that were full or even two-thirds full. He went on to affirm that "youth can be blessedly resilient, hopeful and enthusiastic; youth knows that the Christian church has survived difficult time before the present and that Jesus has said 'I will build my church.'"

It was clear that training for ministry and ministry itself was changing, and so it is appropriate to ask just how big the shift was to including open option students as a core component. With the loss of numbers within the churches and a growing concern for seeking the work of God beyond the traditional description of church, it could therefore be argued that training people to think theologically and to understand their work in whatever context as Christian work, did involve a broadening, but was not in fact a fundamental shift *per se*. It was an appropriate response to the changing context in which the College was operating.

If this is so, it is clear that it was a broadening with which Dr West was deeply in sympathy. When he was president of the Baptist Union in 1973 his presidential address had the title "For What We Have Received." Among other things in this address, he argued that

> in the celebration of our new beginning in Christ comes witness in everyday things. Our lip service to this conviction needs translation into life service [. . .] I am not simply to be a Christian proclaiming in the pulpit and then a citizen in society. I am to be a Christian preacher and Christian citizen. Christian worshippers on one day are Christian citizens on every day. We need to help each other far more than we do. To share together more groups which face similar situations. To talk these things through more in Bible study, in home groups, in church meetings. To recognize that this way leads to involvement in making known the Gospel of Jesus Christ in places where apart from us it will not be heard.

This address demonstrates a conviction that while the minister has a particular role, which we will reflect more on below, the role of each believer is to be part of the activity of mission and service in whatever context they are in, not simply in "church activities". The Bristol Tradition is to train able, evangelical, lively, zealous ministers of the gospel. For many years, this was primarily aimed at those who took the title 'minister' within a local church. However, with the significant changes of the first half of the twentieth century, and the reflection on these changes and discernment of the way forward for the churches and so the College, there is clearly a sense that some of what had been a minister's role was now also to be carried by other church members. So, the development of lay training, both through short courses and more intense study, and, in particular, the possibility of a theological context in which to offer other forms of service in society—that is, training that would produce those who were able, evangelical, lively, and zealous in all sorts of contexts—was a very proper development of the College life and intention.

TERCENTENARY CELEBRATIONS

As part of the affirmation of this, during Dr West's time, the College celebrated its tercentenary. As we have seen in the early part of this discussion, the dates on which we might say the College 'began' is not as clear as we might assume. The Terrill gift is dated 1679 but in fact was not 'activated' until 1720.

However, taking that earlier date, a three hundredth anniversary was celebrated in 1979. There was a celebration lunch in the Great Hall of the University, with city dignitaries in attendance. Dr West noted in his speech of welcome how the place of the College in the life of the city had moved in three hundred years: in welcoming the Lord Mayor, he remarked,

> If our founding fathers were present with us, and from the point of view of our faith it may well be that they are at least overhearing what is going on, they might be surprised that you are singled out to be the first to be welcomed. I am quite sure that Edward Terrill and his contemporaries would not have put the Lord Mayor at the top of the list but at the bottom.

Dr West went on to highlight the involvement of the College both ecumenically and civically in the present age, and he particularly emphasized the connection with Bristol University. Welcoming the vice-chancellor, he recalled how Andrew Gifford had suggested that the College ought to apply for a University Charter. He also recalled that the reasons why this did not happen was, according to the minutes of the College, because of the "modesty of the Tutors." However, by the time of this tercentenary celebration, the College along with other theological Colleges in the city were now part of the Theology Faculty of the university, a position that "helped to maintain the proper academic standing of the College."

Representatives from the Baptist Union and from the other Colleges were also present and welcomed as were former students, reaching right back to 1919. The representatives of the Community included those who had had served overseas, had served in academic capacities, and had served in local pastorates; what Dr West called

> the types of service offered by the College over the years [. . .] and tomorrow we shall begin again doing what all those responsible for the College have tried to do from the time of Terrill onwards, namely preparing men and women who will be able and evangelical ministers of the gospel.

Sidney Hall, who was then secretary of the College managed to track down details of fifteen hundred men and women who had studied in the College, and this remembering was deeply encouraging to the current generation of students and staff.

By 1979, funding that had previously been available through Local Education Authorities was beginning to decline, and so the College also set up a fund, the Terrill Memorial Fund, the interest of which would be distributed through the denominational scholarship committee to support students at each of the Baptist Colleges.

There were other celebrations too, one of which was the publication of Norman Moon's history, *Education for Ministry*, which told the story of the College's life through the years. Staff and students were invited to speak in various contexts, and pictorial exhibitions were available to illustrate the history of the community. The Founder's Day service was held at Broadmead Baptist Church, and broadcast on BBC Radio 4, and BBC1 televised a Celebration Service. At the beginning of October, nearly two hundred members of the College Community, past and present staff, and students, gathered at Broadmead for a reunion on the Monday evening, addressed by several speakers. On the Tuesday morning meetings were held at Tyndale Baptist Church and in the evening, Dr David Russell addressed the community with a "powerful challenging address."

Regardless of what the actual date of founding might be determined as, this celebration of the ongoing life of the College, reflecting both continuity and change was an important affirmation and reaffirmation of the tradition which has shaped the way the College has functioned through the centuries: training men and women for service to God among the people of God as those who will be able, zealous, lively, and evangelical, who will function in a broad ecumenical context. The links with the city and the university as well as with other communities across the country and the world had emerged as appropriate responses to changing situations over the centuries and were firm and life-giving. Above all, as shown in the numbers who returned for the reunion, the sense of community among those who were part of the College, as students, as staff, as friends and supporters, had been nurtured and encouraged and remained strong and vibrant.

To have reached this point, and still to be within a recognizable identity without being ossified was an achievement worthy of celebration—and celebrate it the College did!

Dr West in the denomination

Dr West, as with all the principals of the College, by no means limited his work, insight, and energy to the College itself. He was deeply involved in wider Baptist life, in the UK and beyond. Between 1982 and 1985, he chaired the Council of the Baptist Union, and even after his retirement continued to be deeply involved in the structural life of the denomination. One of his major roles after retirement was to chair the search committee for the new general secretary of the Baptist Union, when Bernard Green retired, and so he was part of the process that appointed David Coffey and Keith Jones in 1991 (he had also been involved in the process of appointing Bernard Green, and his deputy, Douglas Sparkes, and on that occasion had been approached to consider both posts, but had refused). He was also chair of the working group that dealt with the move of the Union offices from London to Didcot.

His involvement in the Union's life was deeply tied up with his ecumenical commitment, and he was the representative of the Union in the British Council of Churches, and was part of the process which culminated in 1995 with the formation of Churches Together in England. Within the Union he chaired the Church Relations Committee as well as sitting on the General Purposes Committee and the Scholarship Committee. He was Moderator of the Free Church Federal Council from 1981 to 1982 (which meant he was one of the guests at the wedding of Prince Charles and Lady Diana Spencer). This also led to a renewal of the relationship he had developed with Robert Runcie, when they had both been ministers in St Albans. And his ecumenical work went beyond Britain. From 1951, he was involved in the World Council of Churches and in 1962, he was elected to the Faith and Order Commission of the WCC, and served on that for twenty years.

A 'Bristol man' through and through, taking seriously the tradition of lively, able, evangelical, zealous ministers of the gospel, he also exemplified the wider issues of ecumenism and catholicity.

Taking theology wider

His emphasis on the need for good theology and the capacity to think about it was also part of the form that the service of other tutors took. In 1975, Neville Clark was appointed tutor at South Wales Baptist College, in an appointment that was made jointly with the College in Bristol. Initially, he taught New Testament and pastoral theology, and later his main work was in theological studies. This sharing of the teaching went both ways, as Dr West also caught in Cardiff. The development and sustaining of the link between the Colleges was an important part in allowing a breadth of teaching that might otherwise have been difficult to sustain. It also ensured that the College did not became too parochial in its outlook. The links between Bristol and Wales, as we have seen, were there in the very beginning, and this form of the link was to prove very fruitful.

Following his retirement as principal of the South Wales College, Neville Clark wrote a series of booklets entitled *Invitation to a Conversation*, which were published by South Wales Baptist College and were intended to encourage readers, whom he hoped would be beyond a "trained inner circle," to grow in "their knowledge of God and understanding of how to live Christianly." This intention to encourage good, non-trivial and theologically educated thinking and understanding among members of churches is another aspect of the pattern of life that was being deeply encouraged with lay training and involvement.

Clark could be quite cutting in his assessment of the lack of theological reflection in the communal life of the denomination, and in his comments on the Baptist Union Report *Meaning and Practice of Ordination*, published in 1958, he noted that it contained "clear signs of the pervasive influence down the years of non-theological factors," and identified its main weakness as its lack of "a sustained attempt to think theologically in a systematic way" which led to a lack of "coherence, profession, unity, and a worthy attainment of its goals." He went on to argue that rather than simply calling for such theology, as the report did, "the group was surely committed to ruthless and relentless theological thinking, however provisional it might be in its conclusions." Sadly, he felt, the report had stopped short of that.

This theological reflection on ministry, its meaning as well as its practice, was one of the themes that shaped Clark's teaching, and while the majority of his service was in and through the College in Cardiff, he was also a significant part of the Bristol teaching team for many years. When Dr West retired in 1987, Clark ceased to teach in Bristol, although Dr West continued in his teaching in Cardiff until Clark's retirement in 1991.

DEMANDING TIMES

In the first part of the 1980s, life in the College was thriving. The numbers were increasing, and included, in line with the policies outlined at the beginning of Dr West's tenure, not only ministerial students, but also open option students. The age range of the students had broadened, and there is no doubt that the depth of reflection brought into the studies and the informal conversations was increased by the life-experience which more mature students brought with them. The College had faced challenging times and had to all intents and purposes done well.

If Dr West's principalship covered a time which was characterized, as we have noted above, as "a challenging and confusing situation," this did not lessen in the late 1980s. This was to be a time across the board when numbers in theological Colleges were dropping rapidly. It was also the period in which the financial support from the state that had benefitted so many was drastically cut, and the issues of finance for training became very difficult to handle. In 1986, students were no longer allowed to apply for benefits during the vacations, and plans began to be made for first the freezing, and then the removal of student maintenance grants, culminating in the beginning of the loan system in 1990. This process has of course continued with the introduction of tuition fees and the ongoing impact on the financing of study.

It was also a time when the denomination itself was decreasing both in size and in resource and the support for Colleges and for the Baptist Union through Home Mission giving was in decline. Theologically and denominationally, it was also a period when the lessening of denominational identity was having an impact. The development of a pan-Evangelical identity, fostered by events such as Spring Harvest, and reinforced by the growth in charismatic style worship across denominations meant that even more than before, people were more inclined to find a church where they were at home in terms of style and theology, and were in fact less concerned about denominational identity. (This was true not only for Baptists of course; we were part of something much wider in this experience.) While this brought with it many benefits and strengths, it also meant that support for denominational institutions, in terms of the denomination itself, and mission societies, Colleges, and other such bodies diminished. Congregations, if they were able to give outside their immediate needs, were often now choosing to give, not to denominational organizations, but to parachurch or explicitly non-denominational ones. It also meant that those who were choosing to pursue theological education could choose to attend Colleges other than those of the denomination. Thus, Colleges such as London Bible College, Moorlands College, Birmingham Bible Institute, and the Glasgow Bible Training Institute were now all possibilities, and a significant proportion of those who were eventually to enter Baptist ministry chose to attend Colleges other than Baptist ones. This was nothing new, but the possibilities available, and the numbers involved did increase in this decade.

This was not an easy time for any of the Colleges of our denomination, nor indeed, many other denominations. It was into this unpromising situation that Dr John Morgan-Wynne stepped, when he was appointed in 1987. Nearly a decade on from the tercentenary celebrations, there was a recognition that while things were still going well, especially in terms of numbers, this was by no means a situation that could be depended on. The issue of what might be called 'supply and demand' was important and although the numbers applying to come to College at this point were holding up, the number of churches and numbers in churches were declining, and therefore, the number of churches who could afford ministers was also declining.

DR JOHN MORGAN-WYNNE

John Morgan-Wynne, having studied at Jesus College in Oxford, moved in 1958 to Regent's Park College to study theology. This was while Morris West was a tutor there, and they developed a friendship. Thus, although Dr West could not, as Dr Dakin and Dr Champion had done, see his successor as one of the men who had come through the College under his care, he did claim him as "a former student." The College Committee was enthusiastic about the appointment and in April 1987, he arrived for a preliminary term as a handover period alongside Dr West.

When he had finished his training at Regent's Park College, Morgan-Wynne had served in Eccles, in New Road in Oxford, and at Botley. He had been appointed to Regent's Park in 1965 and had been dean of the College for five years. He was also honorary pastor at Wolvercote during this time, as well as teaching Greek in the University. He gained a Master of Arts at Regent's Park, and while he was tutor there, he earned the postdoctoral Bachelor of Divinity—and he competed his doctorate at the University of Durham while he was principal at Bristol. His particular interest was in the historical and theological issues associated with the Passion—an interest sparked by the principal of Regent's Park, Henton Davies, when Morgan-Wynne was first a tutor there. Morgan-Wynne also worked with Barrie White when he was principal, though does not appear to have been as easy a relationship.

Tradition and custom were important to Morgan-Wynne, and he showed this when he came to Bristol by continuing to wear his clerical collar and academic gown. Although some had worn gowns to teach, not all had, and not all did consistently. The wearing of a clerical collar has long been a matter of debate among Baptist ministers, with a variety of practices in evidence over the years, and in different contexts. For Morgan-Wynne, the collar was important as a badge of office, and it had been part of his practice since his first pastorate. In this, as it turned out, he was different from his predecessor, who was not a fan of the clerical collar. As Brian Haymes, a later principal was to remark about various things when the question of 'the Bristol way of doing things' was raised, "the Bristol Tradition is that there isn't a tradition about it."

Teaching and Bristol University

As is always the way when a new member of staff is appointed to a role, the teaching is adjusted around it. Morgan-Wynne was a New Testament scholar and he took on that role, and it may be that he hoped to teach in the university department as well, in the way that the other College tutors had. At this point, the College tutors were Keith Clements and Mike Wotton, both of whom were teaching in the Faculty of Theology. However, the faculty was well-supplied with New Testament scholars, since both Dr John Zeisler and Dr Meg Pamment were there, and so there was not actually a role for another teacher. One of the results of this was that John Morgan-Wynne had no teaching contact with the students who were doing the Bristol Bachelor of Arts, which is a frustrating position for a College principal to be in.

As it happened, within the next few years, all teaching contact with the university ceased; Keith Clements left College to work with the Council of Churches of Britain and Ireland as coordinating secretary for International Affairs, where he remained until 1997, and Mike Wotton resigned for personal reasons. Thus, for the first time, there were no staff from the College teaching in the university. This meant, as Morgan-Wynne pointed out, that there were some students going through the College and into ministry who received no teaching from their own principal and tutors. He and others recognized this as a very unsatisfactory state of affairs.

This, taken together with the change of direction of the university department, following the retirement of Dennis Nineham as head of department and the appointment of Dr Ursula King, made it clear that things needed to change. The university department was refocused to concentrate more on religious studies, and thus was less appropriate as the main training context for those who were going into ministry. This was to become a major issue for all theological Colleges and ministerial training contexts toward the end of the twentieth century.

Continuing a university context remained important however, and since the London Bachelor of Divinity was a much more traditional theology degree, it was decided to enrol those students who already had a degree and therefore were not in receipt of grants (which meant they were not constrained regarding their course) for that degree. The subjects they covered there were almost the same as the earlier Bristol Bachelor of Arts. During the six years that Morgan-Wynne was principal, two students gained first class honours in this degree, and all the others who studied it were awarded second class honours.

The beginnings of what was eventually to become a happy and fruitful relationship with the Anglican College that had been formed by the bringing together of the previous three was also begun at this time. Trinity College, which had also previously been involved in Bristol University, was instrumental in persuading the university to establish an alternative theology degree to be taught through the theological Colleges. But the relationship between Bristol Baptist College and Trinity College did not really come to fruition until a change of principal at both Colleges.

Contact was also made with the University of Wales with a view to doing their degree, a route that Spurgeon's College had taken, since London University was not happy with external institutions teaching their degree course.

This separation from the university was unfortunate. The relationship between the College and the university went right back to the very beginning of Bristol University, and was an important part of the College's identity, as had been seen in the tercentenary celebrations. The change as it were, happened to the College, because of internal decision of the university department, but nevertheless, it had profound implications for the College's direction and identity. The College Committee or at least, some members of it, much regretted the break, and tensions that were to make the next years hard ones in the life of the College began to emerge.

However, in other ways, life continued much as before; students left and settled, new students came, tutors lectured, addressed conferences and retreats, and served the denomination as well as the College in various ways. The lay training course continued and was well supported.

Student life

Although for some years there had been student pastors in a variety of forms, the main form of pastoral experience at this time was in the practice of placements, often in the summer vacations. Some of these placements were with another minister in a church different from a student's former experience, some were working alone in a smaller church. There were hospital chaplaincies, being part of a team at the hospice or taking part in the work at a drug rehabilitation centre.

The academic and community aspects of life also helped with personal development, including for example, encouraging the "mutual acceptance of different viewpoints and personal enrichment through discussion and debate"; a long tradition of robust discussion over the meal table and in the common room as well as in formal learning settings is always an important part of any College life, and it had always been part of the life in Bristol.

The accounts we have been able to give in earlier sections of this account of who the students were and where they came from and where they went prove, for this period, to be much harder to include; not because there are no records or memories, but because we are now moving, as noted at the beginning of this chapter, into the section of our work for which research proved so hard. As outlined above, the impact of both the COVID-19 pandemic of 2020 and 2021 and the personal circumstances of Dr Cross mean that although there are rough notes about a few of the students, there is nothing like the detailed material that has been provided for earlier part of the story. The full recording and analyzing of this period of the College's history must await later historians.

Dr Morgan-Wynne's concept of training and ministry

When he was asked who it was he hoped that the College would serve and care for as students, Dr Morgan-Wynne identified four aspects he believed vital for any student: that students loved the Lord with all their heart, personality, mind and strength.

- *Heart*—that they had experienced God's love in Christ and responded to it.
- *Personality*—that they were emotionally stable, were people of rounded personality.
- *Mind*—people who took learning seriously at whatever was their capacity.
- *Strength*—that they were not lazy but were also not workaholics, but instead would work with their particular strength.

Having outlined this, he invited the churches to "send us men and women who can do as Jesus bade us. We pledge to do OUR best to prepare them for a lifetime of service."

Again, here is a principal and a College working within the Bristol Tradition: seeking to prepare those who will be able, lively, zealous, evangelical ministers of the gospel.

As well as identifying these aspects needed for ministry, in 1992, Dr Morgan-Wynne reflected on changing patterns of ministry. He recognized that when he had entered ministry in 1960 it was a time of crisis: "Many left the ministry for other work, while many who remained were often perplexed as to their role." He went on to comment that "another crisis has crept up on us" to do with "models of ministry." He remarked that "we are being offered models largely drawn from the secular world" attractive because "they fit the temper of the age," but he believed they were "dangerous and misleading." He identified two models, the first from *entertainment* to do with establishing rapport and focused on a horizontal connection between minister and congregation, and the second, the *managerial* model, "using techniques to measure goals and performances." Morgan-Wynne argued instead that we "re-affirm the concept of the Minister as Servant," explaining that

> he/she serves God's people in ministering the words and presiding at the Supper. He/she serves God's people by loving pastoral care; he/she helps to lead God's people out in mission of proclamation and service to the world. In serving we reflect, however brokenly and imperfectly, the Lord who emptied himself and took the form of a servant. [...] I cannot think of a higher form of calling than to reflect our Lord himself.

Although he was by no means alone in making this argument (and indeed, was continuing the call of Neville Clarke for a theological reflection and underpinning of an understanding of ministry), his diagnosis of models for ministry and the power they were exerting was to be shown to be accurate in many ways over the next decades.

Worship had remained deeply important in the communal life of the College, and in shaping those who would seek to be ministers according to the kind of model that Dr Morgan-Wynne was arguing for, based on reflecting the Lord. The student House president wrote about it in the report for 1988 in this way:

> WORSHIP [sic] is at the very heart of the College life in Bristol, it is the response to everything that is leaned about God in the Bible, in history and in the world [...]. The worship which begins each day and the prayers which are offered each evening are therefore highly valued experiences, Similarly the Communion Service each Wednesday brings together round the Table students and staff, their wives and sometimes families in celebration of the life which all share through Jesus Christ.

Here is a pattern that served to sustain life and faith. It also gave a rhythm to life together even when separation through different courses, and stresses known and hidden, threatened the fabric of the community.

Difficult times

However, this was not an easy time for the College. In addition to the stress of the changing patterns at the university, in 1990, as we have seen above, there were changes of personnel which made life in College difficult. The strain of losing two colleagues at the same time, one unexpectedly, meant that while the principal spoke positively in the College Report of that year of good things, he acknowledged that there was also a great deal of stress and anxiety present. His report opened with the words,

> Of 1989–90 I am tempted to use part of a hymn "change . . . in all around I see." Who would have thought in the Summer of 1989 that so many changes would sweep across the College scene? These were not sought or engineered but they happened [. . .] but in the kaleidoscope of change we hold firm to the belief that the world of the College is God's work, not ours, and this He is working his purposes out in the midst of change.

One of the changes was the need to appoint two new members of staff. Both appointments were former students: Hazel Sherman, whose principal areas of responsibility were Christian doctrine, mission, and sharing in the teaching of New Testament Greek, and Tony Turner, to share responsibility with the principal for the pastoral training program and to teach Old Testament to the first-year students.

Tony Turner's role also involved being pastor at Hillesley, Gloucestershire, which enabled him as pastoral tutor to maintain links with the pastorate. This pattern of serving both College and a congregation is one that has appeared in various forms over the years, and it is an interesting counterbalance to the important drive to highlight the academic aspect of the College's life. The vast majority of tutors have spent some time at least in the pastorate, and as we have seen, many have combined the roles. This groundedness in a local congregation brings something important to the life of the College and to the context of teaching. As we will see in the decades still to be covered in this history, it is a pattern that has now become a norm for students as well. For all the undoubted strains of combining the role of student and pastor, there are also important gains, as we will see. When Tony Turner retired, one of the appreciations of him spoke of him having "brought all the skills and knowledge of the years of pastoral experience." From the very beginning, this link between pastoral presence and the teaching of the next generation has been central to the Bristol practice, taking different forms in different eras, but bringing with it a richness and a depth that has been invaluable.

Financial strain

But there is no disguising that these were years of strain. We have seen some of the personal strains, but there were also strains caused by circumstances. Local Education Authorities were becoming much less inclined to give grants for vocational training, and money was becoming an issue in a way it had not been for many years. The increasing number of married students meant that accommodation had to be addressed in different ways; no longer would the majority of students be able to live in the single study bedrooms around which the Woodlands Road building had been designed. Appeals were made for accommodation; and a suggestion that perhaps houses could be left to the College in people's wills. Two houses were bought in the new estate of Bradley Stoke in 1991, and the College Committee felt that more would be needed soon.

And the building itself was costly in terms of maintenance. A gale in 1990 caused a great deal of damage in the West Country and the College building did not escape. Repairs were made, but they were expensive.

In 1990, for the first time in many years, the College had a working deficit of £12,000. The question of how to deal with this, and what changes needed to be made, not least to the building, was to dominate the life of the College for many years.

One of the reasons for the drop in income was the lack of grants. Another was the undoubted drop in numbers of students. This was an experience of all the Colleges. This was partly because there were, as we have seen above, more options available for those who wished to train for ministry, even as the numbers presenting as candidates was declining. One of the other undoubted factors in this was the increasing differentiation in the types of training, and the conception of ministry that emerged at this time among Baptist Colleges. For very many years (we have seen it taking place in the College reunion in 1846), discussion has taken place about whether a denomination of the size of the Baptist Union of Great Britain needs four Colleges in England and two in Wales, especially when it is acknowledged that there are those who are candidates for its ministry who train in other institutions and in other ways. There have always been differences of identity between the Colleges, the very recognition of something called the Bristol Tradition is an aspect of this. However, with the pressure on numbers that all the Colleges were feeling, this decade is one in which the differences between them were emphasized in a particular manner, which meant that their employment as ways to increase students in one College turned out to be at the expense of others. This brought strain between the Colleges in forms that had not been seen for decades. There had always been differences in theological emphasis, and there had been times when this had caused suspicion and bad feeling between institutions. However, even in those times, a rough geographical division of the country had held: each College had an area that always felt like a 'natural' constituency. However, as means of recruitment changed, this undefined, but very real *modus vivendi* broke down, and relationships suffered.

Personal strain

Quite apart from concerns about the building, relationships with other Colleges, and struggles with numbers, it was clear that Dr Morgan-Wynne was not well, and that things were not well in College life. In 1993, after only three years as a tutor, Hazel Sherman decided to move; her duties had been extensive, not only in teaching, but also in administrative work, and her own research had suffered. Her intention (duly fulfilled) was that while remaining living in Bristol, she would both do some teaching at Birmingham University, the institution at which she was studying for her doctorate, and devote time to finishing those studies. In that year as well, Dr Morgan-Wynne had a heart attack, and later in that year it was reported that he had told the College General Committee that he was going to move to another sphere. When football managers leave clubs, sometimes it is reported that they have been sacked, and sometimes it is reported that the decision to move is by 'mutual agreement'—but just who makes the first move in these circumstances? Exactly who decided first that Dr Morgan-Wynne should move to another sphere remains one of those episodes about which various stories are told and various perceptions held. Dr Morgan-Wynne himself has said that his understanding is that he was sacked by the committee and that his heart attack was used as an excuse. It is certainly clear that there was a breakdown in relationship and in confidence between the principal and the committee, and, sadly, that this involved very painful breaks in what had been longstanding friendships. His leaving was presented in as positive a light as possible, with Dr West offering words of appreciation and honour, and then encouraging the Community and the College supporters to look ahead and to trust in God's leading. However, it remains clear that this was not a good ending, and that hurt and mistrust remained.

In his own writing *Reflections in Retrospect* (an unpublished memoir), Dr Morgan-Wynne raises some interesting questions about what was expected and indeed required of a principal. Certainly, he came to understand that one of the important aspects of the role is a denominational presence, which he did not feel he had, and although he worked to develop it while in Bristol, he was not at home in that role.

It is also apparent from his own reflections that relationships with the other members of staff, both teaching and administrative, were not always easy. It is a reminder that a College community is just that; it is above all rooted in, and reflects, relationships. That there were tensions, differences of understanding about priorities, and confusion about expectations in the whole of Dr Morgan-Wynne's period of office, and in particular in its ending, is one of the very painful episodes in our community's life. Dr Sean Winter, who was a student at the time, that the whole thing felt "very, very messy," and also that it was made harder because of pre-existing friendships. Dr Roger Hayden, then superintendent of the association, was a long-term friend of Dr Morgan-Wynne and had been instrumental in bringing him to the College as principal. He was also one of those who was deeply implicated in the ending of his tenure, and this strained their friendship, causing distress to both Dr Hayden and Dr Morgan-Wynne.

This remains a story that is not yet fully told. Not all the files of the time were available to Dr Cross as he did his research, largely for practical reasons of lockdown and inability to travel. Some of the anxieties about what was happening have not been fully explored for this history for that reason. We have here, as in other places, an area in which further research is needed, at an appropriate time.

Dr Morgan-Wynne moved from Bristol to a pastorate in Ilkley Baptist Church in Yorkshire, where he remained until his retirement. He made it a priority to continue with study, and so avoided taking on other roles. He has written a history of the church, and has published his thesis and various other books in the area of New Testament Studies. Dr Morgan-Wynne died in October 2021, while this book was in preparation.

Living with and through difficult times

Every institution has episodes and periods of life that are painful, and this is one of the College's. As well as questions about the nature of principalship to which Dr Morgan-Wynne refers, there are other questions. He was not somebody trained in Bristol. Did this matter? The previous three principals were shaped by and, perhaps more significantly, known by the Community as 'one of them'. The next principal was Bristol-trained, and although he faced the same issues, he was able to make the radical changes that had originally not been easily accepted by the committee, in particular with regard to the building and the relationship with Bristol University. Certainly Dr Morgan-Wynne thought that being an outsider was a difficulty for him.

Another question is about the nature of making mistakes. It is clear that everybody involved in the appointment believed that they had discerned together the will of God. What happens when, after such a decision is made, some come to believe it to be the wrong decision? This of course is something we can struggle with in local churches as much as in Colleges . . . people do not set out intentionally to make the wrong decision. But the fact is that we are fallible humans and make mistakes. And sometimes those mistakes can result in great pain for individuals and for institutions. And if we can stray from history into theology for a moment, it is why central to any practice we have for discerning the mind of Christ we must also insist on the immensity of God's grace to us in Jesus, and our calling therefore to seek and to offer forgiveness.

Did people get things wrong in this episode? Clearly, they did. Whose fault is it? That depends on where you are standing. Is it possible to believe that people acted in good faith and yet ended up hurting one another? We can certainly affirm this while still saying that there must have been a better way to handle what were evidently very tough issues. And so we come back again to the comment that a College is a community, and not simply an institution, a business, or an organization. The emphasis of the Bristol Tradition on community has been noted in several places: the role of what was once called the Brotherhood and is now the Community the place of the gesture fund (gifts given to members of the community, or their families, in times of difficulty, grief, or stress), the significance of news shared at the reunions, the current patterns of linking students together through social media; all of this is witness to an ongoing reality of the centrality of relationship. When relationships break down and when conversations are taking place that are not appropriately transparent or fully reported, when resentments are allowed to build up, when expectations are not well communicated, then people get hurt and the hurt can last for a long time.

It is important that we recognize that Dr Morgan-Wynne committed himself, both because he believed this was the Christian approach and for his own appropriate well-being, to a position where he "would not harbour resentment." He demonstrated this by continuing to give to the College financially. We rejoice that in 2021, he preached at the induction service of the latest appointment as tutor in biblical studies, Dr Helen Paynter. This has meant a great deal to him, and he understands it as the College saying, "we embrace you."

There is a particular pain attached to telling this part of the story because we are not simply in the realm of history, but also in the area of memory; the two writers of this book remember this part of the story because we were both involved in various ways with the College at this time. Many of those who are reading this history in its first publication will also remember, and may remember it differently from the way in which we have tried to tell it. As has been noted above, there is a particular challenge both in writing and in reading 'history' that is also 'memory'. It is clear from the whole of the story so far, that this is by no means the only difficult or painful event in the College's history, nor the only time when relationships broke down, and decisions were made that might have been different or been better made. But this is the difficult one to tell because we remember it.

In his letter in the College Report in 1993, which he wrote following Dr Morgan-Wynne's departure, Morris West quoted from Norman Moon's closing paragraph in *Education for Ministry*.

> If history teaches anything, it is that the College has changed with the times, but that its basic tasks and its underlying assumptions have remained the same. The sovereign grace of God, the centrality of Christ, crucified and risen—these do not change and will not change.

These words about both the unchanging nature of the God the College is established to serve, and the changing shape and structure of the College's life were both to be seen clearly in the next few years.

DR BRIAN HAYMES

At the end of 1993, the decision was made that Dr Brian Haymes, then principal of the Northern College in Manchester, would be the next principal of Bristol Baptist College, and he was inducted in autumn of 1994. In this appointment, the Committee and Community had decided once again to appoint one of their own, since Haymes had been a student between 1960 and 1965. After leaving College, he had served in Bristol, in Exeter, and in Nottingham before moving to Manchester to teach in the Northern College, and eventually to become its principal. On the way, he had completed a Master of Arts degree in 1973, and his doctorate in 1976, where his topic was "The Concept of the Knowledge of God." This reflected his growing conviction and fascination that "in the Bible intellectual, experiential ways of knowing God were all of a part with a strong emphasis on practice. Knowing God was something you did!"

Theology, and theological reflection as the undergirding for practice had been central to his ministry, and so to his involvement in ministerial training, and this was the emphasis that he brought to his understanding of what it meant to be principal in Bristol. Wrestling with theology, and above all wrestling with Scripture, in particular to enable preaching, has been, and remains, central to the ministerial task both in his own calling and in what he understood to be the formation process of those called to ministry. The role of the preacher in talking of and about God and enabling a congregation to encounter God through the Word was something he took with the utmost seriousness and expected students to do so too.

Colleagues

At the same service, a new tutor in biblical studies, Dr Ernest Lucas, was also inducted. A degree in chemistry, followed by a doctorate in biochemistry and then post-doctoral research took him to North Carolina in 1970. While there, he continued a previous involvement in teaching Christians to think, leading a Sunday School class in the church at which he and his wife Hazel were involved. Returning to Oxford, he sensed a call to study theology, and was accepted in 1973 at Regent's Park. Leaving there (with a top first-class degree) he became pastor in Durham City Baptist Church, and then moved in 1986 to be Old Testament tutor in Liverpool Bible College, and for some years, honorary minister at Cottenham Street, Liverpool. In 1986, he became education director at the London Institute of Contemporary Christianity, moving to be director of studies, and then associate director. While he was in Liverpool, he started his second doctorate, on the book of Daniel in its Mesopotamian context, and completed it in 1989. His teaching of Hebrew, of biblical studies, of issues in faith and science, and increasingly in ecological issues was of huge importance for many of the students both within the College and beyond. Almost as soon as he arrived in Bristol, he was invited to teach Hebrew at Bristol University, something valued by both College and university. His writings in various areas and subject matters, and at different levels of accessibility from A-level students through to technical work for experienced scholars, meant that his contributions went far beyond the teaching of students in College.

Tony Turner was still a member of the academic staff when Haymes and Lucas began, and the three formed an effective team, helping the Community to recover its nerve after the distresses of the previous year. In 1995, Tony Turner finished his time as tutor, and Ruth Gouldbourne was appointed to the post of tutor in history and doctrine. Having completed a Bachelor of Divinity at King's College in London, after a previous degree in English, she had entered Baptist ministry through the Residential Selection

Conference route, rather than the more normal College route, although there had been some formation as part of a cohort at Spurgeon's College to complete a diploma in pastoral studies, and then almost eighteen months placement at Bloomsbury Central Baptist church in London. From there she had moved to be assistant minister at Bunyan Meeting in Bedford, working part-time while she began a doctorate in Reformation history, which she eventually completed during her time as a tutor. She came being the same age as, or younger, than the majority of the students when she started, and with limited pastoral experience, and she was to be very grateful for the patient support of colleagues (in particular Ernest Lucas's willingness to let her in the first morning, when she could not work out how to open the door!) and for the significant support of former tutors, especially Tony Turner and Morris West.

Tony Turner was not the only person who bridged the gap between the principals. There were also several students who came into the College under Dr Morgan-Wynne's leadership, and who then had an interim year under the care of Dr West, and were still present when Brian Haymes became principal. When things go wrong there are always those who suffer consequentially—and the students of the transition were among those who bore the most significant cost of this difficult period. They lost out on so much. Their continuation as students, rather than leaving or moving to another College is noted here with gratitude, and with an acknowledgement of the cost that they paid for others' choices and decisions.

Making new connections work

There were substantial changes happening; not simply new members of staff, but a new partnership and therefore degree course, as the relationship with the Anglican Trinity College was made formal in the session of 1994 to 1995. Between the two Colleges there was now an arrangement to teach a degree course jointly, validated by Bristol University, in theology and biblical studies. As the larger partner, Trinity College brought more into the relationship in the way of resources and numbers, both of staff and students, but there was still an insistence that this was to be a partnership of equals—and in large measure, that was what it proved to be. For a couple of years there was a transition period, as students who had started under one pattern of training completed that course, while others began the new one as the pioneers of a degree that was being developed. For those students who were the first to be part of this cohort, there were moments of learning that were not on the curriculum: finding Trinity College, for as the larger institution, it was the place where larger classes were held; negotiating Anglican assumptions (the necessity of reminding one tutor who started a lecture "as we all say in the creed each week . . ." that this was not necessarily to be taken for granted); calculating the time needed to get from one building to another (those writing timetables needed to learn this too!); and developing the ability to speak up in class when the ratio of Baptist to Anglicans might be 2 to 30 (this was felt to be an appropriate ratio, given that Baptist students on the whole did not find it hard to speak up!). There were inevitable blips and collisions, but with good will and good humour, these were worked through.

In 1995, the College Newsletter (the new format of the previous Report) reported that as a result of "increasingly close links with Trinity College, students were no able to choose from over 100 modular courses, and draw on the wisdom and experience of a staff of over thirty." It also led to an increasingly complex timetable, with different requirements needing to be balanced, and appropriate denominational studies fitted in as well; as dean of studies, Ernest Lucas added the drawing up of the timetable to his duties, much to the relief of his colleagues.

The appropriate denominational formation was fitted in, and Wednesdays became the days when students were based in the Baptist College for explicitly denominational aspects. Sermon class which involved the whole student body took place on a Wednesday, as did sessions on ministerial practice, spirituality, and in some years, Baptist history and identity—however, as a course for academic credit, this module was normally taught at other times in the week. Wednesday was also the day when College Communion took place in the evening, and staff and students attended, and families of both were also present. These were important times of fellowship and worship, and were well served with preachers from within the College staff, and significantly, visitors from among local ministers, or visitors from further afield.

In 1995 the Bristol Federation for Ministerial Training was agreed; this was not simply the partnership of the Baptist College and Trinity College. It also included Wesley Methodist College and in due time, the West of England Ministerial Training Course, which was a training course taking place in evenings and weekends specifically designed for those, largely Anglican and Methodist, who were continuing in paid employment while undertaking training for some form of ministerial work. The Federation was a significant resource in theological education, but it was much more than this. There was joint worship at least once a term, where students and staff had the opportunity to share in the worshipping life of another tradition. There were joint Quiet Days each term, providing opportunity for extended reflection and prayer, and offering a wide range of means of doing this, which was valuable both in itself, and as a way of broadening the experience and expectation of students about what might be available in terms of forms of spirituality. The possibilities of discovering each other's traditions in their integrity was a vital part of the ecumenical intention of the Federation.

Weekend and evening teaching as well as daytime teaching became the pattern for the next years, something that was to put a strain on both students and staff. When he retired after eighteen years, Ernest Lucas began his farewell letter by remembering this: the average term-time day was 8 a.m. until 6 p.m.; on Wednesdays, dinner and chapel stretched this to 8 p.m.; there were periods of evening teaching and of Saturday teaching; there were Sundays visiting churches to observe students, to lead and to preach. He did not say this to boast or to gain sympathy, but simply as an indication of the kind of load both staff and students had to sustain. His comment was that it had been a very satisfying job. His memory was that five students started the new course in 1994, but by the time he finished there were thirty-six across the degree course, alongside the over fifty enrolled in the Youth Ministry course and somewhere in the region of forty attending the Prepare for Service course that ran on Saturdays.

Dr Lucas's comment indicates the breadth of forms of teaching at this time. Of course, there has always been a whole variety of ways in which the College has served the constituency. For very little of its life has it been solely and exclusively concerned with training people for only one form of pastoral ministry since, equally, of course, there has been no time in our churches when ministry has taken only one form. The development of Prepare for Service as a Saturday course was the latest in an ongoing pattern of resourcing that was offered to those taking on various roles in church life: perhaps lay preaching, teaching children or new converts, leading in various ways, or those who are simply interested in learning more about the faith. We have seen, for example how, during the Second World War, classes were offered to chaplains and lay preachers, and again under Dr West's principalship, there was an emphasis on working with congregations as well as with ministerial students.

For some years, the Baptist Union had a series of distance learning modules grouped under the title "Christian Training Programme," which allowed people to develop knowledge and deepen skills that would be helpful in their life and service. When this came to an end, the Colleges agreed together that the variety of courses which each catered for those who did not come to College full time could be coordinated and the levels of engagement and of marking could be standardized across the Colleges, so that the 'national' offering of lay training could be maintained. It is probably true to say that this had mixed success, but it worked well enough to be of service to the churches, and in Bristol, it took the form of Prepare for Service. The various courses ran on a rolling program on Saturdays, and it was possible to complete a Certificate in Theology over three years in this way. It was also made possible, partly because some of the degree courses were taught in the evenings and because employers were often supportive in the area of personal development and allowed some time away from work, to progress to a full degree through this part-time mode, as several people have done. It has been one of the strengths of all the Colleges that the riches available in learning, in library resources and in community reflection have not been limited to those who are there full time, but have been offered in a variety of creative ways to all who are interested. This engagement has also helped to develop and maintain a sense that the Colleges are not separate entities somewhere in a rarefied seclusion but are part of the whole community of churches. Quite apart from the importance of developing and sustaining relationships of prayer and friendship, this also helps with financial support. When a College is 'our College' because all sorts of people have engaged with it in a variety of ways, then people are more inclined to offer practical as well as vocal support.

Wider involvement

Another way in which such support is and has been given is through the voluntary work that people have offered in a variety of ways. Service on College committees is perhaps the most obvious, as people bring various skills and offer time and interest to helping the College to live well and fulfil its purposes. But there have also been those who have volunteered in the library, in the office, as receptionists in the building, and as archivists. All of this weaving together of the life of the College with the lives of the local congregations has been a strand that has run through the life of the institution from the very beginning within the life of a local congregation until the present. It has taken various forms, but without it, the College would not have survived—and indeed, would have had no purpose. The tracing of those involved in this way in the life of the College, and the noting of their stories and contributions is another area in which further research is required. There are currently anecdotal memories of those who have served and enriched the life of the community in this way, and there are passing comments in the published Reports and Newsletters. But the role of local church members in serving on committees, offering their expertise in support of the College's life, and ensuring that the College as a community did not become isolated from congregations is deep and rich, and as yet untold.

Another significant strand of such a linking of lives has been the invitations that local congregations have offered to students to preach. It has been a form of service which has offered the churches a particular ministry, especially those congregation which have not had a full-time pastor. Inviting students (and on occasions tutors) to fill the pulpit has eased the load on lay preachers and enabled many a preaching secretary to know that at least some Sundays were covered some months in advance. It has also been a gift to students, since such invitations have provided the context in which a preaching gift can be tested and also developed—the opportunity to preach in front of congregations made up of people, some of whom might not be known, offers a particular opportunity to explore what it means to preach, and the different aspects of that.

For many years, the local congregations have also offered the possibilities of deeper involvement, in the form of placements: times when students were welcomed to work alongside a minister in pastoral charge and explore different aspects of the task—sharing in meetings, in planning, in dealing with administration, in pastoral care, and in the whole ongoing life of a fellowship. This was of course present in various forms in the earliest days, when the students lived alongside the minister of Broadmead Baptist Church and were involved in the life of that fellowship (and others) as well as serving congregations for extended periods, for example, in the summer months. There was a period when it appears less in the description of life as a student, though preaching has always featured. In the middle of the twentieth century there was a very intentional organizing of long-term placements, called Pastorate Teams, involving senior and junior students serving a church over two years This pattern too came to an end and other models emerged. But the organizing of placements continued to be a feature of students' time in College and was often supplemented by time spent in hospitals, rehabilitation centres, or prisons, sometimes during term time, but often as part of a vacation task.

Developing models of training

Another pattern, in some ways an extension of the placement scheme, was the model of student pastorates. This was when a student divided their time between serving a congregation in a pastoral role and coming to the College for teaching sessions and fulfilling assignments. Again, this model had existed alongside the more assumed model of full-time residential studying for many years, and there were several churches that offered such hospitality and support. Taking such a route was often as much a practical as a theory-driven decision: serving a church in such a way could provide accommodation, which was important if the student had a spouse and children, and therefore would have found life as a full-time residential participant inappropriate. But it is also a model that offers particular strengths. For those whose learning style, for example, is best served by practical experience and then reflection upon it, this is a very good pattern of training. Of course, it has its drawbacks, not least the constant need to balance time and demands. The times when students following a more conventional model might have opportunities for extra reading, reflection, or even diverse experiences, for example during vacations, are just the times when life in a congregation can be especially busy, namely Easter and Christmas. And the needs, especially pastoral needs, of a congregation rarely time themselves to fit in with essay deadlines and tutorial preparation. There is also, especially when the majority of students were engaged in the more College-centred studies, a definite lack of time for reflection and informal interaction which has always been such an important part of the College experience. When the timetabling caters for the majority of students being full-time in College those who were in-pastorate students had to fit in as best they could, and it was not always easy. The sense of being perpetually rushed, and perpetually on the way to somewhere else did mean that for students who trained through the student pastorate model, there was a sense of incompleteness and missing out on certain things. While there might be time for coffee between classes, there was little time for conversations over the snooker table, or late-night discussions in the common room.

For several reasons, partly to do with changing models of education, but also significantly shaped by the changing demographic of students as well as the financial realities of undertaking a vocational course in mid-life rather than straight from school, as the 1990s progressed, as we have seen, more and more students chose the church-based model. By the end of the 1990s, this was the dominant form of training. This was not only true in Bristol; it had been pioneered in Northern Baptist College in the 1980s as a main way of training and Brian Haymes had been involved in that in his time there. It was also becoming much more the norm in the other Baptist Colleges. In Bristol, the development of the new degree course with Trinity College made it much more accessible. The pattern of modules taught in blocks rather than a course taught through a whole three terms allowed the flexibility that was needed for students to come into the College on two or three days a week rather than every day. In addition, with the majority of students in this kind of training, it became much easier to build in the times that students needed for reflection on the activities in the church; since most people were in the same position of trying to balance competing demands, and were dealing with similar real-life situations in congregations, the mutual learning as students reflected together and shared insights, frustrations, and delights became a real strength. The time challenges remained very real, and this is by no means a light option for training.

As well as time pressures, there were other questions to address. The loss of 'informal community time'—the conversations late at night, or over the snooker table—diminished one of the formative aspects that is not easily quantified but is very real. The loss of daily prayers together meant that the times of worship that were still part of the week had to bear an even greater weight as part of the development of a sustainable spirituality.

In response to a shared timetable with another College and as one way of addressing some of the issues raised above, a pattern developed in which all students were in College on a Wednesday for 'Baptist time'—sessions on spirituality, on preaching, on the practice of ministry, time in small groups for reflection, conversation and support, time in worship in the morning, and College Communion in the evening. Church-based students would then also be in the College on one other day, either Tuesday or Thursday (making them consecutive days allowed those who were based at a considerable distance to stay over, often in accommodation in Trinity College rooms, or in a room in one of the student houses) and that day would be very full of academic classes—all day and evening, starting with prayers at 8.30 a.m. and ending the last teaching session at 9.30 p.m. To complete a full degree in this model took four years, while those who did the course would complete their studies in three years, for they would also have teaching on a Monday and/or Friday.

The task of managing the timetabling of all this complexity fell to Ernest Lucas, and in the one year when because of illness he was unable to do it, those who did it in his stead were even more reminded of the skill and grace which he brought to his tasks!

Expanding the tutorial staff

The care of students and churches whom they served rapidly became a task in itself, and it was one that was part of the job description for Tony Peck when he arrived as a tutor in 1998. He had originally trained as a musician at the London Guildhall and then trained for ministry at Regent's Park College. He served as minister in the Central Bradford Fellowship and then was Association secretary for the Yorkshire Baptist Association for seven years. He arrived in the College, having served on various denominational reviews and been part of the Baptist Training Partnership, to serve as tutor in ministry and mission studies, and church partnerships.

His work involved what in other contexts might have been called 'extra-mural studies' as well as the care and support of students and churches in church-based training. He developed the outline agreement which structured the expectations and requirements of the church, the student and the College in the partnership involved in church-based training, and also worked with churches and students to enable good fits between the two and support them through the training period. He took the lead in the redevelopment along with the other Colleges of Prepare for Service and also helped to develop the pattern of courses offered at a distance from the College for groups of churches and ministers. He taught on mission and ecumenism modules for students across the Federation and as we will read below, was instrumental in the development of the Thomas Helwys Institute.

Tony Peck had always had an interest in relationships with Baptists in Europe, and in his time as Yorkshire Association secretary, he had been part of a growing partnership between Yorkshire churches and churches in Latvia. When he came to the College he brought these connections, and a partnership with the seminary in Riga was developed, which involved staff visiting and teaching (both Ruth Gouldbourne and Ernest Lucas visited and taught at various times), and some student contact, most notably when Enoks Neilands came to study advanced Hebrew with Ernest Lucas as part of his involvement in translating the Old Testament into Latvian. Peck also served on the Baptist World Alliance Christian Ethics Commission, succeeding Brian Haymes, as one of the British representatives, and in that role, he attended the Congress in Melbourne and the Council in Havana. In the home context, he convened the National Steering Group for the Baptist Union and also spoke at various ministers' conferences over the years. In 2004, during the principalship of Chris Ellis, he was appointed General Secretary of the European Baptist Federation and was farewelled from the College with the recognition that he was being called to serve in a larger sphere.

The links established by Peck were not the only ones with Europe. Another significant link has been with what is now the International Baptist Theological Study Centre in Amsterdam. When he arrived as principal, Brian Haymes was already involved in the Board of Trustees of what was then the International Baptist Theological Seminary, which had for many years been located in Ruschlikon, Switzerland, and had been relocated to Prague in the mid-1990s. This was a challenging time for this institution, and on coming home from one particularly difficult board meeting, Haymes had remarked to his colleagues that they should stay uninvolved. However, despite such warning, Ruth Gouldbourne accepted appointment to the Board of Trustees and served on it for several years, including some years as chair. This was never easy work, but was a valuable insight into the breadth of Baptist life in Europe, and was another of the ways in which the links for the College with the international Baptist world were kept open.

DR CHRIS ELLIS

In 2000, Brian Haymes moved from Bristol to become the minister of Bloomsbury Central Baptist Church in London, and Revd Chris Ellis came to be the principal of the College. He had spent time in the College during his sabbatical in 1987 and spoke of being struck by the warmth and acceptance that he experienced. He learned something of the Bristol Tradition, which he came to value, and which he readily embraced when he returned in this new role. He came from many years in the pastorate, most immediately in Cemetery Road, Sheffield, and had also been involved in different ways with the Baptist Union and the Baptist World Alliance, as well as having a rich ecumenical experience, since he had served in an ecumenical congregation in Swindon, where he was also a part-time city centre chaplain.

He had published on ecumenism in the 1990s, and been part of the Churches Together in England Working Party on Baptism and Church Membership during much of the 1990s. He also served from 1982 to 2005 as part of the Baptist participation in the Baptist-Church of England conversations.

His writing was not only academic, but included hymn-writing, and he had hymns published in Baptist Praise and Worship and elsewhere. While he was at Cemetery Road, he had begun a doctorate in liturgical theology, which he finished in 2002, after starting at the College. The popular version of his thesis was eventually published as *Gathering*. In 2005, together with Myra Blyth, he published *Gathering for Worship*, a resource and liturgical book for the Baptist Union. In 2009, *Approaching God: A Handbook for Worship Leaders*, which was based on his lectures, was published.

So, it was as an ecumenist, a liturgist, a practical theologian and as an experienced pastor that he undertook the principalship. He came to what was in some ways a quite different College from the one he had met in 1987. It was now in a new building, and was a bigger and more diverse community, since the CYM students were now a full part of the College community. In the current structure, ministerial students were in the building some days, CYM students in on other days, and on some—very full—days, everybody was in.

Building an effective community

For Ellis, his vision of how this would become a meaningful community was based on the community knowing itself in the following ways:

- As a community of learning in which we offer God the searching and diligence of our minds.
- As a community of discipleship in which we offer God the devotion of our hearts and the obedience of our actions.
- As a community of service in which we offer back to God the gifts of ministry with which he has entrusted us.

Alongside this, he put the three inter-related areas of formation that were at the heart of the College's intention.

- Knowing: learning and academic study to resource people who were called by God to "feed my sheep."
- Serving: skills that are to be learned and developed, including preaching, counselling, leadership in mission, and administration.
- Being: growing in discipleship, following Christ and growing into spiritual maturity.

Ellis was keen to emphasize that these areas were not topics to be delivered by tutors to students, but areas in which the whole community, students and tutors alike, were continually developing and growing.

Learning to live together in new ways

Because the overwhelming majority of students were now church-based rather than College-based, and there was no longer a residential space in the College building (though there were shared houses in which single students lived in community), there was a particular determination to find creative ways of sustaining mutual support and encouragement. Areas of practice and life that had been taken for granted as part of life in College—sharing meals, being together in the common room at coffee time, attending College Communion—were now treated not as more important (they had always been important), but as that to which attention would have to be paid, since it would be all too easy for such contacts and the space they allowed to wither. Inevitably, the community aspect of life was to be different in this new world, but students and staff alike were delighted and surprised at the level of community life that was possible with due care and attention, even with these new circumstances.

Central to this life was the commitment of the students to one another, and their support and care for each other. Reflection groups, which were part of the Wednesday program, allowed time for students to bring to a peer group questions, struggles, and joys that they were experiencing in the churches that they served, and to offer wisdom, care, experience and above all the commitment to pray for one another. This sharing of 'real time' reflection on ministry was not always easy; there were struggles to find focus and to make time and the level of mutual trust needed for in-depth sharing of issues was not something that was achieved in one term. But most of the students were committed to the process, and these reflection groups could become spaces of significant care and mutual support.

This connection with the life of a variety of local congregations has allowed the congregation to retain and to develop in new ways its rootedness in the gathered fellowships which are the heart of Baptist life. Another way in which this was expressed was through the contribution of local ministers to the teaching community of the College. For some, this involved offering one or two specialized sessions: for example, Revd John Houseago, who had graduated from the College in 1979 and had come back to Bristol to be minister of Broadmead Baptist Church, offered sessions in administration and organizational skills.

Renewing governance

During Ellis's time, there was also yet another of the changes in governance that need to happen at various points for the College as a legal body to exist as appropriately as possible. These governance questions can seem dry and uninspiring, but the legal make-up of the College, how it stands in law, and how it is to be cared for, overseen, and supported is deeply important. We have already seen, for example, how the move from being part of a local church's life into the Bristol Education Society enabled the clarifying of the Bristol Tradition that has shaped the continuing life of the community. The relationships with Bristol University, based in legal documents and bringing different people into the committees that, for example, appointed staff, was a broadening of a base that the first founders could not have imagined. In 2001, because of changes in charity law, and in good practice for the management of charities, the decision was taken to formally incorporate the College as a Private Limited Company, which would allow it to become a charitable company limited by guarantee.

The most visible change as a result of this move was to change the composition of the AGM and the process by which trustees were appointed. The result of the change was that membership of the College was now by invitation, and all local Baptist churches in the various Associations to which the College most immediately related were invited to become members. Members were empowered to send representatives to the AGM, and members also appointed the trustees who formed the governing body. This took the place of the old Council. One result of this was that decisions now lay with a smaller group of people, since the previous Council had been somewhere just over fifty members. This allowed for the clearing up of various legal anomalies created because charity law was not designed to deal with the particularities of theological training institutions. But it was also hoped that such a trustee body would be representative, and, because it was smaller, those who served on it would feel more involved. Changes to charity law and guidance led to a further revision of the governance structure, and new Memorandum and Articles were agreed by the members in 2015.

Finances

Alongside governance, the other recurring, and not apparently inspiring, strand of the story is always that of money. As we have seen all the way through, there has rarely been a time when there has been no anxiety about finances, and there have over the years been various creative attempts both to realize assets to fund ongoing life, and to raise money. Consistently, the College has depended on such fees as could be paid by students, or on their behalf by churches (and for short periods, through statutory grants) and on direct giving from churches. By 2006, for various reasons such as drops in giving from churches, struggles to finance students, challenges of investments, the College Council found it necessary to agree to a running deficit of £40,000 a year simply to maintain staffing levels. This had been met through investment income, but there was also the threat that if this dropped (as indeed it did), capital would need to be used.

One way of tackling this was the beginning of the Friends' Scheme. This model is one used by many organizations and institutions, and it initiation was an attempt to build a particular group of loyal supporters who would pray and give financially, and who would be sent news of students, events, and opportunities, including opportunities to study. The College was developing an understanding a vision of "the people of God equipped for service." In line with renewal of the emphasis throughout the churches on the place of all in the call of God, there was a broadening in the understanding of what ministry might look like.

New Patterns of ministry

One of the results of the charismatic renewal that affected Baptists along with others in the latter part of the twentieth century was a change in the pattern the one-person ministry, where one, set-apart individual did everything. Instead, there was a recognition that worship leading could be, and should be multi-voiced. Indeed, in line with a Baptist conviction that the church is a gathered community rather than one centred on a priestly activity, it can be argued that this is a return to our earliest practice. Thus, people throughout congregations became involved in leading the musical aspects of worship, in leading prayers, in sharing in preaching, as well as giving testimony, or telling stories of life, so that services had several or many voices. There was also the growth in patterns of "whole-body ministry," which again meant that rather than one person doing it all, people had responsibility for particular aspects of the life of a congregation such as the youth work, evangelism and outreach, community care, and pastoral work.

Alongside this, albeit slowly, came the recognition that such multiplicity of ministries could work best when people were well resourced and grounded theologically as well as in skills. So, all of the Colleges including Bristol began to be more conscious not simply of offering lay training—which had long been part of the life of the College—but of training for distinct kinds of ministry.

Centre for Youth Ministry

In Bristol, this was most clearly visible in the presence of the Centre for Youth Ministry, which we have mentioned several times. This training, at the stage when it first became part of the Bristol College, was validated by Oxford Brookes University and was a multi-site course, that is, students were enrolled in one of the centres, and each centre delivered the same degree course in youth work with theology. Rather in the way that the ministerial courses had developed, this was a placement-based course where students were in College two days a fortnight, and the rest of the time involved in work in a variety of placements.

The arrival of CYM as part of the College community brought a new dynamic. There was not as much integration across the courses as had been hoped—though there were opportunities for tutors to teach both ministerial and CYM students, and all students who were in College on a Wednesday were invited to share in attending and leading College Communion, as well as being together at meals, and in the common room. As a separate educational establishment, sharing resources and space, Bristol CYM also had its own staff, and to start with, the work was headed by Iain Hoskins, previously head of Youth Work for the Baptist Union. There was also a separate administrative office and staff. However, there were attempts to overcome the separation: Iain Hoskins attended the meetings of the tutorial staff, for example, and the administrative and tutorial staff were all treated as one community, and staff and students from each strand were invited to each other's valediction and graduation services.

Other forms of differentiation also emerged, as the denomination developed recognition of those who were youth workers, evangelists, pioneers, and chaplains as well as pastoral ministers. For each of these, the process of discerning a call, developing a course which matched specific needs and also offering appropriate contexts for reflection, personal growth in discipleship and spirituality, together with grounding in Baptist identity and a broadening of awareness of the wider Christian story and context needed to be offered and supported.

Postgraduate studies

In addition to undergraduate and vocational training, there continued to be a steady stream of postgraduate students, supervised by staff both at the Baptist College and at Trinity College. Thus, for example, Simon Perry, while minister of Fiveways in Somerset, undertook his doctorate under the supervision of Robert Forrest, one of the tutors at Trinity, while Ernest Lucas in particular had a constant procession of biblical studies research students, both Anglican and Baptist.

There were also those who, having trained in Bristol went on to offer academic teaching at other institutions—for example, Revd Dr Simon Woodman, who, on completing his time in the College became assistant minister at Counterslip Baptist Church in Bristol and then moved to be biblical studies tutor in the South Wales College in Cardiff for eleven years, before becoming co-minister at Bloomsbury Central Baptist Church. Some came back to teach within Bristol: Revd Kerry Birch, for example, who taught Baptist history for several years, and later was appointed part-time community tutor, in which he worked to support students who were at a significant distance from the College, visiting them in their churches and offering pastoral and mentoring support, as part of the team that worked with Ken Stewart.

Keeping the Tradition?

As we have asked before, it is appropriate to ask was this a change in purpose for the College? Yes, at one level it was—it was a deepening and broadening of purpose, as the resources that had once been on offer to those who were training for local pastoral ministry were now offered to those who would be serving the churches in a wide variety of contexts, not all of which might be identified with pastoral oversight of a local congregation.

But in another way, of course, it can be seen as an appropriate growth in line with the trajectory of the College's intentions. Rooted in a local church and begun in order to serve the ministry of local churches, the same thing, it can be argued, is still being offered in a context of both church and the life of faith that has altered radically in the last three hundred years.

These are changes on a large scale—there have also always been changes on the personal and immediate scale. In 2004, as we have noted, Tony Peck left his tutor's post to become General Secretary of the European Baptist Federation. He was succeeded by Revd Ken Stewart, who had been minister at Horfield Baptist Church in Bristol, and involved in teaching in the College in various ways over the years. He took over and developed the role that Peck had pioneered of supporting students and churches in the arranging of and sustaining of placements as part of the training project.

This work was growing ever more significant as easily 85 percent of the students at any one time were now church based. Stewart visited churches interested in a student minister, visited candidates interested in developing a training post in the church in which they were already in membership, visited students in place to understand their contexts and to reflect with them *in situ* about the work, as well as helping churches to set up support groups, and helping them to work out what their role should be. As students could be based anywhere up to two hundred miles from Bristol, he worked alongside local ministers who were involved in the support of students in an area, developing a network of local Tutors. He also undertook teaching in the joint College curriculum and was involved with CYM in several ways.

Further staff changes

In 2004 the College also said goodbye to Pearl Woolnough, who had been involved in numerous ways in the administration of the College's life for twenty-seven years. As we have noted above, issues of finance, governance, and administration can seem workaday and somehow of less significance than some of the other more 'heroic' forms of service, but as anybody who has had to cope with life in contact with somebody whose administrative skills are not high, good administration, secure finances, and well managed and transparent governance are all important; when things are going well, they are not noticed, and that is as it should be. They are there to make life go well, and in saying farewell to Pearl Woolnough, the College recognized that she had sustained the life of the College in many and various—often hidden—ways.

She was succeeded by Phil Hindle, who had been an area BMS coordinator and team manager for eight years. Starting officially in 2005, he was responsible for overseeing the non-academic aspects of the life of the College, including students, staff, buildings, technology (an ever-growing area) and finance. He was employed four days a week to do this, and certainly was not short of tasks to fill his time.

In 2006, Dr Ellis announced that he was seeking settlement as a local pastor, and in the same year Ruth Gouldbourne was called to succeed Brian Haymes as pastor at Bloomsbury Central Baptist Church in London. Ellis was called to West Bridgford in Nottingham.

REVD DR STEPHEN FINAMORE

As has already been noted above, it is too soon to make an assessment of this present time, and this section cannot be a comprehensive analytical account to match those on former principals. However, without some coverage the story would be less than adequate. Stephen Finamore's time in office already significantly outstrips that of his immediate predecessors and this brings a sense of stability which has made continued development possible.

Personal background and vision for the College

Following the return to pastoral ministry of Chris Ellis in 2006, the College Council appointed Stephen Finamore as principal. He brought a range of experience and gifts, a variety which in some ways echoed the different paths by which so many of today's students arrive in College. Some come from established Baptist families, others, like Stephen, do not. Many, like him, have had a number of jobs and varied life-experience which has prepared them for the demands of education and ministry.

After studying law at the London School of Economics and the College of Law, Stephen qualified as a solicitor. Soon, however, instead of pursuing a career in the law he was involved in a community development project in London. By this time there was a strong connection with Northcote Road Baptist Church in south Battersea, where compared with his experience of other churches he recalls a strong feeling that this was like 'coming home'. Here he also met his future wife, Becca, and after marriage explored a call to work overseas. In 1986 they moved to Peru to support a project in the Andes through Tearfund (the start of Stephen's long connection with the charity, latterly as a trustee). During these formative years he sensed a call to pastoral ministry which was tested in the ministerial recognition and interview process during a period back in the UK.

Having been accepted for training, he chose Regent's Park College because of the stimulating academic opportunities offered by study in Oxford. His own scholastic gifts were confirmed by the opportunity to remain in Oxford after training to complete a doctorate (awarded in 1997), during which he also served for a time in the Mission Department of the Baptist Union. He then entered the settlement process, and in 1996 was called to the pastorate of Westbury-on-Trym Baptist church in Bristol. He ministered there for ten years before discerning the possibility that it might be right to apply for the principalship of the College where he had already done some teaching.

Reflecting on his training and formation at Regent's, at interview Stephen proposed three themes in his vision for Bristol's future—discipleship, mission, and spirituality. These have been worked out in the years which followed, alongside other significant changes in the life of the College.

With varied experience, but little immediate knowledge of the College's life, Stephen remembers with gratitude the support offered by other colleagues as he settled into the role—the business manager Phil Hindle, vice-principal Ernest Lucas, and other tutors, along with treasurer Edward Duffield. Such help was very necessary, since in addition to fulfilling College responsibilities the position also leads to other commitments.

Wider involvement

All principals have been deeply engaged with the wider Baptist world and with organizations beyond it. Something of this has already been seen above, in the long-term involvement with Tearfund, and time spent at Didcot while studying at Regent's Park College. A trustee of the Baptist Union, Finamore has also served on the steering group of the Futures Project. As a member of the Baptist Union Council in virtue of his office, and as a trustee, he additionally is part of the Baptist Union of Great Britain Core Leadership Team. As principal he is a trustee of the Regional Association, and more locally has been involved in ecumenical activities when minister at Westbury-on-Trym.

Needless to say, along with the College workload this reduces the opportunities for academic writing, but he pens articles and papers and is also a regular contributor to *festschriften* for friends and former colleagues.

Staff changes

Tutors

With the departures noted in the previous section, there was an immediate need for a new member of staff. The Revd Sian Murray Williams was appointed as tutor in 2006, bringing a deep knowledge of BMS World Mission as well as of the British Baptist scene. Serving first as tutor in worship and as College chaplain, on the retirement of Ken Stewart in 2014 she took over the role of coordinator of ministerial formation. Lis Pearce, who had trained at Bristol, became chaplain, leaving in 2020. When Ernest Lucas retired in 2012, the need for an Old Testament specialist was filled by the Revd Dr Peter Hatton, a Methodist minister who combined academic skills with long experience of pastoral ministry. Previously serving at Wesley College, its closure released him for this new role. Peter retired in 2020 having made a stimulating contribution to many areas of the College's life. His place was taken by the Revd Dr Helen Paynter, who had trained in Bristol, later teaching biblical languages at the College, and who had served as a part-time tutor since 2015. In addition to her teaching and tutorial commitments, Helen is founder and director of the Centre for the Study of the Bible and Violence.

The Revd Dr Tim Welch joined the team in 2016 as coordinator of the ministerial programme and tutor in practical theology. He has formed close links with local associations and churches, especially those where ministers are in training or on placement.

Not all appointments have worked out as hoped. Dr Anthony Reddie became tutor in theology and coordinator of community learning in 2014 but left after one year because of a need to fulfil commitments in Birmingham which proved impossible to combine with duties in Bristol. His contribution to College life, though short, was much valued. His role in community formation was taken over by Helen Paynter, and later by the Revd Lindsay Caplen.

Administrative staff

The administration of the College was becoming more complex due to the growing regulatory demands upon higher education establishments, and when Phil Hindle stepped down as business manager a review concluded that a full-time College manager was needed to oversee this whole area. Fran Brealey, previously in an associated role at Trinity College, was appointed in 2008. Supported by an able team, her role and responsibilities have expanded over the years to ensure that the College's governance, policies and processes comply with all legal and regulatory requirements and are adequate for the fulfilment of its mission. Successive inspections by the churches' Quality in Formation Panel, and more recently the Baptist peer review process, the Higher Education Funding Council for England, the Quality Assurance Agency, and the Office for Students have proved this work to be wholly effective. (This list shows something of the demands of the modern culture of standards and compliance.) She has also undertaken tutorial responsibility for groups of students and been a regular preacher in the College chapel.

The finances of the College are critically important. Here the contribution of Edward Duffield (retired 2012) and Malcom Broad as treasurers has been very significant. In recent years a finance officer, working closely with the treasurer, has been responsible for the day-to-day financial administration—firstly Peter Young and now Paul Holland. Careful management of investments (which include the proceeds of the sale of the Tyndale New Testament) has been necessary, since income from other sources has in recent years been insufficient to produce a balanced budget. The cost of meeting regulatory requirements is itself considerable and falls particularly heavily on small institutions. The generosity of former students is a constant reminder of the value of the work and reinforces the commitment needed to carry it forward.

The governance structure of the College remains as detailed above, but the Revd Michael Docker, the long-serving chair of the College Council, stepped down at the end of 2018 and the current chair is the Revd Ruth Bottoms.

Students

Teaching and learning takes place in a number of contexts and at various levels. It is not confined to the purpose of ministerial training, but rather aims to equip men and women in all sorts of roles as effective disciples, able to make their own unique contribution to church and society.

The extra-mural "Prepare, Feed, and Sustain" Saturday morning course (recently re-named "Equipping Missional Disciples") is designed for people wanting to serve more effectively in their churches, and to stimulate their own faith. Feedback has been very encouraging, showing that students and churches benefit considerably. Several students have progressed from PFS to undergraduate and postgraduate study, and to ministerial formation.

"Disciple Makers" is a more recent initiative, aimed at supporting those wishing to develop their gifts to become effective disciples of Christ who are in turn able to encourage others in faithful lifelong discipleship. It is currently led by the Revd Maki Miço and his wife Ruth; Maki is a graduate of the College and minister of Cairns Road Baptist Church, Bristol.

The growth in independent theology students has been a marked feature of recent years as people seek to explore and understand their faith better. Sometimes it leads to a call to ministry, or to further study. Many are part-time, as are the wider community of doctoral students who are often at a distance. Despite the different patterns of attendance, students from the various groups repeatedly testify to the significance of the conversations which take place in the College, as well as the value of more formal opportunities to meet together.

Ministerial students continue to be mainly based in churches as ministers in training and gather in College on Wednesdays for the ministerial programme. The forming of able, zealous, lively, and evangelical ministers—as our eighteenth-century forebears described it—continues to guide the College's work with this group, alongside the specific requirements for ministry set out by the Baptist Union of Great Britain. Attention to the varied contexts within which ministry is expressed has become an important feature of the ministerial programme.

In order to serve the south-west region more effectively, a hub has been established in Exeter in partnership with the South-West Baptist Association for ministerial students unable to travel easily to Bristol. This new venture is being spearheaded by the Revd Eleanor Moffatt. The use of technology to support online learning which has been so necessary under COVID-19 restrictions has here again proved its worth by allowing Exeter students to join remotely in Wednesday activities taking place in the College.

These mixed cohorts, now predominantly part-time, produce a stimulating and diverse student body, which still gathers under the traditional name of 'The House' to regulate the life of the community. The annual Community Day continues to welcome former students to Bristol and reinforces the sense of belonging within a long history finding new expression in each generation.

The shared life of the whole community is informed by the three themes that inspire Stephen's vision for the College.

1. Discipleship

This aspect is now woven through all student activities, and is represented, for example, in the current content of the ministerial programme, in the shared life of prayer and worship, and in the Disciple Makers initiative.

2. Mission at home and overseas

The second theme is the emphasis upon mission, and the work of God beyond the church walls, reflecting the contemporary importance of the concept of the *missio Dei*. A module, initially called "Integral Mission," introduces students to a variety of contexts, such as prison chaplaincy, inner-city work with families, with the homeless, and so on. Individual and corporate reflection on these different initiatives stimulate fresh thinking, something particularly important with the rise of pioneer ministry.

A deep interest in cross-cultural engagement is another significant outworking of the focus upon mission. The historic partnership with the Baptist Missionary Society has been re-imagined in annual trips to share in the life of churches linked with the Society. These have so far included India, Nepal, Lebanon, Zimbabwe, Mozambique, Jamaica, Brazil and Peru. Not limited to ministerial students, the rich experiences provided have deeply affected many. For some it has confirmed a call to work abroad, while for all it has brought a new understanding of participation in the mission of God.

3. Spirituality

Spirituality is explored in tutor groups, formal teaching, and through other aspects of the Wednesday programme such as the regular "Still Point" days of creative engagement in prayer and reflection. The range and depth of Christian spirituality is recognized, and practical techniques to nurture it shared. Personal spiritual development is understood as essential for healthy ministry.

Academic links

The partnership with Trinity College endures and has been further cemented by joint participation in the Church of England's national "Common Awards" programme since 2015, under which the University of Durham has replaced the University of Bristol as validator of the academic programme (with the exception of MTh and doctoral level students, now registered with the University of Aberdeen).

Teaching continues to be integrated between the Colleges delivered across two sites by staff of both Colleges with some academic support services in common. For practical reasons, it was necessary to create a new umbrella legal entity, "Trinity College Bristol with Bristol Baptist College," to sign the Common Awards agreement with the University of Durham, but this has not effaced or replaced the separate legal and charitable status or governance arrangements of either College. There have been continuing discussions about the most effective ways of joint working, including site-sharing, and various forms of convergence, but the conviction remains that both Colleges wish to retain their separate institutional existence. Each naturally is also fully responsible for the distinctive ministerial formation required for their respective denominations.

The link with the University of Bristol has not been entirely lost, since some Hebrew teaching is offered to their students, an echo of the College's traditional emphasis upon the teaching of biblical languages.

The long-standing connection with the South Wales Baptist College (renamed Cardiff Baptist College in 2021) remains, with Peter Hatton and Helen Paynter both lecturing to their and other University of Cardiff students in recent years.

The Development of Study Centres

The College has developed a number of specialized centres which address the needs of particular ministries or deal with issues of contemporary concern in the churches and society.

While the Bristol Centre for Youth Ministry was a separate entity rather than a College project, it did spawn a Centre for Family and Childhood Studies headed by Sian Hancock in 2013, which was active in nearby Lawrence Weston. It ceased to operate when Sian left the College in 2017.

A concern for mission in different contexts was reflected in the Urban Life centre which was established by the Revd Dr Mike Pears in 2014 and supported by a grant from Baptists Together. On Mike's move to take up the post of director of the International Baptist Theological Study-Centre in Amsterdam, Urban Life formed a partnership with St Hild's College in Sheffield and continues successfully there.

The College has long had a connection with Anabaptist groups, notably through Dr Stuart Murray Williams. When the London Mennonite Centre closed and offered its library to the College the opportunity was taken to form a Centre for Anabaptist Studies, which opened in 2014 with Stuart as director. The Centre offers a number of Master of Arts modules in addition to supervision for doctoral students in this field. An annual lecture is held in the College.

The newest venture is the Centre for the Study of the Bible and Violence, established by Helen Paynter in 2018. It promotes the academic study of biblical texts associated with violence, and seeks to challenge misguided interpretations which might lead to the endorsement of violence and abuses of power, in human relationship and elsewhere. Regular symposia and lectures are held, and Helen has written and spoken often on this subject.

The library

The donation of the London Mennonite Centre library made necessary changes in the arrangement of the College library, which had already undergone several transitions. The collection still contains some books which can be traced to the library formed at Stokes Croft, but each move of building has necessitated much reorganization. It began to take its modern shape in the Woodland Road years, though it was not until 1982 that a professionally qualified librarian was employed. Previously staff, volunteers, and students had in various ways contributed to its operation.

Stella Read worked tirelessly to bring order to the collection, which at that time included a good deal of older material in poor condition, as well as books on many subjects no longer taught. Some of these had been offered to other libraries from the 1960s onward, but many a cupboard or dark corner was explored as her labours continued. Particularly valuable historic items were considered for sale, a process culminating in the purchase of the Tyndale New Testament by the British Library in 1994. She retired in 1997, succeeded by Mary Barker, who oversaw the move to The Promenade, and was in turn followed by Shirley Shire. She consolidated the collection, and added material necessary for new teaching needs, especially in the field of children's and youth work. Michael Brealey was appointed librarian in 2014, coinciding with the Mennonite gift. This created the need and opportunity for a wholesale reorganization, helped by a generous grant from the Mennonite Trust for new shelving. With additional funding from the College over the next couple of years the whole library was equipped with metal shelving. At the same time the in-house classification system was largely replaced with the Library of Congress system already used in the Trinity College library, and so familiar to our students.

The basement vault was also re-shelved and the historic material within rearranged. The holdings include many records of the library in earlier days, which can now be exploited for research purposes. Interest in them has been prompted by the Dissenting Academies Project under the auspices of the Queen Mary (University of London) Centre for Religion and Literature in English. Their remit covers a wide range of institutions, with Bristol the sole survivor of the academies remaining in continuity with their foundation. The Project's 'Virtual Library' system allows those interested to track the use of books in the Bristol library, and to identify their borrowers.

Modern learning, especially for students living at a distance from Bristol, relies upon electronic as well as physical resources. The COVID-19 pandemic produced a sudden need to enhance what could be offered, and the College now subscribes to the Digital Theology Library, a jointly-owned consortium which provides a huge range of content to its members.

PRESENT-DAY CHALLENGES

Student recruitment, staffing, managing the finances, maintaining the building—these are staples of the College's story and in different measure each remain challenges for the future. Every part of the College's work comes under regular scrutiny to see what scope there might be for improvement. This looking forward and planning in trust is characteristic of the College's life and takes its lead from the principal.

While his term in office is not yet complete, surely nothing to come can exceed the current severe test which, with other sad circumstances, has made the production of this history as we would have wished it to be so difficult. The COVID-19 outbreak and associated restrictions on everyday life have represented the most serious peace-time challenge to the College's ability to function. However, with the help of technology, the flexibility of staff, and the patience of students, it has proved possible to carry on the academic and ministerial programmes throughout the pandemic.

Such resilience embodies the best features of this principalship—a staff team working harmoniously together, students graciously making the best of things, and overall a determination to foster the formation of competent, passionate, Spirit-filled, and evangelical men and women for the service of Christ in the church and society. These four qualities re-express in modern idiom the earlier ones of able, zealous, lively, and evangelical, and thus exemplify the mixture of continuity and contextual adaptation which marks the College and the Bristol Tradition in the twenty-first century.

AFTERWORD

EVERY ATTEMPT TO TELL history must choose not only a time to start but also a time to stop. Circumstances, as we have seen, have meant that we have stopped this history, at least in this version, earlier than we would have liked to. Stopping at this point means that none of those who came to work in the College or to study as part of the community after 2006 are really talked about. Indeed, even those who were part of the College in the years between 2001 and 2006 are not as fully spoken of as we would have hoped.

For this I apologize—but it is also the life-giving reminder that no history is complete; there is always more to tell, and a fuller richer story to explore.

As you read this, especially if you know the College well, you will find an incomplete story. I ask your pardon if I have missed something that you value, or something that you know to have been of first importance. We have worked with such records as we have been able to access, and are grateful to those who have made them available to us. We are also grateful to those who have offered memories and reminiscences. We have tried to be as faithful to what we have been told as we can be.

But it will still be incomplete.

And in the end, I will not apologize for that. For no story is complete until the whole story is told. And the whole story will not be told until we are in glory. I cannot tell in this book, the full story of the relationships, the conversations, the prayers, tears, laughter, and discovery that are at the heart of the life of the community. I cannot tell the story of the ways in which the Kingdom has been served, the churches nourished and hearts moved and lives opened to a Saviour's loving call through the ministry and service of those who are and have been through the years, the College. I cannot tell, for time would fail, of the faithful ministries, the sermons preached, the prayers offered, the sacraments presided at that have been the result of the College's vision of training lively, able, zealous, evangelical ministers of the gospel.

For indeed, such functions and tasks are not a result, but a privileged calling through which our Lord in mercy deigns to invite we incompetent ones into the life of God's ministry in the world.

And so this story is incomplete.

But I hope that it gives glimpses and prompts memories, that it raises smiles, and heals some bruises, that it puts in context some aspects of the life of this institution that are valuable and continuing, but not always obvious. I dare to hope that in a small way, it will offer the authors' thanks to a community which has embraced them, and from which they have gained far more than they have offered. And above all, I pray that in the reading of this history, incomplete as it is, you will be moved again with wonder at the work of God with people, and the faithfulness of God to the people of God, continually calling, challenging, blessing, enabling and above all, loving.

A NOTE ON SOURCES

AT ANTHONY'S REQUEST, THIS volume was produced without the footnotes and references which grace the fuller work on which he was engaged. Nonetheless, readers may wish to be aware of some of the sources upon which this account draws. (Anthony's work includes a full list of sources and archives.)

A number of published histories of the college and its work already exist, as listed below. The account by Norman Moon, senior tutor and librarian, was produced to the mark the tercentenary of Edward Terrill's 1679 deed of gift.

PRIMARY SOURCES

Rippon, A. R. *A Brief Essay toward a History of the Academy at Bristol*. A lecture to the Bristol Education Society, reproduced in Rippon's *Annual Register*, vol. II, 1796.

Swaine, S. A. *Faithful Men; or, Memorials of Bristol Baptist College, and Some of Its Most Distinguished Alumni* London: Alexander & Shepheard, 1884.

SECONDARY SOURCES

Bristol Baptist College. *Bristol Baptist College: 250 years, 1679–1929*. Bristol: Bristol Baptist College, 1929.

Moon, N. S., L. G. Champion, and H. Mowvley. *The Bristol Education Society, 1770–1970*. Bristol: Bristol Baptist College, 1970.

Moon, N. S. *Education for Ministry: Bristol Baptist College, 1679–1979*. Bristol: Bristol Baptist College, 1979.

Hayden, R. *Continuity and Change: Evangelical Calvinism among eighteenth-century Baptist ministers trained at Bristol Academy, 1690–1791*. Milton under Wychwood, UK: Nigel Lynn Publishing for the Baptist Historical Society, 2006.

FURTHER SOURCES

In addition, the printed annual reports of the Bristol Education Society from 1770 and later College newsletters provide much useful information, especially on staff changes, student arrivals and departures, property matters, and finances.

The annual reports summarize fuller manuscript records of meetings, but under the circumstances of the writer's illness and COVID-19 travel restrictions it was impossible to fully exploit this material. Similarly, correspondence and committee minutes have been used only in part.

INDEX

Aberdeen, 23, 26, 34, 58, 103, 205
Academies, 46
Adelaide, 100, 152, 153
Australia, 100, 152, 153

BMS, 14, 31, 40, 41, 42, 45, 62, 65, 75, 75, 77, 84, 85, 103, 137, 140, 144, 145, 149, 150, 152, 163, 199, 201
Boxer Uprising, 96
Brealey, Fran, 202
Brealey, Michael, 207
Bristol Education Society, 12, 13, 14, 16, 19, 23, 28, 29, , 31, 45, 56, 58, 87, 114, 120, 129, 196
Bristol Federation for Ministerial Training , 125, 185, 186, 191, 198
Broadmead Church, 9, 11, 16, 18, 19, 20, 22, 23, 26, 28, 29, 34, 39, 40, 41, 50, 56, 57, 70, 83, 106, 113, 114, 129, 168, 188, 194
Brotherhood, 72
Brown University, 26, 27
Burchell, Thomas, 42, 97–101

Calabar, 42, 152
Calabar College, 83, 97, 99, 100–102
Calvinism, 17, 18, 19, 20, 21, 24, 29, 30, 31, 32, 36, 161
Cambridge, 3, 35, 58, 59, 110, 135
Cardiff, 95, 169, 170, 197, 205
Carey, William, 13, 17, 45, 85-, 88, 90–92, 149
Centre for Anabaptist Studies, 130, 206
Centre for Family and Childhood Studies, 206

Centre for the Study of the Bible and Violence, 201, 206
Cheeloo University, 97
China, 55, 85, 93–97, 101, 150
Christian Training Programme, 186
Clark, Neville, 169–70, 176
Clements, Keith, 161, 173
Clifton, 123, 126
College Lane Church, 35
Community, 72, 126, 142, 167, 168, 179, 180–83, 192, 204
Conference of Former Students, 72, 111, 145
Cotham Grove Church, 138, 159
Counterslip Church, 197
CYM, 130, 192, 196, 197, 198

Ecumenism, 29, 53, 133, 135, 142, 159, 169, 191, 192
Ecumenical, 29, 53, 71, 142, 146, 148, 153, 158, 159, 167, 168, 169, 186, 192, 201
Edinburgh, 23, 88, 90, 91, 105
Equipping Missional Disciples Course, 203
Estonia, 138, 152

Finland, 152

General Baptist Academy, 106
Germany, 94, 105, 155
Gifford, Andrew, 16, 129, 167
Gifford bequest, 130
Gouldbourne, Ruth, 183, 191, 199

Hall, Sidney, 167

Hall, Robert, 19, 20, 24, 34, 36, 39, 56, 83, 87, 106
Hancock, Sian, 205
Hatton, Peter, 201, 205
Hindle, Phil, 199, 200, 202
Horton College, 103
Hubble, Gwyneth, 80, 144

India, 55, 85–93, 97, 102, 204

Jamaica, 41–42, 83, 85, 97–100, 102, 103, 152, 204

Kingston, 100
Kyiv, 152

Latvia, 138, 191
Library, 67, 80, 95, 114, 117, 126, 128, 129–31, 187, 206–7
Lucas, Ernest, 183–86, 190, 191, 197, 200, 201

Manley, Ken, 153–54
Marshman, Joshua, 83, 85–86, 90–92
Melbourne, 152, 153, 191
Modern Question, 24, 29, 45
Montego Bay, 97
Moon, Norman, 159, 168, 182
Moravian College, 142
Moscow, 152
Murray Williams, Sian, 201
Museum, 67, 82, 97, 117, 123, 130

Nassau, 101
North St Manse, 113

Old King St Church, 71, 82, 92
Oxford, 3, 56, 87, 94, 110, 142, 150, 151, 159, 161, 163, 172, 183, 200
Oxford Brooke's University, 196

Particular Baptist Fund, 29
Paynter, Helen, 181, 201–2, 205–6
Peck, Tony, 130, 119–91, 198
Pithay Church, 26
Placements, 52, 137, 174, 188, 196, 198
Promenade, The, 50, 51, 67, 123, 125, 126, 130, 206

Reddie, Anthony, 201
Regent's Park College, 101, 105, 142, 148, 159, 161, 163, 172, 183, 190, 200
Richards, Timothy, 95

Salters Hall, 32, 35
Serampore, 85–88, 90–93
Shandong Christian University, 95, 97
Sherman, Hazel, 177, 179
Sierra Leone, 40
St Andrew's Hall, 102
Stewart, Ken, 198, 201
Stokes Croft, 46, 47, 56, 58, 66, 73, 77, 80, 97, 114–22, 130, 206
Student pastorates, 157, 188

Terrill, Edward, 8–12, 40, 82, 113, 167
Terrill Fund, 29, 167, 168
Trestrail, Frederick, 57, 61, 62–63, 65, 70, 118–19
Trinidad, 101–2
Trinitarianism, 32–36
Trinity College, 51, 53, 127, 130, 174, 184–85, 190, 197, 202, 205
Turner, Tony, 177, 183–84

United States of America, 26–27, 37–38, 39, 86, 91
University of Aberdeen, 23, 205
University of Birmingham, 137, 179
University of Bristol, 48–49, 72, 77–78, 80, 82, 100, 108, 120, 121–23, 125–26, 127, 130, 137, 142, 144, 155, 160, 167, 172, 173–74, 177, 181, 183, 184, 194, 205
University of Cardiff, 205
University of Durham, 155, 172, 205
University of Edinburgh, 88, 90, 91
University of Glasgow, 92
University of London, 71, 93, 100, 137, 159, 160, 207
University of Wales, 174
University of Zurich, 163
Urban Life Centre, 206

Wales, 2, 26, 28, 56, 105, 136, 169, 170, 178, 197, 205
Welch, Tim, 201

Wesley Methodist College, 51, 125, 164, 185, 201
Western Association, 20, 33–34, 39, 149
Western Congregational College, 48, 77, 82, 120, 123, 125, 130, 137, 138, 142, 160, 164
Whitewright, John Sutherland, 96–97
Women students, 79–80, 123, 144–45, 154, 156, 157, 163, 167, 168, 175, 203, 208
Woodland Road, 48–51, 77, 80–83, 96, 120, 121–23, 125–26, 127, 130, 206
Woolnough, Pearl, 127
World War, 1, 55, 79, 83, 133, 136, 151, 162
World War, 2, 132, 133, 134, 138, 141, 149–51, 159, 162, 186
Wotton, Mike, 173.

www.ingramcontent.com/pod-product-compliance
Lightning Source LLC
Chambersburg PA
CBHW062025220426
43662CB00010B/1472